Language and Ethnography Series

Language in Education: Ethnolinguistic Essays

by Dell Hymes

Center for Applied Linguistics

Library of Congress Cataloging in Publication Data

Hymes, Dell H.
   Language in education.

      (Language and ethnography series; 1)
      Includes bibliographical references.
      1. Anthropological linguistics--Addresses, essays,
   lectures. 2. Language and education--Addresses, essays,
   lectures. I. Title. II. Series.
   P35.H88   401'.9   80-27439
   ISBN 0-87281-134-4

December 1980
Copyright © 1980
by the Center for Applied Linguistics
3520 Prospect Street, N.W.
Washington, D.C.   20007

Printed in the U.S.A.

contents

introduction

These essays were written for different occasions but do have a perspective in common. I shall try to point out some of the common features and implications, but first want to thank the Center for Applied Linguistics for the opportunity of inaugurating this series. It is particularly a pleasure because of a long personal association with the Center. Let me thank Dora Johnson and Marcia Taylor for bringing the book to print so rapidly and effectively and Courtney Cazden for suggesting the collection to them.

The term "ethnolinguistic" in the subtitle may be a bit surprising, yet it expresses the common perspective of the essays better than any other term known to me. One alternative would be "sociolinguistic" and, indeed, I have written about this perspective under that heading (Gumperz and Hymes 1972, Hymes 1974, 1979). The history of such terms, indeed, would suggest that "sociolinguistics" should be the general term for all involvements of language in social life. The success and importance of certain lines of work and certain issues, however, have led to a widespread connotation for "sociolinguistics" as having specifically to do with variation and change, studied along the lines developed so inventively and successfully by William Labov. And part of the domain of this book, especially the first two chapters, would more easily fit what Joshua Fishman prefers to call the "sociology of language." It seems best to admit that the inspiration for the perspective of these essays is mainly anthropological tradition, and to use a term, "ethnolinguistic," that openly suggests anthropological concern for human culture throughout the world, for open-ended inquiry of the sort best termed "ethnography," and for cumulative comparison of cases of a sort best suggested by "ethnology."

These essays can be considered a contribution to the nascent fields of "educational linguistics" (cf. Spolsky 1978), but in that context their perspective seems distinctive enough to make a qualifying label useful. The focus is only partially on what happens in schools and what is taught there. To a considerable extent, the focus is on the societal context that shapes what can happen in schools. The concern is with some of the ways in which we think about language and knowledge in our disciplines and in society at large.

The first essay, "Functions of Speech," is the first essay in which the perspective known as "the ethnography of speaking" was publicly advanced and was also the occasion of my first formal visit to the university of whose Graduate School of Education I am now a member. In retrospect that visit, then an isolated occasion, seems to have been premonitory. I hope that readers will excuse the roughness, even crudeness, of the chapter. The fundamental point is sound and essential. We need to be able to think of language situations and educational situations as part of the evolution of human societies. We need to be able to think of languages and personal competencies as specific sets of communicative means, shaped by particular histories and adaptive niches. We need to transcend the liberal assumption built into so much of linguistic thought, that all sets of communicative means are equal in the eyes of linguistic theory. They are not equal in the eyes of history.

We inhabit a world whose languages are stratified in terms of roles and lexical scope, broadly speaking, as world, national, and local. (For example, English, Danish, Frisian.) Of course a particular speaker of English may be linguistically inferior to a particular speaker of Danish or Frisian, in command of a primary language and in scope of repertoire. It remains that English, as the name for a set of lexical and discourse resources, and a body of materials employing them, has a different scale. It may be that a person whose command of English was limited to just those resources of technical terminology and routine in which English was distinct would be a communicative monster, were that command complemented by no other. And the fact that a rapid-loading gun can defeat a bow and arrow confers no normal superiority on those with the gun (although they may think it does), and it may be important to point that out. As analysts of armament, nonetheless, we would be remiss if we ignored the technical difference.

With regard to persons, what reason can there be to alter circumstances if the circumstances have no substantive effect? How can inequality be injustice if it does no injury? We must be vigilant against false stereotypes and ascription of deficit, but vigilance itself is insufficient. It postulates tacitly a natural equivalence, as if social life could only interfere. The truth is otherwise. Social life shapes communicative competence and does so from infancy onward. Depending on gender, family, community, and religion, children are raised in terms of one configuration of the use and meaning of language rather than another. The particular configuration will affect the opportunities and access they have for other uses and meanings of language. Depending on social, economic, political factors, they will come to be able to use and experience language in some ways and not in others. Often enough, the result will be less than justice or vision would require. It is my considered judgment that Indian children raised in certain circumstances today suffer injustice with regard to language. The past hundred years has seen the demise of the Indian language with which they might identify, which they might share, into whose cognitive and literary richness they cannot enter, yet they mostly do not have the opportunity of mastering the corresponding dimensions of English. The cultural autonomy of the Indian language, a century ago, allowed a richness and satisfaction through language that subordination to an educational system they do not control does not allow today. Even the vitality of idiom and pronunciation in their Indian English is losing out in the younger generation, together with the carrying over into English usage of narrative patterns and etiquette unconsciously cultivated and enjoyed. Domination does do something to the life of language in a community, and we must face the fact. The last embodiments of an ancient linguistic art of narrative die, and we write, theoretically, as if nothing had been lost. We escape into an Edenic vision of the equality of languages and their uses that is contradicted by everything we know about the history of the past hundred years, probably the most vicious and destructive hundred years in the history of the human race. We must despair a little if we are to do much good.

The theme of diversity, inequality, and evolution is elaborated in the second essay where the original article is expanded by new sections on writing and on the views of Bernstein and Jurgen Habermas. The third essay addresses in part the development of linguistics. I hope that it will help bring to the attention of educators the importance of linguistics as embodiment of a methodology that is something of a third force, so far as the usual contrast between qualitative and quantitative methodologies is concerned. Indeed, the essay was written because a conference devoted to that contrast ignored linguistics in that respect. So much for the fame of French structuralism, one might say. But the first fount of French structuralism, Claude Levi-Strauss, acquired his sense of the qualitative rigor of linguistics in New York City during World War II, and it was in American linguistics and anthropology during the 1940s and 1950s that the extension of linguistic methodology to the rest of cultural life was first explored. The work of men such as Hockett, Smith, Trager, Pike, Goodenough, Lounsbury, and others in this regard is not widely known today, perhaps, but it is part of a development to be traced to the very roots of American linguistics in Sapir and Bloomfield, and a development that informs the "ethnolinguistic" perspective of this book. Models and formats apart, it is the heritage of an understanding of what it means to establish units and structure through commutation aid distribution that underlies the belief in these essays and in the work of other educational ethnographers, such as David Smith, that the openness of ethnographic inquiry is not an invitation to subjectivity but a path to intersubjective objectivity of a particular kind.

Chapter 3 also address what can be called the "arc" of linguistics, from its separation out of philology, language departments, and anthropology earlier in this century to its interdependence with psychology, computational sciences, philosophy, and social science studies of discourse today.

The main direction of the development of linguistics as a separate discipline has been from phonology (in the 1930s) through morphology and syntax to discourse. This direction has been founded on what may be loosely called the "referential" function of language. The crucial aspect of phonology has been the organization of speech sounds to distinguish and express elements of the lexicon and grammar. The crucial aspect of grammar has been its organization in relation to propositional content. The most cultivated aspect of lexicon has been its categorization of experience.

In recent years there has been growing attention to the organization of discourse beyond the level of the sentence and to the interdependence between the organization of discourse and features of situations, including the identity and roles of participants in situations. Perspectives for such attention are old, but a considerable body of empirical work is recent. Interest in the ways in which the use of language by and to men and women differ; in the properties of discourse between professionals (lawyers, psychiatrists, doctors, and teachers) and clients; in politeness as a dimension of conversation; in literature; in what is variously called "pragmatics," "semiotics," "conversational analysis," "ethnography of speaking," according to focus and context, is rife. It appears to lack, however, a comprehensive grounding in a view of the organization of linguistic means in the service of such ends.

Much of what is done in the study of politeness, speech acts, and the like is done on top of, or alongside of, standard conceptions of the formal analysis of grammar. The formal models are used, ignored, or rejected, but, apart from the work of Michael Halliday, new, thorough-going models of the organization of language are not discussed.

Such models would seem to be indispensable. When one starts from the standpoint of talk by and to women, for example, one must take into account more than is accounted for by standard formal models. The relevant features of speech may include details of articulation, intonation, pitch, tempo, lexical choice, syntactic choice that go together in a fashion or way of speaking, a style. Yet some of those features may not be part of a standard description of the language. The features are part of the conventional speech of the persons in question, to be sure, but a part that focuses on the organization of language in terms of the "referential" function has set aside. It is the start from a "higher" level, the organization of language in terms of interaction among persons, that brings the other features into view and finds them essential parts of what language is and does.

In my own opinion, a comprehensive model of the organization of language from the ground up, adequate to such inquiry, would systematically recognize and investigate two complementary elementary functions. One is that which can be called "referential" (or anything else), and the other is one which can be called "stylistic." The same methodological foundation pertains to both. Out of the stream of speech we identify certain features of sound as structurally relevant to the "referential" function by showing that they "contrast" in distinguishing the features distinguishing words. "Pig" and "big" are relevant in the structure of English (but not necessarily of another language) because the substitution of the initial sound of one for that of the other results in a different English word. Just such a commutation test applies to features whose substitution results in an utterance being conventionally taken as more formal or self-conscious, more forceful in intent, the speech of a person of one kind rather than of another; "bi:::g" as different in degree from "big," but not a different morpheme; "p^{h}ig" (with heavily aspirated p) as more forceful than "pig" with ordinary aspiration; whereas the difference between "p" and "b" in "pig" and "big" is not expressive or stylistic since it does make them different morphemes. The two kinds of commutation test and feature are interdependent. A feature that serves the one function cannot simultaneously serve directly the other: the difference in vowel length in "big," like the difference in aspiration in the two forms of "pig," can be expressive just because it does not make the two forms different morphemes. The difference between "pig" and "big" cannot be expressive just because it does mark a difference of morpheme. On the other hand, a feature grounded structurally in the one function can be employed indirectly in the pragmatic service of the other: "Not that one, the bi:::g one" (expressive length used to discriminate a referent); "Not beautiful, but certainly bootyful" (said of a rich attorney's elderly ugly daughter, referential difference enlisted in speech play). Together, the two kinds of elementary diacritic function provide the true basis for analysis of language, whether one's concern is with discourse or with universals of structure.

With regard to the latter: it would commonly be held that aspiration of consonants is not a universal of language structure. It distinguishes words "referentially" in some languages (Hindi, for example), but not others (English, for example). I would suggest that aspiration is contrastively relevant in stylistic function in those languages in which it is not relevant in referential function. If this suggestion proves valid, then aspiration is functionally relevant in all languages. Its relevance is universal; it is the function in which it is relevant that differs. The same thing may hold true for vowel length and perhaps other features. The very goal of formal analysis, a demonstration of what is universal, would seem to depend on returning to a more comprehensive functional starting point in order to leap further.

With regard to analysis of discourse: if it is necessary to attend to "stylistic" features in order to understand socially interesting use of language, then we must encourage a broader base of training in linguistics itself. The Chomskyan "revolution" led to a widespread disparagement of phonetics and associated

kinds of phonology. The ability to transcribe speech has not
been a standard part of linguistic training for some years. And
training in each level of language has been understandably
focused on analysis of its place in models of language conceived
in terms of the "referential" function. Organization in terms of
the "stylistic" function has been set aside as something that
might be dealt with later on. We need people trained to identify
features serving "stylistic" function and to trace their distribution, interpret their configurations, in relation, not to grammar,
but to the organization of activities, events, and social relationships.

The tradition of dialectology and sociolinguistic variation can
contribute much. The frame of reference, however, would not
be language change but the varied ways in which varied means of
speech are organized and charged with meaning in community life.
A crosscultural and comparative perspective will be essential. It
is striking, for example, that the work of the Milroys in Belfast
discovers patterns of communication in some working-class neigh-
borhoods that are quite similar to patterns known from some
American Indian groups. The common element would appear to
be people whose several networks of relationship reinforce each
other. Those who live in the same neighborhood also work together to a great extent and to a great extent are kin. The
finding suggests that recurrent social structure may be as much
or more an explanation of ways of speaking as geographical
separation and cultural tradition.

These considerations can be brought to a head by contrasting
two formulations of the fundamental questions of linguistic theory.
Much of the work of Chomsky and others has been associated with
the questions: How is it that a child can acquire a grammar of
(technically) infinite capacity on the basis of finite experience?
What form of grammar can account for all the grammatical sentences of a language while distinguishing them from the ungram-
matical? The perspective suggested here would address the questions: How do members of a group use language in order to conduct a certain activity? How do members of a group use language
in order to be taken as a certain kind of person, status, role, or
the like? The second set of questions entails a mode of organization of linguistic means and a set of capabilities on the part of
speakers, just as does the first. Many linguists might accept
both sets of questions as pertinent, but think that the work
associated with the first set must be accomplished before there
can be answers to the second set. My argument is that one
cannot get from the one to the other. The work associated with
the first set leaves out of account features and relationships that
are essential to the second. In order to deal with the second set
of questions, one needs a broader starting point.

When one adopts the broader starting point, one finds, I
think, that the other starting point appears as a specialization
within its framework. The specialization establishes the nature of

many, but not all, the resources made use of in the organization
of speech in social life. One way to summarize the difference is
to contrast the organization of speech in terms of *levels* with
organization in terms of what may be called "lenses" (the term is
taken from my colleague, Claire Woods-Elliott). When we review
the development of linguistics as a discipline, focused around
issues first of phonology and then later of syntax, and still
later, now, of discourse, we see an evolution in terms of levels.
The connections between levels occupy much of our attention.
We do not much think of phonology, for example, as a sphere of
the organization of language which might be involved in social
and cultural life in interestingly different ways in different
places. We do know that some languages seem to revel in
onomatopoetic and sound symbolic possibilities and others to be
chary of them. We know that the differences between men and
women enter into the very phonological shape of words in a few
languages, although not in most. We are aware that it seems
possible to describe the phonology of some languages almost without regard to the grammar, whereas in other languages the two
seem inextricable. Sometimes it seems necessary to rely on something phonological to delimit something grammatical, and sometimes
the other way round. Sometimes particular sectors of the lexicon
appear to have partly their own phonological character. When
languages are written, whether or not phonological shape is
represented, and if so, what portion, varies from culture to culture (cf. Chinese, Arabic, English). Such considerations point
to a view of phonology as a sphere of its own, a "lens" of its
own, as it were, through which to view the interaction of language and social life, a "lens" that may have a greater part in
some societies, a lesser part in others. The fit of phonology
into a grammar, as one level among others, is itself something
that seems culturally variable.

    A universal model of language is necessary to account for the
parameters of organization present in all languages. The fit
among spheres of language appears as more than a matter of relations among levels. The spheres themselves seem to differ from
one case to the next in terms of the amount and kind of attention
given them over time by different communities and in terms of
the way and degree to which they have been integrated into the
rest of grammar, other modes of signalling, such as writing and
the symbolic and expressive activities of concern to the group.
Morphology, syntax, and lexicon appear as partly autonomous
lenses as well. The degree of independence and interdependence,
the degree of elaboration, the relation to writing and other forms
of signalling all vary in ways that say something about the place
of language in social life.

    From this point of view, the description of the phonological
sphere or lens in a given case would comprise four aspects: the
inventory of phonological means, of course, including features
relevant both "referentially" and "stylistically"; attitudes and

beliefs towards speech sound, including interest in sound symbolism, speech play, correctness of pronunciation, and the like; the
organization and integration of phonological features in relation to
each other and in relation to the rest of the language; the organization and integration of phonological features in relation to kinds
of events, activities, and participants in them. The same four
aspects would apply to the sphere or lens of morphology, or syntax, and of lexicon.

    The middle chapters, 4 to 6, are concerned in complementary
ways with what counts as legitimate knowledge and who is counted
as entitled to know. The tempo of ethnography is in some respects conservative; its results are the better for ripening in the
mind; insofar as it makes local practice intelligible, it may lessen
impetus or optimism for change. By legitimatizing the knowledge
of the participants in educational settings and by giving weight
to the universal human need for self-worth, ethnography is likely
to make it difficult to argue solutions that take for granted the
fault or failure of teachers, of parents, or of some other category
of scapegoat. Ethnographic inquiry is likely to show people doing
the best they can with what they have to work with, given what
it is possible and reasonable for them to believe and do. The
ultimate result of ethnography, of course, may be radical. It
may suggest that some desired outcomes are impossible, given
what the society is willing to spend on schooling, and the consequences in what children must find in schools, in terms of resources, meaningful activities, minutes of meaningful guidance,
and communication. To empower teachers as having legitimate
knowledge may disrupt some practices. Just so, too, for principals in systems where principals are treated by those above them,
not as instructional leaders, but as hired hands. By making
particular situations palpable, credible, a living part of the imagination, ethnographic accounts may make it more difficult to impose
uniform general solutions that are arbitrary in local settings.
When some charge that ethnography does not permit generalization, they may be shrewder than they know. Whose power is
hurt if the pretense of theoretically generalizable results is
stripped away? If educational practice is found to require, not
the application of general theory, but the discovery of new,
local knowledge?

    In any case, the question of methodological preference is
secondary to the question of what we want to know. In anthropology itself, ethnography comprises a wide variety of techniques
and methods and is combined with a variety of modes of comparative analysis. If one truly wants to know about a culture, a
society, a way of life, one uses all there is to use. One does not
refuse to know something because it is known in a certain way.
Just so with schools and the educational configurations of neigh-
borhoods and communities. If we truly want to know them, we
will welcome and use every approach that can contribute.
Ethnography is indispensable and, to my way of thinking,

fundamental, but it is not the name of a methodological virgin undefiled. It can embrace anything useful so long as it can make the bed it lies in.

It remains that ethnography makes frequent use of narrative accounts and itself is often cast in narrative form. The status of narrative as a form of knowledge is addressed in chapter 7, and I am indebted to the co-author, Courtney Cazden, for letting me include it here. (I would also like to thank Lisa Delpit for her thoughtful comments on it.)

Chapter 8 weaves together many of the themes of the book. It and the preceding chapters should make clear that I share the concern of Ray Rist (1980) and Elizabeth Brandt (1980) that an ethnographic, or ethnolinguistic, perspective not be trivialized and vulgarized. I am far from holding that educational ethnography should be restricted to what ethnography means to one or another anthropologist. Indeed, the history of ethnographic inquiry is checkered enough to provide precedent for a great variety of practices, including sending students out with a checklist or having informants brought to the veranda of one's hotel for interview. The roots of ethnography in anthropology remain important because they anchor educational ethnography in a commitment to cumulative knowledge and comparative analysis of particular cases. Such roots tie educational ethnography to a rhythm of inquiry dictated by the nature of what it is one seeks to know, as against the arbitrary timing of other forces. Valid knowledge and successful change are both likely to require long-term involvement and continuing relationships.

Chapter 8 ends by emphasizing the role of Schools of Education, as those parts of institutions of learning and inquiry where the problems of language in education can most readily and steadily be addressed. Let me close this introduction with a few additional words on the long-term strategy that should inform such efforts. (I use "strategy" in its standard sense of long-range plans toward a goal, the sense in which it translates into English concerns such as those of Mao Ze Dong when he assessed the future of his country in the midst of its war with Japan and of Antonio Gramsci when, gradually dying in one of Mussolini's jails, he reflected on "wars of movement" and "wars of position" in relation to the ultimate liberation of Italian society. This comment is made necessary by the degenerate use of "strategy" in linguistics sometimes to denote a single choice or device.)

I assume a shared concern to change schooling, and education generally, for the better, and a willingness to consider an ethnographic way of working an essential part of such change. Given such assumptions, it is essential that our strategy for change concentrate our energies on the true obstacles to be overcome, the limitations of our knowledge, and the limitations of what can be accomplished within the existing resources and organization of education in this country. Our strategy must minimize diversion of energies to conflict over labels, over disciplinary proprietorship of a given method or perspective, over the propriety of certain techniques or fields or persons contributing to knowledge. It is of course an inveterate characteristic of colleges and universities to experience tension along such lines of fault in the scholarly terrain. But if our energies are diverted to conflict between liberal arts departments and professional school faculty, between academic personnel and practitioners in schools, between "ethnography" and other modes of inquiry, we harm our major purpose, and do the work of those who would prefer that what we can discover not be known, and certainly that it not lead to change.

Let us avoid, for example, christening our insights with noble names so that the contribution to our work of sociology, for example, is taken as divided among "ethnomethodology" or "neopraxiology," "cognitive sociology," "wild sociology," "reflective sociology," "critical theory," "dramaturgical approaches in sociology," "sociological behaviorism," "phenomenological sociology," "sociological introspection," "existential sociology" (see Douglas and Johnson 1977:xiii for this catalogue and differentiations among its elements). Such distinctions and tensions are to be taken as secondary to the "principal contradiction" that confronts us. That contradiction is between the dominant form of legitimate knowledge and legitimate knowers, with respect to education and schooling, and the legitimation of kinds of knowledge and knowing that "ethnography," "ethnomethodology," and many other trends in the philosophy and practice of social science encourage. The fundamental point in common is an understanding of social life as something not given in advance and a priori, but as having an ineradicable aspect of being constituted by its participants in an ongoing, evolving way. Those who accept this point can agree on giving priority to discovery of what is actually done in local settings and of what it means to its participants. The concomitant of that priority is an empowering of participants as sources of knowledge. What is ultimately known about a situation may not match the view of any one participant, but its validity and value will be compelling. And the concomitant changes in practices of inquiry and in relations between knowers and known may themselves be quietly radical, an essential step toward larger change. Work of this kind is already going on in a number of places, and it is a reason for hope, rather than despair, about the future of education. In changing what goes on in our own work place and in its relationships to its immediate context, we clear and cultivate a soil from which much may grow.

References

Anderson, Perry. "The Antinomies of Antonio Gramsci." *New Left Review* 100:5-80, 1976-77

Brandt, Elizabeth. "Popularity and Peril: Ethnography and Edu-
    cation." Paper presented at 40th annual meeting of the
    Society for Applied Anthropology, held March 19-22, 1980,
    in Denver, Colorado

Douglas, Jack D. and John M. Johnson, eds. *Existential
    Sociology*. Cambridge, London, New York: Cambridge Uni-
    versity Press, 1977

Gumperz, John J. and Dell Hymes, eds. *Directions in Socio-
    linguistics: The Ethnography of Communication*. New York:
    Holt, Rinehart and Winston, 1972

Hymes, Dell. "Introduction." In Courtney Cazden, Vera Johns,
    and Dell Hymes, eds. *Functions of Language in the Class-
    room*. New York: Teachers College Press, 1972

_____. *Foundations in Sociolinguistics: An Ethnographic Approach.*
    Philadelphia: University of Pennsylvania Press, 1974

_____. *Soziolinguistik. Zur Ethnographie der Kommunikation.*
    Eingeleitet und herausgegeben von Florian Coulmas. Frank-
    furt am Main: Suhrkamp, 1979

_____. "Blitzkreig and Protracted Warfare; or Wars of Movement
    and of Position; or Rist-slapping." Keynote address delivered
    at the Ethnography in Education Research Forum, March 14,
    1980, Philadelphia, Pennsylvania

Mao Tse-Tung (Mao Ze Dong). *On Protracted War*. Peking:
    Languages Press, 1967. (First edition, 1954; from a series
    of lectures, May 26-June 3, 1938.)

Milroy, Lesley. *Language and Social Networks*. (Language in
    Society, 2.) Baltimore: University Park Press, 1980

Rist, Ray C. "Blitzkrieg Ethnography: On the Transformation
    of a Method into a Movement." *Educational Researcher* 9:8-
    10, 1980

Spolsky, Bernard. *Educational Linguistics: An Introduction.*
    Rowley, Mass.: Newbury House, 1978

Woods-Elliott, Claire and Dell Hymes. "Issues in Literacy:
    Different Lenses." Commissioned paper for Stephen Reder,
    Northwest Regional Educational Laboratory, for report to
    National Institute of Education, 1980

functions of speech: an evolutionary approach

Let me begin by stating the thesis that lies behind my title. I want to controvert two widely accepted views, first, that all languages are functionally equivalent, and second, that all languages are evolutionarily on a par. I want to maintain that the role of speech is not the same in every society, and that the differences can best be understood from an evolutionary point of view; that we must understand speech habits as functionally varying in their adaptation to particular social and natural environments, and recognize that there are ways in which some languages are evolutionarily more advanced than others. Letting "speech habits" stand for the gamut of linguistic phenomena and "functions" for the varied roles these play, I am arguing for an evolutionary, comparative approach to functions of speech. Such an approach does not now exist in anthropology. I shall indicate reasons for the present neglect, and try to show that by overcoming it, anthropology will contribute to both its own theory and the foundations of education.

There can be, particularly, a contribution to some problems of education in the rapidly changing modern world, especially in underdeveloped and linguistically complex areas. We are all aware that, given the great surge throughout the world toward social and economic progress, the only feasible goal is for all to share as equitably and peacefully as possible in the fruits of industrialized civilization. To attain this goal in many areas requires the introduction of new educational forms and content, and we must help in this introduction while maintaining and enhancing the quality of education as part of a democratic way of life in our own country. And while success depends much upon problems which are political and economic, it also involves problems which have to do with the functions of speech.

As an instance of a problem encountered widely, we can cite the Mezquital Otomi of Mexico. The need here is through education to enable a group to overcome its poverty and isolation from the national society. Dr. Manuel Gamio, father of applied anthropology in Mexico, once commented that Otomi cultural character had changed very little during the twenty-five years of his active work among them. Part of the problem is an arid environment, but a missionary linguist writes that "the comparatively high degree of monolingualism in the tribe, forming an immediate barrier to fusion with the official system of education executed in Spanish, a language foreign to most of the members of the tribe, is an obstacle to progress tantamount to the imposing economic one."[1] And the obstacle of monolingualism in such a case can best be overcome with the help of an adequate analysis of the functions of

1

speech from a general point of view. Let us do this by considering what it means for a child (or an adult) to master the speech
habits of a group, to function as a linguistically normal member of
it.

FUNCTIONS OF SPEECH

When we think of learning a language, we may think first of
rules of pronunciation, grammar, and vocabulary, but there is
clearly more than this to the acquisition of a form of speech. A
person could master these rules but still be unable to use them.
He could produce any possible utterance but not know which
possible utterance to produce in a given situation, or whether to
produce any. If he spoke, he might say something phonologically,
grammatically, and semantically correct, but wrong, because inappropriate. He might find hearers (or correspondents) "taking
him the wrong way" or responding in ways that indicated that,
although understood, he was not a normal member of the speech
community.
In a society speech as an activity is not a simple function of
the structure and meanings of the language or languages involved.
Nor is the speech activity random. Like the languages, it is patterned, governed by rules, and this patterning also must be
learned by linguistically normal participants in the society. Moreover, the patterning of speech activity is not the same from
society to society, or from group to group within societies such
as our own.
The nature of such patterning, as well as its cross-cultural
variation, can be brought out by considering four aspects of it:
(1) in terms of the materials of speech, there is the patterning of
utterances in discourse; (2) in terms of the individual participants,
there is the patterning of expression and interpretation of personality; (3) in terms of the social system, there is the patterning of
speech situations; and (4) in terms of cultural values and outlook,
there is the patterning of attitudes and conceptions about speech.
Let us briefly take up each in turn.
1. Beyond the syntactic structure of sentences (with which
grammars usually deal), utterances have an organization into what
we may call *'routines.'* By *'linguistic routine,'* I refer to sequen-
tial organization, what follows what, either on the part of a single
individual or in interchange between more than one.[2] Routines
range from reciting the alphabet, counting, and greeting, to the
sonnet form, the marriage ceremony, and the direction of a buffalo
hunt. Obviously, societies and groups differ both in the content
of equivalent routines, such as those for greeting, and in the
kinds and numbers of their routines. The more complex the
society, the greater the number and variety of routines, and the
greater the variation in control of routines by individuals.[3]
2. Persons who participate in speech activity learn the patterning of its use as medium for personality and role-playing.

Cues expressed and perceived in speech may enable individuals to place, and to adjust quite subtly to, each other. This complex process ranges from tempo and general handling of voice dynamics to choice of expressions and over-all style. The individual learns both signaling patterns outside language proper and the integration of these in speaking (and, correspondingly, in writing). Such signals differ from group to group, of course, and can be misinterpreted, either in themselves or as part of other behavior. Thus, as James Sledd observes:

> British speakers have far more final rising pitches in
> statements than do Americans, whose favorite intonation
> pattern /231#/ sounds brusque to British ears. British-
> ers are also likely to use a greater range of pitches than
> Americans, more frequent and extreme pitch changes,
> and more numerous expressive devices....In some
> parts of the United States, an adult male who talked so
> would be suspect.[4]

In a school for Mesquaki Fox Indian children near Tama, Iowa, many white teachers who probably regard their classroom behavior as normal have had loudness of voice, together with verbal directness, interpreted by Indian pupils as "mean"-ness and a tendency to "get mad."

The relative importance of speech to personality, vis-à-vis other modes of activity and communication, varies from person to person and group to group, and so do the range of expression and interpretation of personality possible in speech, the extent to which speech is a form of gratification (oral or other), and the importance of speech for role performance and attaining rewards, especially those depending on personal interaction. Among the Ngoni of Africa, rules of speaking etiquette are strict, and skill in speech is greatly encouraged, for such skill is considered part of what it means to be a true Ngoni.[5] Contrast this to conceptions of the "strong, silent type," the "man of few words," etc. in sectors of American society.

3. Social systems are often regarded as patterned relationships among roles and among groups such as families, lineages, and corporations, and there are speech patterns diagnostic or characteristic of particular roles and groups, just as there are speech patterns diagnostic or characteristic of particular personalities. These of course differ cross-culturally in content and relative importance. If we also look at a social system in terms of the behavioral activity involved, we can see it as a network of interaction in situations or behavior settings, and can discover related patterns of speech. For example, societies differ in the settings in which speech is prescribed, proscribed, or simply optional. We so commonly think a social situation requires something to be said that writers have described this as a universal need.[6] Certainly, were someone to come to your or my house,

sit silently for half an hour, and leave still silent, we should not
consider it normal. In some American Indian groups this would
constitute an acceptable social visit. For them, physical presence
is enough; the situation is defined as one in which speech is not
necessary when one has nothing to say.

If we look at a social network in terms of speech settings,
we can discriminate a set of factors whose interrelations may serve
to describe its patterns of speech activity, and so provide a basis
for comparing the functions of speech in different social systems.
These factors can be termed: a *sender* (or *source*); a *receiver*
(or *destination*); a *message* (viewed in terms of its form or shape);
a *channel*; a *code*; a *topic*; a *context* (setting, situation, scene).
All are compresent in speech activity. Societies differ in what can
function as an instance of each factor, and in the relations of
appropriateness which obtain among the factors in given cases.
There is a system of speech activity in a society, then, because
not all possible combinations of particular senders, receivers,
message forms, channels, codes, topics, and contexts can occur.

A teacher in a school for Navaho children may discover that
one boy cannot speak to a girl classmate because she stands in
a certain kinship relation to him. A society may traditionally permit only certain individuals to use the channel of writing, and
among the otherwise non-literate Hanunoo of the Philippines, writing is used only among young people in courtship and love affairs.
Education for birth control may encounter the barrier that such a
topic cannot be discussed among or in the presence of both sexes,
including husbands and wives. A teacher may misinterpret an
ornate and allusive style in an examination as an attempt to con-
ceal ignorance of the answers, not realizing that Puerto Rican students may deem it the only style appropriate to such an occasion.
One teacher in a project of fundamental education may find it hard
to teach children to define the classroom situation as one in which
they do not talk to each other, and in which they speak to her
only when asked or acknowledged. In another society a teacher
may find it equally difficult to bring children to define the classroom situation as one in which they can speak at all, they having
learned to regard instruction as a situation in which they function
as receivers only.

These scattered examples must suffice here, except to note,
under the *code* factor, the importance of levels, styles, and functional varieties of a language, and in some societies, of entirely
different languages, in relation to particular settings, channels,
senders, and receivers. Here rules of appropriateness may make
a great difference, especially if they differ for teacher and students because of differences in class or cultural background.

4. Cultural attitudes and conceptions regarding speech differ
notably from society to society and also from class to class. The
pattern of such attitudes and conceptions permeates the role of
speech in personality and social structure. Reciprocally, differences with regard to the interest in and valuation of speech (or of

a particular linguistic code) may have correlates in differences with regard to how speech enters into the socialization and early education of children.   It is clear from ethnographic sources that societies differ as to their conceptions of children as users of language, and of the process of language learning; as to the stage in children's speech development at which major socialization pressure is exerted; as to the extent to which interest in speech and speech play is encouraged or discouraged; as to the extent to which speech is a mode of reward and punishment for children; and as to the portions of culture which are linguistically communicated.   Some societies are permissive about eating and toilet training until the child can understand verbal explanations, whereas others conceive a newborn child as capable of understanding speech, and lecture it from the cradle.   Adult skills are transmitted verbally for the most part in many societies, but among societies such as the Kaska of northwestern Canada, children learn them almost wholly through observation and imitation. Differences as to the functions of speech in adult life probably are related to such differences as these in the functions of speech in childhood, but there has not been the systematic comparative study which would permit us to be sure.

In any event, although we tend to think first of cases in which language has been integral to a group's sense of identity and unity, and in which it is thus a focus of pride, it is clear that here also the function of speech may vary.   Four distinct functions and three correlated attitudes have been differentiated by students of the development of standard languages, and these can be applied generally to all languages.[7]   The first two functions are *separatist* and *unifying*, jointly associated with an attitude of *language loyalty*.   There is a *prestige* function associated with *language pride*, and a *frame of reference* function associated with *awareness of a norm*.

Two South American peoples contrast sharply with regard to the separatist and unifying functions.   The Fulnio of Brazil have abandoned their homes several times in the past three centuries to avoid assimilation by Brazilian national society.   The preservation of their language and an annual religious ceremony have been the basis as well as the symbol of their distinct identity.   The Guaqueries, a Venezuelan group, seem to have abandoned their language and native religion perhaps as early as the eighteenth century, but the society thrives as a distinct identity within the Venezuelan nation, through maintenance of a special socio-economic base.[8]

Two North American groups contrast sharply with regard to the prestige function.   Three centuries ago a Tewa-speaking group fled from the Spanish to find refuge on one of the Hopi mesas in Arizona.   There, as the Hopi-Tewa, they have maintained a position as a specially regarded and privileged minority--a situation in which attitudes toward language have been a major factor.   Loyalty to their Tewa dialect has had a separatist and unifying role, as

has their persuasion of the Hopi, through the reiteration of a
myth and constant ridicule, that no Hopi can learn their language. They in turn have a reputation as polyglots for their
own knowledge of Hopi, and often of Navaho and English; they
have maintained pride in their language, and have won linguistic
prestige for it and themselves.[9] In contrast, the Eastern Cherokees of North Carolina, a remnant group, retain their language in
large part, but without pride. It is a source neither of prestige
nor of unity, persisting only in a separatist function with a negative, anti-White language loyalty.[10]

In Mexico the Zapotecs of the Isthmus of Tehuantepec resemble the Hopi-Tewa in the fact that, as a group bilingual in Spanish and Zapotec, they retain pride in their first language and
national identity, and these are accorded prestige by those
around them. In contrast, language has been salient in the cultural persistence of the Otomi against Spanish pressure, but the
Otomi have accepted an outside valuation of their language as inferior to Spanish, and feel no prestige in its use. Language
loyalty to Otomi makes imposition of education in Spanish alone
impossible, but acceptance of prestige for Spanish alone makes
education in Otomi alone unacceptable; it suggests an attempt to
keep them in an inferior status. Bilingual education, using diglot
texts, wins acceptance, by reassurance that knowledge of Spanish
is the end in view. (Such bilingual education may, of course,
come to enhance the prestige of Otomi.)

How groups differ in the degree to which a language serves
as a frame of reference in the sense of awareness of a norm is
noticeable in attitudes among themselves towards incorrectness or
slovenliness of speech. Among some American Indian groups such
as the Washo and Paiute, a child might receive as a nickname a
word it frequently mispronounced. Attitudes towards correctness
among foreigners may depend upon the identity of the speaker.
Many Frenchmen find a Spanish or Italian accent charming but a
Germanic accent unbearable. The choice of teaching personnel
and procedures obviously would pose a different problem among
linguistic sticklers, such as the Ngoni of Africa, from that posed
among linguistically more laissez-faire peoples.

The functions of writing systems in these respects are often
significant for attempts to introduce literacy and new education.
Often, as among the Otomi, a successful orthography for the
native language, if it is to be easily accepted, must depart from
scientific accuracy to resemble a prestigeful other written language. Native conceptions (folk-linguistics) enter too, as when
the writing of tones with accent marks was found impractical
among the Soytaltepec Mazatec of Mexico. They conceive of tones,
not as high and low, but as thick and thin, and it makes no
sense to try to teach them the rule that the mark for the "high"
tone slants up and that for the "low" tone slants down. Printing
expense and legibility make the use of their own metaphor of thick

and thin impractical also, but superscript numbers for tones have
proved successful. [11]

Even in this cursory survey, we see that the role of language
and linguistic activity can vary greatly from group to group, and
we can begin to see more clearly how this variation matters for
practical problems of raising the educational level of the world. In
programs of fundamental education such as UNESCO has sponsored,
for example, literacy must often be introduced. To this end, one
among several dialects or languages often must be chosen as the
medium of education, and often an orthography must be selected
or constructed. Whether literacy is already present or not, new
speech habits and verbal training must be introduced, necessarily
by particular sources to particular receivers, using a particular
code with messages of particular forms via particular channels,
about particular topics and in particular settings--and all this from
and to people for whom there already exist definite patternings of
linguistic routines, of personality expression via speech, of uses
of speech in social situations, of attitudes and conceptions toward
speech. It seems reasonable that success in such an educational
venture will be enhanced by an understanding of this existing
structure, because the innovators' efforts will be perceived and
judged in terms of it, and innovations which mesh with it will have
greater success than those which cross its grain.

There is direct analogy with the fact that one perceives the
sounds of another language in terms of the structure of sounds in
one's own. [12] This phenomenon--perception of another system in
terms of one's own--has been studied by linguists as *interference*
between two systems, most notably by Uriel Weinreich of Columbia
University in his book *Languages in Contact*. [13] When both systems
in question are known, it is possible to predict quite accurately
where and what kind of interference will occur, and what kinds of
substitutions and interpretations will be made, as speakers of one
language learn the other. In consequence, it is possible to design
materials for the teaching of one language specifically for speakers
of another, and to anticipate the particular advantages and disad-
vantages their own system will confer in the task.

This suggests the nature of the contribution that anthropology
can make to such problems in education. It would be a matter of
applied anthropology, defined as "the formal utilization of social
science knowledge...to understand regularities in cultural processes and to achieve directed culture change." [14] An adequate
comparative study of the functions of speech would imply a descriptive science of the functions of speech, just as there is a
descriptive science which deals with language structures. Such a
science would provide a basis for detailed analysis of the differing systems of speech activity which meet in an educational situation, and such analysis would make it possible to predict or at
least to anticipate more effectively the interference which a program of literacy, bilingual education, and so forth would encounter. Even the broad conceptual analysis outlined above can

help by calling attention to aspects of the problem, such as the Mesquaki children's perception of teachers as "mean," or the need for a successful written form of Otomi to resemble that of Spanish. But there must be detailed empirical studies, from which can emerge a more refined theory and the descriptive science I have advocated.

It is remarkable that no such comparative study of speech functions exists. Anthropology is noted for just this sort of cross-cultural perspective when it is a matter of religion, of kinship, of sexual behavior, of adolescent crisis. Why not when it is a matter of the functioning of speech in society?

The answer lies in the theoretical perspective on the functioning of speech now usual in anthropology, a perspective which is non-evolutionary and minimizes cross-cultural variation. So I must now sketch an evolutionary perspective, as framework for a short critique of current anthropological views and a basis for a broader concluding interpretation of the educational aspects of functions of speech.

AN EVOLUTIONARY PERSPECTIVE

There is no single or monolithic body of evolutionary theory in anthropology and biology, but there is a body of recent literature from which we can single out some essential features for application to speech.[15]

First, there is an essential distinction between two kinds of evolutionary study, namely of *specific* evolution and of *general* evolution. Specific evolution is concerned with individual lines of evolution, the development and adaptation of particular groups in particular environments. General evolution is concerned with the course of evolution as a whole. It abstracts from and often cuts across individual lines of evolution to consider types, as these have emerged and as these represent broad levels of evolutionary advance. General evolution might consider the relation between the mammal and marsupial types, and the advance which led to the dominance of the former. Specific evolution would examine such questions as the adaptation of the whale to marine existence, the bat to flight, and the radiation of the kangaroo line of marsupials into various ecological niches in Australia. In terms of specific evolution, advance means improved adaptation to the particular environment relevant to a group and in relation to those with whom it is in direct competition in that environment; outside this context it is relativistic. In terms of general evolution, advance means progress which emerges in the course of specific evolution and has consequences for it, but considered in a broader spatial, temporal, and environmental context. Thus a familiar case is the successful adaptation to a specific environment which proves fatal in the long run. Criteria for general evolutionary advance include "change in the direction of increase in range and variety of adjustments to its environment" and succession of dominant types.[16]

When we study evolution specifically, we find that its focus is upon a population, and a set of traits associated therewith; that it analyzes the variation in traits within a population, and the differential retention of traits within the population over a period of time; that it interprets this process through the adaptation of the population within its environment (and of the traits to one another), in connection with the pressures which selectively affect the retention of traits and hence this adaptation. It sees a population and its characteristics as participating in a continuous process of change, and it interprets the change and the characteristics of the population in broadly contextual and functional terms.

It is easy enough to see linguistic change in these terms: a speech community has a certain set of speech habits, whose incidence varies within the population and which are differentially retained, as a result of selective pressures (such as the social and natural environment, prestige of speakers, customs such as tabu and word-play, and internal requirements for maintenance of the linguistic code), the whole being adaptive both to the environment of the speech habits and to the maintenance of the code.

If we carry through such a view, however, we can find ourselves in a stance quite different from that typical of the attitude toward language today. Our broad category of *speech habits* in relation to a *population*, as the unit of primary focus, does not in the first instance isolate the formal structure of the linguistic code, the usual object of linguistic attention, from the patterning of the uses of speech. Both would equally be analytical abstractions from the same phenomenal reality, the speech activity of the population. We begin by considering the totality of the speech habits of the population, and so subsume at first the presence not only of different types, varieties, and dialects, but even of different languages as parts of the whole.

Since one readily takes a functional view of traits involved with selective pressures, it becomes quite natural to analyze individual speech habits or sets of habits, including those of separate languages, in terms of competition within the environment of a population, and to see this competition as turning partly on the merits of the habits themselves. Such a view requires one to consider what the relevant environment for the adaptation of a population's speech habits really is at present, and is necessarily concerned with the real locus of change of such habits in the speech activity of definite individuals living in a definite society. Such an evolutionary view will direct attention toward the variation within and between the speech habits of populations, and will give due importance to the differences in the functions of speech associated with a set of speech habits of a population, to the consequences of this variation, and to the evolutionary survival, development, or disappearance of traits or sets of traits. [17]

In short, the evolving units are sets of speech habits as characteristics of populations--units which sometimes will, and sometimes will not, coincide with the historical units known to us as languages. We begin by examining natural totalities of speech habits firmly embedded in environmental context, cultural and physical, as adaptive to that context, as an integral part of the whole socio-cultural adaptation of the population.

If we examine our recurrent example, the Mezquital Otomi, from this perspective, we find that an Otomi child grows into, and acquires its education as a member of, a population whose speech habits comprise a majority of Otomi provenience, a minority of Spanish origin. The child becomes well aware of the competition, selection, and specialization among these two sets of habits. The Otomi habits are dominant in the sphere of subsistence and in most of social life, occupying a privileged position in the early socialization of young and the loyalities of all, and generally in the tribal environment within which its adaptation has almost wholly taken place. But Spanish habits are dominant in certain situations such as the market and the classroom, and as the relevant environment of Otomi life and speech habits shifts and enlarges, the position of Spanish speech habits is enhanced, and more situations are encountered in which Spanish has selective advantage. The prestige which all accord to Spanish speech habits, and the experienced relatively greater utility of these situations in the expanding sphere of the environment, underlie the general expectation that the relative function of Spanish will continually expand--an expectation which in turn helps bring about the expected state of affairs. As for development towards filling the enlarged environment on the part of Otomi speech habits, this occurs only indirectly as a by-product of bilingual education and the inculcation of Spanish.

Although the published analysis of the Otomi case is one of the few such, it is brief, and its focus is not upon the kinds of questions and of data which an evolutionary perspective requires.[18] The discussion is cast in terms of the proposition that all languages are functionally equivalent and equal, neutral in their own cultural settings, and Otomi is seen as having been forced into a status of ascribed inferiority, because of inferiority ascribed to its associated culture. This is considered to be entirely a social-psychological matter of prestige, having no basis in anything connected with Otomi as a language. Now this assumption is remarkable, since the discussion does mention concrete *linguistic* differences in the functional value of Otomi and Spanish in certain situations, and despite the declared equality of Otomi, the possibility that Otomi can be developed to meet the modern educational needs of its speakers is not considered.

While the superiority of Spanish in the situation is partly a matter of attitude and prestige, it is at best ingenuous not to see it as also partly a matter of the actual linguistic superiority of Spanish. The failure to see this is in part due to heavy reliance on the view that there is no evolutionary superiority among languages, while in fact the superiority of Spanish in the situation is in part a consequence of its being one of a type of evolution-arily more advanced language. Let us now turn to the study of general evolution, which deals with this question.

We mentioned "increase in range and variety of adjustments to environment" and succession of dominant types as two criteria of evolutionary advance as between general types. When such cri-teria are applied to culture, it is generally agreed that some cul-tures are technologically more advanced than others. Vocabulary is the linguistic analogue of technology...." Clearly the lexical con-tent of standard languages shows increase in range and variety of adjustments to environment in comparison to dialects or regional or minority languages, where these are not supported by a standard language outside the situation. World languages such as English, French, Spanish, Russian, and Chinese show such increase, and have spread as representatives of a dominant type, quite apart from military conquests. The existence of linguistic science itself, and of the self-consciousness and awareness and control which go into the construction of logics and systems of mathematical manipu-lation, argue for the advanced status, as a type, of languages which participate in, and indeed make possible, such activities. The same holds for linguistic routines in philosophy, literature, religion, and science. It has been argued that mathematics, logic, et al., are not language itself, but "post-language."[19] Even if this view is taken, it remains that ordinary language is the medium in which "post-language" systems must ultimately be interpreted, and not all natural languages can perform this function. Indeed, differentiation and specialization of function is an important aspect of evolutionary change in languages, as has long been recognized by students of the development of standardized languages. Of course, increase in number and diversity of functions of a lan-guage is a response to change in other aspects of a culture. This is true also of increase in the content and complexity of the vocab-ulary of a language. Some scholars may point to this fact as a reason for disregarding such changes as not properly a linguistic problem, or as not part of language. The argument does not hold. Many, if not all, linguistic changes have sociocultural roots. Lexi-cal borrowing, a standard topic in linguistics, is a case in point. As part of general evolution in language, then, increased complex-ity in the lexical content and functions of a language cannot be disregarded. The response is linguistic, even if the stimulus is not.

We may bypass the question of evolutionary advance in gram-matical features, a question raised especially in this century by leading French linguists, and also the question of increased efficiency and economy in language evolution.[20] Both possibilities may be regarded, not as disproved, but as unproved. The reality of general evolutionary advance in the sphere of language seems clear.

It may be pointed out that any set of speech habits is capable of expanding in content and functions sufficiently to serve a

complex civilization and its associated systems of thought.   Yes,
of course, *potentially* it can so serve, but we must distinguish
between potential and actual development, recognizing that some
languages are actually of the more advanced type while others
are not.

If this distinction is valid, why is it not part of the common
perspective of linguistics and anthropology today or at least a
subject of discussion?   Particularly now that an evolutionary perspective toward culture is being renewed in anthropology, how
can a part of culture, language, be omitted?   The answer lies in
a dominant outlook, whose focus is upon the single language and
its most highly formal, structured aspect, its grammar and phonology considered in abstraction in the first instance apart from
cultural and natural context.   Vocabulary, the aspect most closely
tied to this context, is likely to be treated as residual.   The
thrust has been to exclude from central concern those realms of
phenomena and bits of data which do not seem to fit into formal
structures.   Such structures are abstracted from variation, the
occurrence of which, though not denied, has been submerged
under the dominant presumption of regularity and homogeneity
throughout a speech community.   As a background against which
to set off the structure of the formal code, speech activity commonly has been considered random, perhaps a matter of individual
and unpredictable choice.   As for the functions of speech, these
have been seen as universally equivalent,[21] while competition between sets of speech habits, languages, or parts thereof, has frequently been taken to be a purely social matter, not a matter involving the adaptive merits of the habits involved, and often interpreted under the blanket term of an unanalyzed differential "prestige."   Thus important questions about linguistic change have gone
unanswered because the focus is not upon the actual locus speech
change, and the relation of language to culture becomes a theoretical problem.

Now there are exceptions to each part of the picture I have
sketched.   It is not a question here of a monolithic ideology.   It
is a question of emphases, a dominant outlook and direction, and
the terms in which matters tend to be couched.   Moreover, one
must understand that these arose in answer to definite needs,
and that with them great advances in knowledge of language have
been made.

I see the dominance of the view just outlined as arising out of
a battle that had to be won early in this century for the autonomy
and legitimacy of formal linguistic structure as an object of study
in its own right, as distinct from historical and psychological problems and explanations.   And this carried with it, especially in
anthropology, the implication of equality of all languages for such
study.   This autonomy of structural linguistics is a theme in two
classics, the *Cours de linguistique générale* of Ferdinand de
Saussure[22] and the *Language* of Edward Sapir.[23]   The need for
this focus carried with it the de-emphasis upon cultural

entanglements that we have noted, and, especially in anthropology, an emphatic non-evolutionary view. There still linger misconceptions about the existence of so-called "primitive" languages, whose meager vocabularies must be eked out by gesture, which lack grammars, definite systems of sounds, and abstract terms, and which are more variable and change more rapidly because of being unwritten. All this was demonstrably untrue, and stood in the way of a general science of linguistics, whose material must be the rich diversity actually at hand in the world's languages. "Equality, diversity, relativity" became a linguistic theme.

The rejected notions about "primitive" languages (along with equally mistaken notions about the superiority of an Indo-European type, or of one of its exemplars, Latin, and the use of such as ideal models for description) were of course evolutionary in one sense. But now the notion of evolution was rejected *in toto*. Whatever differences might obtain between simpler and more advanced cultures, no correlative difference was found to hold between the structures of their languages. "When it comes to linguistic form, Plato walks with the Macedonian swineherd, Confucius with the head-hunting savage of Assam."[24] No measures which would satisfactorily rate language structures as more or less advanced appeared that were free from cultural bias. One evolutionary typology would have put Chinese at the bottom of the scale--a patent absurdity. Also, efforts by distinguished scholars, such as Jespersen, to show trends toward progress in efficiency, suffered from limitation in data to two language families, Indo-European and Semitic, and from inadequacies of conceptual analysis. In view of these inadequacies and errors, it is not surprising that the evolutionary notions of the day dropped out. And, despite present-day attacks on that generation of cultural anthropologists for being anti-evolutionary, we must remember that evolutionary theory in biology then was rather disunited and uncertain, not at all the vital force and stimulus it is today, and that to be against certain evolutionary stereotypes was to adopt a democratic and progressive stance.

Now that the battle against the mistaken evolutionary ideas has been won, and the study of formal structure well established, it is time to take up the evolutionary question again. And we can see that the fight against notions of "primitive" languages, whose echoes still reverberate today, confused three levels of evolutionary advance, and so jumped too quickly to the conclusion that all languages are evolutionarily equal. There is the level of "primitive" languages, proto-forms below the status of full languages, then the status of full languages, and finally, the advanced status we have indicated as occupied by world languages and some others. The fight against misconceptions about "primitive" languages did not distinguish the two latter stages, so that to deny the equality of all languages was taken to imply that the less advanced were "primitive." No known languages are. All known languages have achieved the middle status. All languages have achieved the level of basic or primary efficiency, such that they can fully adapt, in time, to the needs of any population. In this sense all languages are potentially equal, as we observed above, and hence capable of adaptation to the needs of a complex industrial civilization. This is just what has happened historically in the case of English, which in its Old English period would certainly not have been adequate to modern technology and science. But not all languages are equally efficient compared with one another, either in terms of specific evolution in meeting particular needs, or in terms of general evolution in meeting the needs of modern complex civilization. Already for many local languages, and ultimately for all, the direction of change in the world is one which is making modern complex civilization part of their relevant environment, within whose context they must compete. The ideal image of a single "neutral" language in a single, homogeneous cultural context hardly holds any longer. For populations such as the Otomi the relevant environment is one in which sets of habits of differing origins compete as means of developing the new forms and content of speech activity--among which education may be included--that successful adaptation requires.

In all this, equality in primary or basic efficiency is not enough, nor is the difference purely a matter of social, non-linguistic factors. In the particular time and place of competition, one set of speech habits is as such functionally superior. Partly the superiority is mutual and relative, specific to particular niches, e.g., that of Spanish routines for the market place, and of Otomi for the usual subsistence activities of tribal life. But partly it is a matter of general superiority, and here the perspective of general evolution provides a sober and realistic attitude. Otomi, like Anglo-Saxon and many languages around the world today, could become a medium of technology, science, and philosophy. Just so, any normal infant, wherever born, could participate in any culture, however complex. But the human infant need only be raised in the cultural environment for the potentiality to be realized in one lifetime, while the realization of the potential of languages often takes much longer. Even granted the will, the cost in money, personnel, and time may be prohibitive for a poor nation or a newly struggling one. This is a poignant fact, for the decisions that must be made in view of it are often hard.

There is a widespread respect for cultural autonomy and integrity. And, as the UNESCO report, *The Use of Vernacular Languages in Education,*[25] shows a child learns to read most efficiently if taught in its native language first, even when it is then to learn to read in a second language. Yet what if, once literate, the child finds that there is nothing to read in this first language, because nothing has been written and the country cannot afford to duplicate the needed educational materials many times over in different languages? (The absence of the needed written materials is a problem even in such places as Egypt and Puerto Rico, where certain aspects of advanced education have had to be conducted in English.) And there are many people of great talent whose efforts to develop a literature in a local language, as for example in Ghana, must, for similar reasons, come to naught. The languages could so have developed, but they have not done so in their existing adaptation, and now it is too late.

So the selective pressure among the languages of the world continues in environments rapidly changing with technological and social revolutions.[26] From a scientific and humanistic point of view, it is a hard loss to see much of this diversity disappear or become constricted in local uses, not because of inadequacy in its own terms, but because the terms have changed, and the chance for development through creative nationalism is lost to all but a handful. The scientific value of a language is independent of its political importance, just as the scientific import of a plant or animal does not depend upon its utility as food, and accordingly, some linguists are devoting their energies to recording and analyzing the languages about to disappear, so that future theories about language can have the broadest possible base, and so that we may come as close as possible to enjoying the full light that language can shed on the range of human nature and creativity. With plants and animals, discovery of a new process or type or rare form is worth more to science than millions of additional pigs and potatoes, and so it is with languages.

The reduction of linguistic diversity is a loss for humanistic educational values too, and perhaps a matter of concern for our own future adaptation. Any one form of language of necessity selects a small portion of the total range of ways of categorizing and analyzing experience that language can embody. To a large extent, the growth of science transcends the framework of any one language, but insofar as the particulars of our first language shape our later thought and use of language, the existence of diverse languages is of value as a means of transcending the perspective of any one, valuable perhaps even to mankind as a reservoir of potential change. And for such transcendence, records of past languages are never so generally effective as living examples. Let us hope, then, that the attrition of the world's languages will leave us not entirely impoverished, but still with some store of diversity.

CONCLUSION

To sum up: I believe that an evolutionary approach to speech can be unifying and vivifying. In linguistics itself it can, by its generality and functional perspective, integrate many separate concerns--genetic classification, linguistic areas, dialectology, bilingualism, standard language studies, linguistic acculturation, and the like--that deal with language change. In anthropology it can remove the embarrassing contradiction between an evolutionary view of culture and a non-evolutionary view of culture's part, language, and point toward integration of linguistic and other

anthropological studies. In education it can, for instance, provide perspective on questions of correctness in speech. But
chiefly, for the problems of education in large parts of the world,
it can contribute to linguistics and anthropology by focusing on
speech habits in relation to populations; by emphasizing a process
of change through variation, adaptation, and selection; and by
providing a framework and incentive for a descriptive science of
the functions of speech. From this, I hope, will come the comparative perspective which anthropology should provide on the
ways in which speech activity enters into the process of education.

NOTES

1. Ethel Emilia Wallis, "Sociolinguistics in Relation to Mezquital [Otomi] Transition Education," *Estudios Antropológicos
publicado en homenaje al doctor Manuel Gamio* (México, D.F.:
Dirección General de Publicaciones, 1956), p. 524.
2. "Repertoire" can refer to the array of resources, words,
phrases, constructions, etc. which are generally available for use
in routines and from which are formed the alternatives available
at particular points in routines.
3. Frequently, different routines are peculiar to different
languages, as in the use of an esoteric foreign language for ceremonial activity, and of a foreign language, jargon, kioné, or the
like for diplomacy, trade, or other communication with members of
other groups. The Otomi use a "market Spanish" in one situation,
but their own language in basic subsistence activities. An essential task of bilingual education among the Otomi is the introduction
of additional linguistic routines in Otomi and Spanish.
4. James Sledd, "Review of R. Kingdon, *The Groundwork of
English Intonation*," in *Language*, Vol. 36, No. 1 (1960), p. 178.
5. Margaret Read, *Children of Their Fathers: Growing Up
Among the Ngoni of Nyasaland* (New Haven: Yale University
Press, 1960).
6. Edward Sapir, "Language," *Encyclopedia of the Social
Sciences* (New York: Macmillan, 1933), Vol. 9, pp. 155-69; reprinted in David G. Mandelbaum (ed.), *Selected Writings of Edward Sapir* (Berkeley and Los Angeles: University of California
Press, 1949), p. 16.
7. See Paul Garvin and Madeleine Mathiot, "The Urbanization
of the Guarani Language," in A. F. C. Wallace (ed.), *Men and
Cultures: Selected Papers of the Fifth International Congress of
Anthropological and Ethnological Sciences* (Philadelphia: University of Pennsylvania Press, 1960), pp. 783-90.
8. W. D. Hohenthal and Thomas McCorkle, "The Problem of
Aboriginal Persistence," *Southwestern Journal of Anthropology*,
Vol. 11, No. 3 (1956), pp. 288-300.
9. Edward P. Dozier, "Resistance to Acculturation and
Assimilation in an Indian Pueblo," *American Anthropologist*,

Vol. 53, No. 1 (1951), pp. 56-66.

10. John Gulick, "Language and Passive Resistance Among the Eastern Cherokees," *Ethnohistory,* Vol. 5, No. 1 (1958), pp. 60-81.

11. For the full account, see Sarah C. Gudschinsky, "Toneme Representation in Mazatec Orthography," *Word,* Vol. 15, No. 3 (1959), pp. 446-52.

12. For excellent analysis and examples, see Hans Wolff, "Phonemic Structure and the Teaching of Pronunciation," *Language Learning,* Vol. 6, No. 3-4 (1956), pp. 17-23.

13. Uriel Weinreich, *Languages in Contact* (New York: Linguistic Circle of New York, 1953).

14. George M. Foster, "Applied Anthropology and Modern Life," in *Estudios Antropológicos publicados en homenaje al doctor Manuel Gamio* (México, D.F.: Dirección General de Publicaciones, 1956), pp. 332-33.

15. See especially Marshall Sahlins and Elman Service (eds.), *Evolution and Culture* (Ann Arbor: University of Michigan Press, 1960); *Evolution and Anthropology: A Centennial Appraisal* (Washington, D.C.: Anthropological Society of Washington, 1959); Julian S. Huxley, "Evolution, Cultural and Biological," in William L. Thomas, Jr. (ed.), *Current Anthropology* (Chicago: University of Chicago Press, 1956), pp. 3-25.

16. See Huxley, *op. cit.,* and George G. Simpson, *The Meaning of Evolution* (New Haven: Yale University Press, 1952), chap. XV.

17. Several lines of fresh interest in speech variation are now emerging, and we can expect a number of significant studies in the next decade. The fresh concern manifests itself in various guises and under various names, but it is especially associated with the revitalization of dialectology. An example is the work of the Linguistic Survey of Scotland; a theoretical approach akin to that advocated here has been sketched by Trevor Hill, a member of the Survey, in his article, "Institutional Linguistics," *Orbis,* Vol. 8, No. 2 (1958), pp. 441-55.

18. It is because Miss Wallis' article is so valuable and stimulating, being a discussion which presents both concrete detail and theoretical assumptions, that it is the focus here for critical analysis of some of these assumptions in terms of a different theoretical perspective. Miss Wallis relies extensively upon the authority of Edward Sapir for her perspective, and, as the discussion immediately following indicates, Sapir for her perspective, and, as the discussion immediately following indicates, Sapir was a principal exponent of the non-evolutionary view which it is now necessary to transcend.

19. Joseph Greenberg, "Language and Evolutionary Theory," *Essays in Linguistics* (Chicago: University of Chicago Press, 1956), pp. 56-65.

20. Evolutionary advance in grammatical features is suggested by A. Meillet, *Introduction à l'étude comparative des langues*

indo-européenes (Paris: Libraire Hachette, 8th ed., 1937), pp.
424-5; Marcel Cohen, *Le Langage, Structure et Evolution* (Paris:
Editions Sociales, 1950), p. 112; and Henri Frei, "Systèmes de
déictiques," *Acta Linguistica,* Vol. 4, No. 3 (1944), pp. 111-129.
Meillet and Cohen cite particularly the association in various Indo-
European languages between loss of the category of dual and development of more complex civilization. Frei writes that "Linguists
agree in attributing the disappearance of the dual to the march of
civilization," citing A. Cuny, *Le nombre duel en Grec* (Thèse de
Paris, 1906) and J. Wackernagel, *Vorlesungen über Syntax*, Vol. 1,
2nd ed. (Bâle, 1926), pp. 74-5, and going on to interpret as a
parallel the tendency of deictic systems to evolve toward a binary
type (such as "here":"there").

The best recent attempt to analyse the development of economy
and efficiency in languages is probably that of W. Koenraads,
Studien über sprachökonomische Entwicklungen im Deutschen
(Amsterdam: Muelenhoff, 1953).   There are valuable comments in
the reviews of the book by H. Hoenigswald (*Language*, Vol. 30,
pp. 591-3 (1954), and Uriel Weinreich (*Word*, Vol. 11, pp. 237-40
(1955)).

21.   For example, "A necessary condition for socialization in
man is the learning and use of a language. But different languages are functionally equivalent in this respect, and one language is comparable with another because human speech has certain common denominators" (A. I. Hallowell, "Culture, Personality,
and Society," in A. L. Kroeber and others, *Anthropology Today*
[Chicago: University of Chicago Press, 1953], p. 612).   Such
statements point out the important common denominator of the
functioning of language in education and socialization, but ignore
the important differences.

22.   F. de Saussure, *Cours de linguistique générale,* published by C. Bally and E. Sechehaye (Paris: Payot, 1916), and
now in English translation, *Course in General Linguistics* (New
York: Philosophical Library, 1959).

23.   Edward Sapir, *Language* (New York: Harcourt, Brace,
1921).

24.   Edward Sapir, *op. cit.*, p. 234.

25.   *The Use of Vernacular Languages in Education* (Paris:
UNESCO, Monographs on Fundamental Education: VIII, 1953).
See the extended review by William E. Bull in the *International
Journal of American Linguistics*, Vol. 21, No. 3 (1955), pp. 288-
94.

26.   Some scholars are directing attention to the linguistic
aspects of this subject, notably (in the United States) Charles A.
Ferguson, Paul Garvin, John J. Gumperz, and Uriel Weinreich.
See Charles A. Ferguson and John J. Gumperz (eds.), *Linguistic
Diversity in South Asia: Studies in Regional, Social, and Functional Variation* (Bloomington, Indiana: Indiana University Research Center in Anthropology, Folklore and Linguistics, Publication #13; Part III, *International Journal of American Linguistics*,
Vol. 26, No. 3, July 1960).

speech and language: on the origins and foundations of inequality among speakers

*I conceive of two sorts of inequality in the human species;
one, which I call natural or physical, because it is established by nature and consists in the difference of ages,
health, bodily strengths, and qualities of mind or soul;
the other, which may be called moral or political inequality, because it depends upon a sort of convention and is
established, or at least authorized, by the consent of men.
The latter consists in the different privileges that some
men enjoy to the prejudice of others, such as to be richer,
more honored, more powerful than they, or even to make
themselves obeyed by them.*

Rousseau (1775)[1]

I use the second paragraph of Rousseau's second *Discourse* as an
epigraph, and adapt its title, because I want to call attention to a
link between his concerns and ours. Like him, we think knowledge
of human nature essential and pursue it; like him, we think the
present condition of mankind unjust, and seek to transform it.
These two concerns, for example, provide the frame for Noam
Chomsky's recent Russell lectures.[2] Unlike Chomsky, but like
Rousseau, moreover, some linguists are beginning to attend to a
conception of linguistic structure as interdependent with social
circumstances, and as subject to human needs and evolutionary
adaptation. And like Rousseau, our image of the linguistic world,
the standard by which we judge the present situation, harks back
to an earlier stage of human society. Here Rousseau has the advantage of us. He knew he did this, and specified the limitations
of it (see the end of note *h* to the *Discourse*). We do it implicitly,
falling back on a "Herderian" conception of the world as composed
of individual language-and-culture units, for lack of another way
of seeing the resources of language as an aspect of human groups,
because we have not thought through new ways of seeing how linguistic resources do, in fact, come organized in the world. Thus
we have no accepted way of joining our understanding of inequality with our understanding of the nature of language.
    Chomsky's Russell lectures are a case in point. The first lec-
ture, "On Interpreting the World," presents implications of a certain conception of the nature of language and of the goals of linguistic research, leading to a humanistic, libertarian conception of
man. The second lecture, "On Changing the World," is about injustice, its roots in inequality of power, and the failure of scholars
and governments to deal with the true issues in these respects.

There is little or no linguistics in the second lecture, just as
there is little or nothing of social reality in the first. Such
principled schizophrenia besets linguistics today; the scientific
and social goals of its practitioners are commonly compartmentalized. Such an alienation from experience and social reality of one
of "the many kinds of segmental scientists of man," against which
Edward Sapir warned years ago,[3] does not mirror either the true
nature of language or its relation to social life; rather, it reflects
a certain ideological conception of that nature and that relation,
one which diverts and divorces linguistics from the contribution,
desperately needed, that it might make to the understanding of
language as a human problem.

The heart of the matter is this. A dominant conception of the
goals of "linguistic theory"[4] encourages one to think of language
exclusively in terms of the vast potentiality of formal grammar,
and to think of that potentiality exclusively in terms of its universality. But a perspective which treats language only as an
attribute of man leaves language as an attribute of men unintelligible. In actuality language is in large part what users have made
of it. Navajo is what it is in part because it is a human language,
and in part because it is the language of the Navajo. The generic potentiality of the human faculty for language is realized differently, as to direction and as to degree, in different human communities, and is useless except insofar as it is so realized. The
thrust of Chomskyan linguistics has been to depreciate the actuality of language under the guise of rejecting an outmoded philosophy of science, but we must be able to see beyond its ideological
use and recognize that one cannot change a world if one's theory
permits no purchase on it. Thus, one of the problems to be overcome with regard to language is the linguist's usual conception of
it. A broader, differently based notion of the form in which we
encounter and use language in the world, a notion which I shall
call *ways of speaking*, is needed.

Let me subsume further consideration of how it is that linguistics is part of the problem, under the following consideration of
some of the other dimensions of language and of some general
sources of inequality with regard to it. In both sections I shall
try to indicate the need for a conception of *ways of speaking*.

Some Dimensions of Language as a Human Problem

It is striking that we have no general perspective on language as
a human problem, not even an integrated body of works in search
of one. Salient problems, such as translation, multilingualism,
literacy, and language development, have long attracted attention,
but mostly as practical matters constituting "applications" of linguistics, rather than as proper, theoretically pertinent parts of it.
There are notable exceptions, as in the work of Einar Haugen, but
for about a generation most linguistic thought in the United States
has seen in the role of language in human life only something to

praise, not something to question and study. Perhaps this situation reflects a phase in the alternation of "high" and "low" evaluations of language to which the philosopher Urban called attention.[5] The skeptical period after the First World War did see leading American theorists of language devote themselves to language problems, such as those involving new vehicles for international communication (Jespersen, Sapir), the teaching of reading (Bloomfield), literacy (Swadesh), language as an instrument and hence a shaper of thought (Sapir, Whorf), and linguistic aspects of psychiatric and other interpersonal communication (Trager, Hockett, in the early 1950's). Perhaps this issue of *Dœdalus* is a sign that the climate of opinion is shifting once again toward a balanced recognition of language as "at one and the same time helping and retarding us," as Sapir put it in one context.[6]

In any case, it is unusual today to think of language as something to overcome, yet four broad dimensions of language can usefully be considered in just that way: diversity of language, medium of language (spoken, written), structure of language, and functioning of language. Of each we can ask,

(1) when, where, and how it came to be seen as a problem;

(2) from what vantage point it is seen as a problem (in relation to other vantage points from which it may not be so seen);

(3) in what ways the problem has been approached or overcome as a practical task and also as an intellectual, conceptual task;

(4) what its consequences for the study of language itself have been;

(5) what kinds of study, to which linguists might contribute, are now needed.

I cannot do more than raise such questions here; limitations of knowledge would prevent my doing more, if limitations of space did not. To raise such questions may, I hope, help to stimulate the development of a general perspective.

Overcoming Diversity of Language. This problem may be the most familiar, and the historical solutions to it form an important part of the subject matter of linguistics itself: lingua francas, koinés, pidgins and creoles, standardized languages, diffusion and areal convergence, multilingual repertoires, and constructed auxiliary languages. The myths and lexicons of many cultures show a widespread and presumably ancient recognition of the diversity of language, although not uniformly in the mold of the Tower of Babel. The Busama of New Guinea and the Quileute of the present state of Washington believed that originally each person had a separate language, and that community of language was a subsequent development created by a culture hero or transformer. Thus it is an interesting question whether it is unity or diversity, within or between speech communities, that has seemed the thing requiring an intellectual explanation.

In Western civilization the dominant intellectual response to the existence of diversity has been to seek an original unity, either of

historical or of psychological origin (sometimes of both). The
dominant practical response has been to impose a novel unity in
the form of the hegemony of one language or standard. The
presence of the Tower of Babel story in the civilization's sacred
book legitimated, and perhaps stimulated, efforts to relate languages in terms of an original unity and played a great part in
the cumulative development of linguistic research. Indeed, some
rather sophisticated work and criticism on this subject can be
found from the Renaissance onward, and the dating of the origin
of linguistic science with the comparative-historical work of the
early nineteenth century reflects its institutionalization as much
as or more than its intellectual originality.[7] The force of Christian and humanitarian concern to establish the monogenesis of
man through the monogenesis of language was felt strongly well
through the nineteenth century, from the dominance of the "ethnological question" in the first part through the controversies involving Max Müller, Darwin, Broca, and others.[8] The special interest
of Europeans in Indo-European origins became increasingly important in the latter part of the century, the idea of a common
linguistic origin stimulating and legitimating studies of common
cultural origins and developments. Humanitarian motives played a
part as well--Matthew Arnold appealing to Indo-European brother-
hood as a reason for the English to respect Celtic (Irish) culture
and perhaps the Irish, and Sir Henry Maine making a similar appeal on behalf of the peoples of India. Sheer intellectual curiosity
and satisfaction must always be assigned a large part in motivat-
ing work in comparative-historical linguistics, and humanistic concern has probably played a part in the major contemporary effort
to establish empirically a common historical origin for languages,
that of the late Morris Swadesh.[9]
    The most salient effort to establish a conceptual unity of
human languages today is, of course, linked with the views of
Noam Chomsky. Concern for such a unity is itself old and con-
tinuous--the appearance of disinterest among part of a generation of U.S. linguists before and after the Second World War was
a local aberration whose importance is primarily due to Chomsky's
reaction against it. He has reached back to the seventeenth and
eighteenth centuries for an ancestral tradition,[10] when he had
only to take up the tradition in this country of Boas and Sapir,
or the European tradition, partially transplanted to this country,
of Trubetzkoy and Jakobson. In both of these traditions some
significant things were being said about the universals of language in the 1930's and early 1940's. It is true, however, that
the history of the tradition of general linguistics stretching back
through the nineteenth century (and, Jakobson would argue, continuing straight back through the Enlightenment to origins in
medieval speculative grammar), had been lost from sight in American linguistics, and a sense of it is only now being recovered.
It is true, too, that since Herder and von Humboldt, the tradition does not much appeal to Chomsky, since its universalism is

combined with an intense interest in typology, that is, in the characterization of specific languages as well as, and as an instrument of, the characterization of language.

Here we touch on the inescapable limitation of either kind of effort to conceive the unity of human language. Although one used to speak of the discovery of a genetic relationship as "reducing" the number of linguistic groups, both the language and the thought were badly misleading. Languages may disappear through the destruction of their speakers, but not through the publication of linguistic papers and maps. The newly related languages remain to be accounted for in their differences and developments as well as in terms of the portion (often quite small) of their makeup that shows their common origin. Likewise, the discovery of putative universals in linguistic structure does not erase the differences. Indeed, the more one emphasizes universals, in association with a self-developing, powerful faculty of language within persons themselves, the more mysterious actual languages become. Why are there more than one, or two, or three? If the internal faculty of language is so constraining, must not social, historical, adaptive forces have been even more constraining, to produce the specific plenitude of languages actually found? For Chinookan is not Sahaptin is not Klamath is not Takelma is not Coos is not Siuslaw is not Tsimshian is not Wintu is not Maidu is not Miwok is not Yokuts is not Costanoan...(is not Tonkawa, is not Zuni, is not Mixe, is not Zoque, is not any of the numerous Mayan languages, or affiliates of Mayan, if one extends the horizon). The many differences do not disappear, and the likenesses, indeed, are far from all Chomskyan universals; some likenesses exist because of a genetic common origin (Penutian), some because of areal adaptations (Northwest Coast for some, California for others), some because of diffusion, some because of limited possibilities and implications (à la Greenberg). Franz Boas once argued against exclusive concentration on genetic classification, calling the full historical development of languages the true problem.[11] A similar point can be made today as against concentration on putative universals. Most of language begins where abstract universals leave off. In the tradition from Herder and von Humboldt through Boas and Sapir, languages are "concrete universals," and most of language as a human problem is bound up with the adjective of that term.

Both of these modes of overcoming diversity of language intellectually, genetic classification and the search for putative universals, locate their solutions in time. There is a past reference, a historical origin of languages or an evolutionary origin of the faculty of language, and there is a present and future reference, one which draws the moral of the unity that is found. Neither speaks to the present and future in terms of the processes actually shaping the place of language in human life, for the faculty of language presumably remains constant and genetic diversification of languages is literally a thing of the past. The

major process of the present and foreseeable future is the adaptation of languages and varieties to one another and their integration into special roles and complex speech communities. The understanding of this process is the true problem that diversity of language poses, both to mankind and to those who study mankind's
languages.

The essence of the problem appears as communication, intelligibility. Some are concerned with the problem at the level of the
world as a whole, and efforts to choose or shape a common language for the world continue.[12] Some project this contemporary
concern onto the past, speaking of a "stubborn mystery" in the
"profoundly startling, 'anti-economic' multiplicity of languages
spoken on this crowded planet."[13] Such a view is anachronistic,
however, for the diversity was not "anti-economic" when it came
into being; it was just as much a "naturally selected, maximalized
efficiency of adjustment to local need and ecology" as the great
variety of fauna and flora to which Steiner refers in the phrase
just quoted. Universal processes of change inherent in language,
its transmission and use, together with separation and separate
adaptation of communities over the course of many centuries, suffice to explain the diversity. Simply the accumulation of unshared
changes would in time make the languages of separate groups mutually unintelligible. There is of course more to it than physical and
temporal distance (as Steiner insightfully suggests); there is social
distance as well. Boundaries are deliberately created and maintained, as well as given by default. Some aspects of the structures of languages are likely due to this. If the surface form of
a means of communication is simplified greatly when there is need
to overcome barriers, as it is in the formation of pidgin languages,
then the surface form of means of communication may be complicated when there is a desire to raise or maintain barriers.[14] This
latter process may have something to do with the fact that the surface structures of languages spoken in small, cheek-by-jowl communities so often are markedly complex, and the surface structures
of languages spoken over wide ranges less so. (The observation
would seem to apply at least to North American Indian languages
and Oceania).

In any case, the problem is one of more than languages; it is
one of speech communities. Here the inadequacy of dominant concepts and methods in linguistics is most painfully apparent. The
great triumph of linguistic science in the nineteenth century, the
comparative-historical method, deals with speech communities as
the source and result of genetic diversification. The great triumph
of linguistic science in the twentieth century, structural method,
deals with speech communities as equivalent to language.[15] Genetic
diversification can hardly be said to occur any longer, and a speech
community comprising a single language hardly exists. The study
of complex speech communities must benefit mightily from the tools
and results both of historical linguistics, for the unraveling and

interpretation of change, and of structural linguistics, for the explicit analysis of linguistic form. But it cannot simply apply them, it must extend them and develop new tools.

The needs can be expressed in terms of what is *between* speech communities and what is *within* them. Despite their well-known differences as to psychology, both Bloomfield and Chomsky reduce the concept of speech community to that of a language.[16] This will not do. The boundaries between speech communities are thought of first of all as boundaries of communication, but communication, or mutual intelligibility as it is often phrased, is not solely a function of a certain objective degree of difference between two languages or some series of related languages. One and the same degree of "objective" linguistic differentiation may be taken to demarcate boundaries in one case, and may be depreciated in another, depending on the social and political circumstances.[17] And intelligibility itself is not only a complex function of features of linguistic form (phonological, lexical, syntactic), but also of norms of interaction and conduct in conversation, and of attitudes towards differences in all these respects. In Nigeria one linguist found that as soon as members of a certain community recognized a related hinterland dialect, they refused to understand it;[18] other communities are noted for the effort they make to understand despite great difference. Such considerations cut across language boundaries. One may be at a loss to understand fellow speakers of his own language if his assumptions as to appropriate topics, what follows what, and the functions of speech are different (as happens often enough in classrooms between teachers of one background and students of another), and many of us have had the experience of following a discussion in a language of which we have little grasp, when the topics, technical terminology, and norms of conduct are professionally shared.

To repeat, communication cannot be equated with a "common" language. A term such as "the English language" comprises all linguistic varieties that owe their basic resources to the historical tradition known as English. That "language" is no longer an exclusive possession of the English, or even of the English and the Americans--there are perhaps more users of English in the Third World, and they have their own rights to its resources and future. Many varieties of "English" are not mutually intelligible within Great Britain and the United States as well as elsewhere. In fact, it is an important clarification if we can agree to restrict the term "language" (and the term "dialect") to just this sort of meaning: identification of a historically derived set of resources whose social functioning--organization into used varieties, mutual intelligibility, etc.--is not given by the fact of historical derivation itself, but is problematic, needing to be determined, and calling for other concepts and terms.

We are in poorly explored territory here. Even with consideration restricted to groups which can communicate, there is a gamut

from "I can make myself understood" at one end to "he talks the
same language" at the other. Probably it is best to employ terms
such as "field" and "network" for the larger spheres within which
a person operates communicatively, and to reserve the term "community" for more integral units. Clearly the boundary (and the
internal organization) of a speech community is not a question
solely of degree of interaction among persons (as Bloomfield said,
and others have continued to say), but a question equally of
membership, of identity and identification. If interaction were
enough, school children would speak the TV and teacher English
they constantly hear. Some indeed can so speak, but do not
necessarily choose to do so. A few years ago I was asked by
teachers at Columbia Point why the children in the school did not
show the influence of TV, or, more pointedly, of daily exposure
to the talk of the teachers. A mother present made a telling observation: she had indeed heard children talk that way, but on
the playground, playing school; when playing school stopped,
that way of talking stopped too.

Community, in this sense, is a dynamic, complex, and sometimes subtle thing. There are latent or obsolescent speech communities on some Indian reservations in this country, brought
into being now principally by the visit of a linguist or anthropologist who also can use the language and shows respect for the
uses to which it can be put. There are emergent communities,
such as New York City would appear to be, in the sense that
they share norms for the evaluation of certain variables (such as
post-vocalic r), that have developed in this century. There are
other communities whose stigmata are variable and signs of severe
insecurity, like those of New York, or the community of *porteños*
in Buenos Aires, comprised principally of immigrants concerned to
maintain their distance and prestige vis-à-vis speakers from the
provinces (who, ironically enough, have lived in the country much
longer). There can be multiple membership, and there is much
scope for false perception; authorities, both governmental and
educational, are often ignorant of the existence of varieties of
language and communication under their noses. An unsuspected
variety of creolized English was discovered recently on an island
off Australia by the chance of a tape recorder being left on in a
room where two children were playing. When the linguist heard
the tape and could not understand it, he came to realize what it
was. That such a language was known by the children was entirely unknown to the school. Indians who have been beaten as
children for using their Indian tongue or blacks who have been
shamed for using "deep" Creole will not necessarily trot the language out for an idle inquirer. In general, when we recognize
that this diversity of speech communities involves social as well
as linguistic realities, we must face the fact that there are different vantage points from which diversity may be viewed. One
person's obstacle may be someone else's source of identity. In
the United States and Canada today one can find Indians seeking

to learn the Indian language they did not acquire as children.
Leveling of language seems neither inevitable nor desirable in the
world today. It is common to mock efforts at preservation and
revitalization of languages as outmoded romanticism, but the
mockery may express a view of human nature and human needs
whose shallowness bodes ill for us.

What is within a speech community in linguistic terms has
begun to be understood better through recent work in sociolinguistics. Empirical and theoretical work has begun to provide
a way of seeing the subject "steadily as a whole." It suggests
that one think of a community (or any group, or person) in
terms, not of a single language, but of a *repertoire*. A repertoire comprises a set of *ways of speaking*. Ways of speaking,
in turn, comprise speech styles, on the one hand, and contexts
of discourse, on the other, together with the relations of appropriateness obtaining between styles and contexts. Membership in
a speech community consists in sharing one or more of its ways
of speaking--that is, not in knowledge of a speech style (or any
other purely linguistic entity, such as a language) alone, but in
terms of knowledge of appropriate use as well. There are rules
of use without which rules of syntax are useless. Moreover, the
linguistic features that enter into speech styles are not only the
"referentially-based" features usually dealt with in linguistics today, but also the "stylistic" features that are complementary to
them, and inseparable from them in communication. Just as social
meaning is an integral part of the definition and demarcation of
speech communities, so it is an integral part of the organization
of linguistic features within them. (Cf. Bernstein's concept of
"restricted" and "elaborated" code, classical diglossia, liturgy.)
The sphere adequate to the description of speech communities, of
linguistic diversity as a human problem, can be said to be: *means
of speech, and their meanings to those who use them.*[19]

No one has ever denied the facts of multilingualism and heterogeneity of speech community in the world, but little has been done
to enable us to comprehend and deal with them. Until now a
"Herderian" conception of a world of independent one-language-
one-culture units, a conception appropriate enough, perhaps, to
a world pristinely peopled by hunters and gatherers and small-
scale horticulturalists, has been tacitly fallen back upon. There
now begins to be work to characterize complex linguistic communities and to describe speech communities adequately. Such description must extend to the place of speech itself in the life of
a community: whether it is a resource to be hoarded or something
freely expended, whether it is essential or not to public roles,
whether it is conceived as intrinsically good or dangerous, what
its proper role in socialization and demonstration of competence is
conceived to be, and so forth.[20] Through such work one can
hope to provide adequate foundations for assessing diversity of
language as both a human problem and a human resource.

"Diversity" could stand as the heading for all of the problems
connected with speech and language, once our focus is enlarged

from languages as such to speech communities--existing diversity
as an obstacle, and sometimes diversity that it is desired to maintain or achieve. Nevertheless, it is worthwhile to comment sepa-
rately on three topics that have been singled out for attention in
their own right. These are problems connected with the media,
the structures, and the functions of language.

Overcoming the Medium of Language. Not long ago one might
have said that most of the world was attempting to overcome the
spokeness of language through programs of literacy, while some
of the advanced sectors of civilization--the advertising and communications industries, and the university--were hailing the im-
minent transcendence of language in graphic form. McLuhan is
less prominent now, but these twin poles of spoken and written
language remain very much with us. A good deal has been said
about speaking and writing, about oral and literate cultures,[21]
and I have no new generalization to add, but I do have a bit of
skepticism to advance. We really know very little as to the role
of the medium of language. Technological determinism is not
generally popular, for good reason, so it is puzzling to find it
avidly welcomed in the sphere of communication. There is no
more reason to regard it as gospel there than elsewhere. Certainly, it is impossible to generalize validly about "oral" vs.
"literate" cultures as uniform types. Popular social science does
seem to thrive on three-stage evolutionary sequences--David
Riesman, Margaret Mead, Charles Reich have all, like McLuhan,
employed them--but if dogmatic Marxism is not to be allowed such
schemes, again for good reason, it really seems a little unfair to
tolerate it in dogmatic McLuhanism.

In such theses, nevertheless, lies a major threat and fascination of media. Is use of one medium of communication rather
than another simply transfer of an underlying competence that
remains constant? Or is there more to it than that? Is the communicative medium itself partly constitutive of meaning, even of
reality, even perhaps of language itself?[22]

Undoubtedly the adaptation of communication to an oral-audi-
tory channel--to mouth, throat, air, and ear--has helped shape
human language [e.g., as to the range in number of phonological
units in languages (a medium with different properties might have
facilitated more or permitted less), and as to relation among units
(sequences, kinds of change) conditioned by the physical characteristics of the sounds]. So much has become a matter of considerable interest to linguists. Not so the adaptation of verbal
communication to a manual-visual channel, to hand, things scrip-
turable, and eye. The origin and history of writing systems has
sometimes attracted interest, but as a separate specialty; linguists
do not think of the written channel as shaping, hence partly ex-
plaining, their object of study.[23] Writing is seen as a record of
something already existing. Interest in the history of writing has
to do with the nature of different modes of representation of

language, their evolution, diffusion, and effect on what one can
know about languages represented by them. Debates about writing have to do with adequacy of different representations (past
or present), and, more generally, with the adequacy of any
written norm as basis for linguistic analysis.

Many modern linguists, reacting against the inadequacies of
conventional writing systems, and the role of conventional writing
systems as symbols of cultural domination, have insisted that
written forms are entirely derivative of speech, entirely secondary, arbitrary, not, as so often thought in traditional cultures,
intrinsic to what is expressed in them. (Hall (1975), for example,
maintains such a view vigorously.) Many linguists associated with
Chomsky's approach have looked more kindly upon conventional
English orthography, reacting against a preceding generation's
reaction against tradition, perhaps, and certainly on general
principle. Whereas the preceding generation emphasized study of
the spoken form of language, Chomsky and others depreciate the
spoken form as a highly imperfect, even "degenerate," manifestation of structure. The net effect is the same. The issue is the
accuracy of a system of writing in representing something else,
the something else being primary. As a secondary realization of
the structure of language (whether in speech or in the mind),
writing has little or no theoretical interest of its own. Independent linguists, such as Dwight Bolinger, H.J. Uldall (1944),
and Josef Vachek (1944-49), have defended the partial autonomy
of writing, as something requiring investigation, but their lead
has been little followed.

The views of American linguists have perhaps been unduly
influenced by the situation of English. The patent discrepancy
between conventional spelling and actual pronunciation helped one
approach dismiss writing; a reaction has led others to profess to
find a close fit between conventional spelling and a phonological
structure imputed to the language (Chomsky and Halle 1968).
(There is of course an interesting fit between conventional spelling and earlier stages of actual pronunciation (e.g., the "gh" in
"right," "night," "light" was once pronounced as in German
Recht, Nacht, Licht).) I am sure this view is mistaken, but no
general principle about writing is at stake, only analysis of English. There are languages whose written form is not a spelling
at all (Chinese), and there are languages whose conventional
written form matches spoken phonology quite well (Spanish).
Wherever English belongs between these two poles, its status is
misleading as a basis for thinking about the relation between
speech and writing.

The point is this: the general issue is not the degree to which
one mode is an accurate expression of the other, or of underlying
structure. Such a formulation limits attention to the relation between speech and writing as one of representation. The general
issue is the relation between speech and writing as *modes of*

action. It is in their status as modes of action that speech and writing fundamentally are related to each other in a society. Diversity and inequality are not manifested in matters of representation alone; they are manifest in what it means to speak, to write (or hear and read), at all, and of course in what it means to do so in one or another way. In sum, the fundamental relation between speech and writing is not that of successive, or correlative, levels of linguistic structure. The fundamental relation is that of choice of means within communicative repertoires. (Clearly my use of "speech," "speaker," etc. in much of this chapter must be understood as surrogate for all communicative modes, wherever speech is not specifically contrasted with others.)

This perspective, that of choice of means embedded in acts, helps keep in view two considerations essential to study of writing: graphic means are not neutral, but have social meaning; graphic means have scope and organization of their own.

As to the first: linguists involved in practical work, such as literacy, standard language planning, and education have long had reason to know that to choose what form of language is to be written, and to choose how it is to be written, are never purely technical matters. Cultural values and social hierarchies are involved. A notable consequence for the situation of language in the world is that many languages, and varieties of language, have not been thought worth writing, or even capable of being written; their written forms, and what exists in them in writing, has come largely from outsiders with a religious or scientific mission. The efforts of outsiders have not always been welcome, and in any case, the sheer fact of the existence of a written form has not been sufficient reason for it to be used. A social interest must be mobilized, as many missionaries have found. (Such facts show that it is silly to explain writing by appeal to its obvious advantages, as if the advantages were self-realizing; more is said on the cultural role of writing below.) Or a social interest may have to be overcome. A technically advantageous form of writing may be rejected because of the prestige of some alternative or to protect some interest. [Thus, the Korean hangul had to wait several centuries and a change of social order to be generally adopted; the government of Somali had to resolve an orthographic impasse by fiat (the solution was indeed in the interest of the country as a whole); Chinese plans for Romanization seem to have been shelved.]

Such questions occur within the United States with regard to the place of varieties of language other than standard English in classrooms, and modes of writing English dialects and Indian languages. A linguist's concern for the efficiency and universality of a phonetic orthography may encounter a Native American's preference for something emblematically different from English symbols, while a linguist taking the standard orthography for granted in his work may unwittingly reinforce social prejudice.

Black parents may react strongly against the suggestion that
their children be taught with materials that represent the speech
of their community, as something distinct from standard English,
while black college students may protest against being penalized
for departures from standard orthographic practice.

Social meaning is not limited to ethnic, regional, or dialect
differences. Joseph Jaquith has pointed out a contrast between
conventional and vernacular spellings, particularly in signs and
advertisements, associated with the durability, cost, prestige of
a product or service. The vernacular spellings employ phonetic
and quasi-phonetic substitutions ("rite," "kwik"), syllabary-like
uses of alphabet letters ("E-Z"), etc. (The vernacular spellings
of words such as "rite," "nite," "lite," incidentally, is evidence
against imputed psychological reality and phonological fit for the
"gh" in the conventional spelling.) Quite within the scope of the
standard language, then, graphic competence in American English
embraces more than one variety of spelling. The relation between
speech and writing has to be discussed in terms of styles of writing, as well as of speech.

The above examples have dwelt on the representational relation of writing to speech, but of course scriptorial competence is
not limited to knowledge of how to represent speech, or structures strictly common to writing and speech alike. In keeping
with a tendency that might be called "communicative plenitude"--
meaningfulness expands to fill available means--the significance of
graphic signs is not restricted to representation of phonic ones or
of an element of structure indicated by both. Nor, of course, is
the significance of a phonic sign restricted to manifestation of a
graphic one, or of an element indicated by both. Users notice
not only the respect in which such signs convey the "referentially-
based" relationships of grammar, but also the respects in which
such signs, and some of their "referentially" indifferent details,
are associated with persons, places, purposes, and styles, are
susceptible to play and aesthetic patterning, etc., and elaborate
these possibilities. Such elaboration gives rise to devices and
relationships that are specific to each medium, having no exact
counterpart in the other, but being part of what one can do with
language only when language is being used in the medium in question. Within the field of language, of competence in language,
styles of speech and styles of writing become partly autonomous
families of symbolic form. Such growth in the range of means is
one respect in which the resources of languages change in scope
in the course of history. Part of the competence in language of
many people is shaped by, must be partly explained by, the
availability and characteristics of graphic channels.

We are often reminded of how much is missed when linguistic
analysis is based on examples that omit essential features of
speech, such as intonation and voice quality. This is indeed a
crucial obstacle to be overcome by linguistics if it is to deal

adequately with language. One seldom thinks of the converse, of
how much is missed when one neglects features specific to writing
and print. It is as if the field of competence in language had the
shape of a butterfly, one wing specific to speaking, one to writing, the body common to both. Linguistic analysis has focused on
the body, as it were, and while that is vital, so are the wings.

Put another way: sometimes to speak is to read aloud, sometimes to write is to transcribe. Such cases of strict equivalence
are special cases, interesting just because of that. Unfortunately,
linguistic analysis has proceeded as if such cases were general.

Having emphasized that speech and writing are not isomorphic,
and have autonomy, I do not want to seem to imply that they are
wholly disjunct. It would be a mistake to postulate a universal,
absolute contrast between styles of speaking and styles of writing.
We need instead to broach the more general topic of *communicative
styles*. The organization of communicative means may follow lines
dictated by modalities, but need not. A style may integrate features from different components of structure (so that a style of
graphic English might select and group together features of
orthography, morphology, syntax, diction, discourse); with regard to any one component, may select some and not other features (e.g., one spelling, alternant, construction rather than another); and may have features uniquely its own (as in a specialized typography); *and* may integrate features from more than one
medium. The integration of spoken and gestural signs within a
communicative paradigm should be well known (for an excellent
analysis of a case, see Sherzer 1973; cf. Hymes 1974a:102). Integration of spoken and graphic signs should not be surprising.
The metalinguistic use of finger-indication of written characters in
the midst of conversation is well enough known from Japan. Ad
hoc hand depiction of letters does occur in interactions in the
United States (quite independently of sign language). The relation between spoken presentation and styles associated with print
(what might be called "scriptive styles") has undergone great
change in the last generation or so, both in lectures and public
talk generally. There has also been a marked rise of engaged
performance, as distinct from prudent reading, by poets. Identification of the social meaning of styles, and analysis of their
appropriateness and effect, must deal with such shifting and
mingling.[24]

In sum, the point of view from which to grasp the relation
between speech and writing, as media or modalities of language,
is function. How are the features of modalities organized for the
purposes of those who employ them?

Having emphasized that speech and writing are to be seen as
modes of action, I do not want to seem to suggest that they are
everywhere the same modes of action. Their degree of autonomy
from each other, their relative hierarchy, their integration into
communicative styles, all these are problematic, and to be

determined ethnographically. As a general principle, one can assume that a difference of means may condition differences in what is accomplished, and that choice of a style specific to speech, or specific to writing, or mingling both, affects meaning and outcome. There is little hard knowledge, however, as to repertoires of choice and strategies for choosing.

As a general principle, one may assume that difference of means will condition differences in what is accomplished; that would seem to hold for the comparative study of symbolic forms as a whole, including those of speech and writing. That speech and writing are not simply interchangeable, and have been developed historically in ways at least partly autonomous, is obvious. There is little hard knowledge, however, as to the degree of autonomy and the consequences of it.

One thing we do know is that a given society may define the role of any one medium quite differently from another society, as to scope and as to purpose. I have elaborated this theme with regard to speaking elsewhere. Here, let me illustrate it briefly with regard to writing.[25] For one thing, new writing systems continue to be independently invented--one was devised in 1904 by Silas John Edwards, a Western Apache shaman and leader of a nativistic religious movement. The sole purpose of the writing system is to record the sixty-two prayers Silas John received in his vision and to provide for their ritual performance. Competence in the system has been restricted to a small number of specialists. Discovery and study of this system by Keith Basso has shown that existing schemes for the analysis of writing systems fail to characterize it adequately, and probably fail as well for many other systems, having been devised with evolutionary, a priori aims, rather than with the aim of understanding individual systems in their own terms. The development of an ethnography of writing, such as Basso is undertaking, is long overdue.[26] Here belongs also study of the many surrogate codes found round the world--drum-language, whistle-talk, horn-language, and the like--for their relation to speech is analytically the same as that of writing,[27] and they go together with the various modalities of graphic communication (handwriting, handprinting, typing, typographic printing, etc.) and the various modalities of oral communication (chanting, singing, declamation, whispering, etc.) in a general account of the relations between linguistic means and ends.

As to ends, the Hanunoo of the Philippines are literate--they have a system of writing derivative of the Indian Devanagari--but they use it exclusively for love-letters, just as the Buan of New Guinea use their writing. In central Oregon the town of Madras has many signs, but the nearby Indian reservation, Warm Springs, has almost none, and those only where strangers impinge--the residents of Warm Springs do not need the information signs give.[28] Recently Vista workers tried to help prepare Warm

Springs children for school by asking Indian parents to read to
them in preschool years. U.S. schools tend to presuppose that
sort of preparation, and middle-class families provide it, showing
attention and affection by reading bed-time stories and the like,
but Warm Springs parents show attention and affection in quite
other ways, had no need of reading to do so, and the effort got
nowhere. The general question of the consequences of literacy
has been forcefully raised for contemporary European society by
Richard Hoggart in a seminal book.[29]

In general, many generalizations about the consequences of
writing and the properties of speaking make necessities out of
possibilities. Writing, for example, *can* preserve information,
but need not be used to do so (recall IBM's shredder, Auden's
"Better Burn This"), and we ought to beware of a possible ethnocentrism in this regard. Classical Indian civilization committed
vital texts to memory, through careful training in sutras, for fear
of the perishability of material things. Classical Chinese cal-
ligraphy, the cuneiform of Assyrian merchants, and the style of
hand taught to generations of Reed students by Lloyd J. Rey-
nolds, are rather different kinds of things. Television may have
great impact, but one cannot tell from what is on the screen
alone. In any given household, does the set run on unattended?
Is the picture even on? Is silence enforced when a favorite program or the news comes on? Or is a program treated as a resource for family interaction?

We have had a great deal more study of means than of meanings. There appear to be many more books on the alphabet than
on the role of writing as actually observed in a community; many
more pronouncements on speech than ethnographies of speaking;
many more debates about television and content-analyses of programs than first-hand accounts of what happens in the rooms in
which sets are turned on. The perspective broached above with
regard to speech communities applies here, since media are a
constituent of the organization of ways of speaking (i.e., ways
of communication). We need particularly to know the meanings of
media relative to one another within the context of given roles,
settings, and purposes, for the etiquette of these things enters
into whatever constitutive role a medium may have, including the
opportunity or lack of it that persons and groups may have to
use the medium. In England a typed letter is not acceptable in
some contexts in which it would be taken for granted in the United
States; the family Christmas letter in the United States is a genre
that can be socially located; subgroups in the United States differ
dramatically in their assumptions as to what should be photo-
graphed and by whom.[30] At Warm Springs reservation last August, at the burial of a young boy killed in a car accident, his
team-mates from the Madras High School spoke haltingly in their
turn beside the grave and presented the parents with a photograph of the boy in athletic uniform, "as we would like to

remember him"--a shocking thing, which the parents stoically let
pass--for the last sight of the dead person, which bears the
greatest emotional distress, had already been endured in the
church before coming to the cemetery. When the rites were complete, Baptist and Longhouse, when all the men, then all the
women, had filed past the gravesite, taking each in turn a handful of dirt from a shovel held out by the uncle of the boy, and
dropping it on the half-visible coffin within the site, when the
burial mound had been raised over the coffin, the old women's
singing ended, and the many flowers and the toy deer fixed
round the mound, then, as people began to leave, the bereaved
parents were stood at one end of the mound, facing the other,
where their friends gathered to photograph them across it. That
picture, of the manifestation of solidarity and concern on the part
of so many, evident in the flowers, might be welcome.

The several media, of course, may occur together in several
mixes and hierarchies, in relation to each other and in relation to
modalities such as touch. Communities seem to differ as to
whether tactile or vocal acts, or both together, are the indispensable or ultimate components of rituals of curing, for example.
In some parts of Africa, languages are evaluated partly in terms
of their greeting systems, and the Haya of northern Tanzania,
who are acquiring Swahili, find it less satisfying than their own
language, for in a Haya greeting one touches as well as talks.[31]

Finally, the use of media and modalities needs to be related
to the norms by which a community takes responsibility for performance and interpretation of kinds of communication. My stress
here obviously is on the qualitative basis of assessing media as a
human problem. Statistics on radios and newspapers and the like
barely scratch the surface. I think it entirely possible that a
medium may have a constitutive effect in one community and not
in another, due to its qualitative role, its social meaning and function, even though frequencies of occurrence may be the same in
both. We have to do here with the question of identities and
identifications, mentioned earlier with regard to varieties of language in schools. We need, in short, a great deal of ethnography.

Overcoming the Structure of Language. Concern to overcome
the structure of language seems to have centered around the function of naming, either to achieve a uniform relation between language and meaning as a semantic ideal, or to avoid it as a spiritual desert or death. Early in the development of Indo-European
studies, when modern languages were thought degenerate in form,
the great pioneer of reconstruction, Franz Bopp, sought to infer
an original Indo-European structure in which meanings and morphemes went hand in hand, reflecting perhaps an original, necessary relationship. Others have sought to realize a semantic ideal
in the present, by constructing an artificial language, or by

reconstructing an existing one to convey the universal meanings
required by science and philosophy. One thinks especially of
the late seventeenth century (Dalgarno, Bishop Wilkes, Leibniz)
and the early twentieth century (Russell, the early Wittgenstein,
Carnap, Bergmann, and others). Still others have thought that
the ideal relationship between meaning and form might be glimpsed
in the future, once linguists had worked through the diverse
structures of existing languages to the higher level of structure
beyond them. Such was Whorf's vision.[32]

At an opposite extreme would be a philosopher like Brice
Parain, who despairs of the adequacy of language, and of course
adherents of the Zen tradition that regards language's inveterate
distinguishing of things as a trap to be transcended. Inter-
mediate would be the conscious defense of other modes of meaning than that envisioned in the "semantic ideal," in particular,
the defenses of poetry and of religious language.[33] And here
would belong conceptions of literary and religious use of language
as necessarily in defiance of other, conventional modes of use.
Much of philosophy and some of linguistics seem to have found
their way back to an open-ended conception of the modes of
meaning in language, and are experiencing great surges of interest in poetics and rhetoric.

Such work is of the greatest importance, but it does leave
the general question of the adequacy of language, or of a particular language, in abeyance. It would seem that the structures of
languages have never been wholly satisfactory to their users, for
they have never let them rest. Shifts in the obligatory grammatical categories of languages over time, like the shift from
aspect to tense in Indo-European, bespeak shifts in what was
deemed essential to convey. Conscious reports of such concerns
may have appeared first in classical Greece, when Plato complained
that the processual character of Greek verbs favored his philosophical opponents, although, at the time, devices such as the
suffix -itos for forming abstract nouns were growing in produc-
tivity. When in the fourth century A.D. Marius Victorinus tried
to translate Plotinus from Greek into Latin, there was no adequate
abstract terminology in his contemporary Latin, and his clumsy
efforts to coin one met with little acceptance, thus inhibiting the
spread of the Neo-Platonic philosophy in that period. Some centuries later "theologisms" had evolved in Latin which quite
matched the terms of the Greek fathers in precision and maneuver-
ability.[34] In the early modern period, English writers lamented
the inadequacies of English and set out to remedy them.[35] At
Warm Springs, some fifteen years ago, a speaker of Wasco (a
Chinookan language), acknowledging Wasco's lack of a term for a
contemporary object, said that when he was a boy, if one of the
old men had come out of his house and seen such a thing, he
would have coined a word for it, "just like that" (with a sharp
gesture). There are no such old men anymore to coin words or
shape experience into the discourse of myth.[36] Such fates are

common, though not much attended to by linguists. The official
preference is to stress the potentiality of a language and to ignore the circumstances and consequences of its limitations. Yet
every language is an instrument shaped by its history and patterns of use, such that for a given speaker and setting it can
do some things well, some clumsily, and others not intelligibly at
all. The cost, as between expressing things easily and concisely, and expressing them with difficulty and at great length,
is a real cost, commonly operative, and a constraint on the theoretical potentiality of language in daily life. Here is the irreduci-
ble element of truth in what is known as the "Whorf hypothesis":
means condition what can be done with them, and in the case of
languages, the meanings that can be created and conveyed. The
Chomskyan image of human creativity in language is a partial
truth whose partiality can be dangerous if it leads us to think
of any constraints on linguistic communication either as nugatory
or as wholly negative. As to the force of such constraints, the
testimony of writers and the comparative history of literary languages should, perhaps, suffice here.[37] As to their positive
side, we seem to need to repeat the development of thought discerned by Cassirer in Goethe, Herder, and W. von Humboldt:

> To them, the Spinozistic thesis, that definition is limita-
> tion, is valid only where it applies to external limitation,
> such as the form given to an object by a force not its
> own. But within the free sphere of one's personality
> such checking heightens personality; it truly acquires
> form only by forming itself.... Every universal in the
> sphere of culture, whether discovered in language, art,
> religion, or philosophy, is as individual as it is uni-
> versal. For in this sphere we perceive the universal
> only within the actuality of the particular; only in it
> can the cultural universal find its actualization, its
> realization as a cultural universal.[38]

We need, of course, ethnography to discover the specific forms
which the realization of universality takes in particular communities, and, where the question is one of speech, we need ethnographies of speaking.

Whorf himself led in describing the organization of linguistic
features pertinent to cultural values and world views as cutting
across the usual sectors of linguistic description, and as involving "concatenations that run across...departmental lines" (that
is, the lines of the usual rubrics of linguistic, ethnographic, or
sociological description that divide the study of a culture and
language as a whole).[39] Whorf referred to the required organization of features as *a fashion of speaking,* and one can see in
his notion an anticipation, though not developed by him, of the
sociolinguistic concept of *ways of speaking.* The crucial difference is that to the notion of speech styles, the sociolinguistic

approach adds the notion of contexts of situation and patterns relating style and context to each other.

Here, as before, the great interest is not merely in diversity or uniformity, but in the possibility that such differences shape or constitute worlds. Do semantic-syntactic structures do so? Sapir and Whorf thought that for the naive speaker they did, although contrastive study of language structures was a way to overcome the effect. What Chomsky describes as the seemingly untrammeled "creative aspect" of language use was treated by Sapir as true, but not true in the same way for speakers of different languages. Each language has a formal completeness (i.e., it shares fully in the generic potentiality of human language), but does so in terms of an orientation, a "form-feeling" of its own, so as to constitute quite a unique frame of reference toward being in the world. A monolingual's sense of unlimited adequacy is founded on universality, not of form or meaning, but of function, and that very sense, being unreflecting, may confine him all the more. The particular strengths of a given language are inseparable from its limitations. This is what Sapir (preceding and giving the lead to Whorf) called

> a kind of relativity that is generally hidden from us by our naive acceptance of fixed habits of speech as guides to an objective understanding of the nature of experience. This is the relativity of concepts, or, as it might be called, the relativity of the form of thought.... It is the appreciation of the relativity of the form of thought which results from linguistic study that is perhaps the most liberalizing thing about it. What fetters the mind and benumbs the spirit is ever the dogged acceptance of absolutes.[40]

I think this is as fair a statement of the evidence and parameters of the situation today as it was a half-century ago when Sapir wrote it. I cite Sapir here partly because I think that linguistics in the United States, having worked its way through a decade or so of superficial positivism, shows signs of having worked its way through another decade or so of superficial rationalism, and a readiness to pick up the thread of the complexly adequate approach that began to emerge in the years just before the Second World War in the work of men like Sapir, Firth, Trubetzkoy, and Jakobson.

To return to relativity: the type associated with Sapir and Whorf in any case is underlain by a more fundamental kind. The consequences of the relativity of the structure of language depend upon the relativity of the function of language. Take, for example, the common case of multilingualism. Inference as to the shaping effect of some one language on thought and the world must be qualified immediately in terms of the place of the speaker's languages in his biography and mode of life. Moreover, communities differ in the roles they assign to language itself in socialization, acquisition of cultural knowledge, and performance. Community differences extend to the role of languages in naming the worlds they help to shape or constitute. In central Oregon, for example, English speakers typically go up a level in taxonomy when asked to name a plant for which they lack a term: "some kind of bush"; Sahaptin speakers analogize: "sort of an A," or "between an A and a B" (A and B being specific plants); Wasco speakers demur: "No, no name for that," in keeping with a cultural preference for precision and certainty of reference.[41]

    This second type of linguistic relativity, concerned with the functions of languages, has more than a critical, cautionary import. As a sociolinguistic approach, it calls attention to the organization of linguistic features in social interaction, and current work has begun to show that description of *fashions of speaking* can reveal basic cultural values and orientations. The worlds so revealed are not the ontological and epistemological worlds of physical relationships, of concern to Whorf, but the worlds of social relationships. What are disclosed are not orientations toward space, time, vibratory phenomena, and the like, but orientations towards persons, roles, statuses, rights and duties, deference and demeanor.[42] Such an approach obviously requires an ethnographic base.[43]

    Overcoming the Function of Language. *Diversity* is a rubric under which the phenomena of language as a human problem can be grasped; the questions which underlie our concern with diversity can be summed up in the term, *function*. What differences do language diversities make through their role in human lives? Some of these differences have been touched upon, and I want to take space for only general consideration here. Linguists have mostly taken the functions of language for granted, but it is necessary to investigate them. Such investigation is indeed going on, but mostly not in linguistics. It is a striking fact that problems of overcoming some of the ordinary functioning of language in modern life attract increased attention from philosophers, writers, and sociological analysts of the condition of communication in society, while many linguists proceed as if mankind became more unified each time they used the word "universal"; freer and more capable of solving its problems each time they invoked linguistic competence and creativity. (This is what I mean by superficial rationalism.)

    Serious analysis of the functioning of language is to be found in England and the continent much more than in the United States. Let me merely mention here Merleau-Ponty on the "prose of the world," Heidegger on speaking as "showing," Brice Parain (already cited) on the inadequacy of language, Barthes on *l'ecriture*, LeFebvre on *discours*, Sartre on precoded interpretations of events such as the Hungarian uprising, and Ricoeur on hermeneutics, and state briefly the significance of two approaches, those of Bernstein and of Habermas.

Bernstein's work has a significance apart from how one assesses his particular studies, which have been considerably shaped by the exigencies of support for practical concerns. His theoretical views, which precede these studies, are rooted in a belief that the role of language in constituting social reality is crucial to any general sociological theory, and that that role has not yet been understood because it has been approached in terms of an unexamined concept of language. For Bernstein, linguistic features affect the transmission and transformation of social realities through their organization into what he calls *codes;* that is, through selective organization of linguistic features, not through the agency of a "language" (e.g., English) as such. He is noted for his twin notions of *restricted* and *elaborated* codes. This dichotomy has not always done the texture of his thought good service, for the two notions have had to subsume a series of dimensions that ought analytically to be separated, and that combine differently in different communities. (See an analysis in Hymes 1974, ch. 4, and discussion below.)[44] Nevertheless, one dimension essential to his work is essential to understanding language as a human problem in the contemporary world. It is the dimension of a contrast between more implicit and more explicit styles.

Let me interpret Bernstein's view of a major importance of the contrast. It is not that one of the styles is "good," the other "bad." Each has its place. The more implicit style, in which many understandings can be taken for granted, is essential to efficient communication in some circumstances, and to ways of life in others. But, and this is an aspect of Bernstein's view that has often been overlooked, the more explicit style is associated with predominantly universalistic or context-free meanings, while the more implicit style is associated with particularistic or context-specific meanings. And, argues Bernstein, the universalistic meanings possible to the more explicit style are essential, if one is to be able to analyze means of communication themselves, the ways in which meanings come organized in a community in the service of particular interests and cultural hegemony, and so gain the knowledge and leverage necessary for the transformation of social relationships.

Bernstein has surely put his finger on a crucial issue. There *is* inequality in command of verbal resources, and in access to them, and it is not the case that inequality would be overcome simply by ending prejudice and discrimination against diverse forms of speech. Some discrimination among verbal abilities and products is not prejudice, but accurate judgment. The transformation of society to a juster, more equal way of life requires transformation of genuine inequalities in verbal resource. But-- here is the crux--we know very little accurately about the distribution of verbal resource and ability in our society. We know too little to be able to specify the nature of the intrinsic inequalities and to judge appropriate remedies. We must be thankful to Bernstein for the courage to insist on an essential truth--within one and the same "language," there are socially shaped contrasts in way of speaking and verbal resource--but we must go beyond his analytic scheme.

The implication of Bernstein's argument is that command of the more explicit style (his "elaborated code") should be made common to all. To apply such a remedy, one would have to enable others to identify reliably the more explicit style, on the one hand, and the desired kind of cognitive power, on the other, and one would have assumed a necessary link between them. Let me suggest some of the difficulties. It would hardly suffice to equate the style with the proprieties of the standard language (although some would be tempted to do so); nor can one equate cognitive power with profusion of words. Certain kinds of analysis of social life no doubt require certain kinds of verbal resource, but we are far from knowing how much of the verbal style in which we couch such analysis now is necessary, how much merely customary. There are verbal repertoires without something of what is necessary--in this I agree with Bernstein. But is the remedy only a matter of lack of certain concepts and terms? Or of certain modes of analytic statement (together with verbal means that facilitate them)? Or of an entire orientation toward meanings, as Bernstein suggests?

There is further difficulty in linking the one style to universalistic, context-free meanings. No use of language, of course, is ever wholly context-free. The indexical function, as Pierce called it, is ever-present and ever essential to interpretation (as Harold Garfinkel has especially stressed in developing the perspective known as "ethnomethodology"). Certainly there are differences in degree of dependence and independence, but their relationship to forms of social life and cognitive power is not self-evident. The distribution of these things within our society is little known. We may think of science and scholarship as dealing in universalistic, context-free meanings, but their work has become highly particularistic and context-dependent, if one thinks in terms of ability and opportunity to share in it. There are large elements of faith and authority, both for those outside these fields and for those within them (as studies in the sociology of science and knowledge show). If public communicability of analytic knowledge is considered, then adaptation to particular contexts of understanding may have an essential role. Some forms of knowledge, indeed, may require "literary" rather than "scientific" methods for their effective transmission, and it is not clear where such verbal methods fit within the contrast in question. The understanding of the perspective of others that is necessary to desired forms of change requires uses of language with narrative and expressive qualities; these qualities often partake of particularistic, context-dependent meanings. It may be that some who

would be said to have an "elaborated code" need greater command
of such qualities, and the devices that convey them, to make
their efforts to change ideas and practices effective. It may be
that some who would be said to have a "restricted code" have
sufficient analytic power, but need command of certain of such
qualities and devices in order to be heard by some they seek to
reach. Finally, we tend to think of explicitness as frankness,
as egalitarian and democratic (at least in public communication),
yet in some societies (cf. Rosaldo 1973) explicitness is experienced as authoritarian, whereas implicitness, allusion, and indirectness is essential to traditional, reciprocal, consensual modes
of resolving issues.

It seems that Bernstein's analytic scheme has inherited a long-
standing tendency to dichotomize kinds of meaning and communication, and to consider kinds primarily in terms of a cognitive
ideal, whereas the actual fabric of relationships among kinds of
meaning, communicative style, and social consequences is intricate.

This is not to depreciate the importance of Bernstein's work.
More than anyone else in sociolinguistics, he has called attention
forcefully to essential dimensions of the organization of ways of
speaking and styles of speech. A contrast or polarity of explicitness and implicitness is probably a universal dimension of means
of speech. The same is true of simplification and complication of
message-form, another dimension associated prominently with the
notions of "restricted" and "elaborated" codes. One or the other
is frequently the salient feature of an important, institutionalized
use of language. There is need for analytic clarification of these
dimensions, as elements of general linguistic theory, and for a
wide range of descriptive and comparative studies. Contemporary
linguistics has given attention to simplification and complication
as aspects of pidginization and creolization, but their universal
relevance has been neglected (cf. Introduction, Part III, in
Hymes 1971; a critical analysis of the notions has been broached
by Mary Hope Lee).

Bernstein himself does not claim validity for his analysis beyond the English situation. The fact that his work attracts
international attention indicates that it corresponds to something
real in other situations; the proper use of the stimulus of his
work is not to impose its categories, or conjure with them, but
to discover the way in which the dimensions to which he calls
attention do come organized in the given case.

In doing so, it is necessary to differentiate dimensions from
one another (e.g., explicitness/implicitness, and complication/
simplification--explicitness may go together with either a complex
or simplified message-form). And it is necessary to disentangle
three factors of communicative events. A broad dichotomy, such
as "restricted" vs. "elaborated" (or some particular dimension),
may easily suggest a contrast that subsumes message-form,

content, and context--restriction (or elaboration), say, in form,
content, and context, all three. The three factors are in fact
analytically, and often empirically, distinct. One must discover
the relationships among them.

In applying the global contrast, or a contrast of dimension,
then, one must not begin with a simple two-fold choice (as many
have done and continue to do). There may be restriction or
elaboration in respect to each factor. Such a contrast (symbol-
ized here R/E) generates eight possible types of relationship, as
the following table shows.

	Message-form	Content	Context
(1)	R	R	R
(2)	R	R	E
(3)	R	E	R
(4)	R	E	E
(5)	E	R	R
(6)	E	R	E
(7)	E	E	R
(8)	E	E	E

The eight-fold framework provides a more adequate, because
more differentiated, starting point, but chiefly it simply illustrates the need of differentiation and needs to be superceded in
the light of empirical work.

Bernstein himself has elaborated his initial dichotomy in
different respects, and it is instructive to consider each critically. One kind of elaboration develops additional distinctions of
content and application (again, cf. reference 44). These distinctions have their own interest; the critical observation to be
made is that the basis of elaboration remains binary contrast in
range of alternatives. At each point, one category has greater,
one lesser, range. Here is the source of a limitation of Bernstein's development of his initial insight, and of applications of
such ideas. First, binary contrasts may be inadequate to the
actual organization of ranges of alternatives. The locally relevant, valid categorization may not be binary, but quantitatively
variable along a scale, may be ternary, etc. If one discovers
local norms, there may be a contrast between two styles, one
more and one less explicit, or complex. There may also be an
unmarked norm, from which a second and third style are distinguished, as markedly more and less explicit, or simple and
complex, respectively. Binary categories, however suggestive,
prejudge.

Second, there is a persistent tendency to interpret the wider
range of alternatives (the "elaborated" category) as more valuable, even though Bernstein himself sometimes cautions against

this. It is hard to avoid such interpretation, especially if one
thinks in terms of a cognitive ideal. "More" suggests more information, more precision, etc. Yet in actual life, forms of
message with the widest range of contexts open to them may be
the least valued, others with a narrower range valued the most.
A message more elaborated in form may be considered more trivial
in content. Evaluation cannot be built into the descriptive framework. Local orientations toward meaning, values, must be discovered. Consider an illustration of rows (5, 6) above. Within
institutions and circles of high prestige, most of the elaboration
of form of a genre of message may be treated as incidental re-
affirmation, even if not predictable in detail, and the key to
interpretation, found in manner or nuance of expression; such
as orientation is very similar to the orientation described for "restricted code" use in Bernstein's initial formulations, and identified there with lower social status. Again, consider an illustration of rows (3, 4). A message may be restricted in form,
highly predictable, context-determined, yet considered rich and
open in content. Men and women of high status, commanding
what their community considers valued elaborated forms, may
give much of themselves to repeated experience of a message, a
piece of music, ritual sequence, literary or religious text, finding, not increase of information so much as increase of connection, resonance, depth. Spareness, predictability, context-
dependence or form may go together with either shallowness or
with depth, with poverty or with richness, of meaning, and so
may prolixity, unpredictability, context-independent of form.
The value of the meaning is analytically independent of the code-
characteristics. There may be a tight connection in particular
cases, but one cannot prejudge what will be connected to what.
        It is indeed an important step toward a pragmatically ade-
quate basis of research just to transect the initial dichotomy with
this one of valued meaning, so as to be able to speak of "deep
elaborated/shallow elaborated" and "deep restricted/shallow restricted" codes, variants, or styles. (Nothing of course depends
on the particular adjectives "deep" and "shallow"; another pair,
such as "thick" and "thin," would serve.)
        This four-fold distinction resembles, but seems different
from, an elaboration that Bernstein himself has made. He has
come to distinguish "codes" from "variants" (Bernstein 1973).
Earlier, some persons had been said to have both elaborated and
restricted codes, and others only restricted codes. Now each
"code" is considered to have both "restricted" and "elaborated"
variants. Obviously this is not to reduce the two codes to
equivalence. "Code" continues to designate an underlying, selective orientation toward kinds and possibilities of meaning. And
it seems that a person is still considered to come to have essentially one code-orientation or the other.
        Now, recognition of parallel variants in both codes does mean

that one cannot readily determine the presence of a "code" from the form of messages. Since much of Bernstein's earlier work sought to identify codes from features of message-form, it is called into question by the change. If the implications of the change are pursued, then future research must concentrate on communicative strategies in natural settings, and employ participant observation fully. Operative orientations toward meanings cannot be assessed adequately from text apart from context. (An apparently "restricted" utterance may be merely practical in a context in which something is known to one's hearer; an apparently "elaborated" utterance may be elaborated from pedantic habit, not cognitive force.) To adapt and revise an assumption once formulated by Martin Joos, by and large "text does not signal its own strategy." Much of what is needed for assessment of orientations is accessible only in persons, not in transcripts. And it becomes essential to speak in the first instance, not of "codes," but of "styles," as I have done earlier in interpreting Bernstein's view of the implicit/explicit dimension. To speak of a "style" leaves open the meaning of the style to those who use it. "Code," in Bernstein's work, does not.

As noted, Bernstein seems to consider that a person comes to have essentially either one code-orientation or the other. The restricted variant of the elaborated code seems intended to account mainly for predictable aspects of social interaction, greetings, casual conversation, and the like (as did the earlier attribution of a restricted code to elaborated code users), rather than for the experience, say, of a middle-class Christian Scientist hearing the Bible and Mary Baker Eddy in fixed text, Sunday after Sunday, and finding new meaning. Bernstein sometimes attends to such situations, but the thrust of his analysis continues to be that the distribution of code-orientations in the society is tantamount to a distribution of people. (Else why distinguish distinct codes as underlying parallel variants?)

I want to suggest that there is something answering to the two types of code-orientation, but not, on that basis alone, two types of people. I want to suggest that *persons in fact have alternative code-orientations*, that such indeed is the common state of affairs in modern society, and that *the central problem is not that some people have one, that others do not* (as most users of Bernstein's ideas have assumed). *The central problem is the management of the relation between the two.* If people differ as types in terms of code-orientations, it is in terms of types of management of the relation. There may be many types of management; there is no reason to assume in advance that there are just two. (For an account of an analogous situation at a national level, cf. Neustupny 1974.)

In sum, each ideal type of code-orientation identified by Bernstein has a necessary part in the life of a person, whatever the person's social origin and experience. Each person must to

some extent project an analysis of the social life and change in
which he or she is caught up, and each must to some extent
"traditionalize" some sphere of experience and relationships.
Both orientations are to some degree inevitable for all. To
understand people in this regard, then, one must think of them
as having *repertoires* of code-orientation, and as having to adapt
to a communicative ecology that favors now one, now another,
element of the repertoire, there being often enough serious tension between person and niche. Many people can be thought of
as having to spend much of their waking life in "verbal passing,"
employing a style constrained by job or group, and unable to
satisfy felt needs for use of language in other ways. Such ecological deprivation may involve lack of others with whom to pursue certain kinds of cognitive elaboration and play, or lack of
others with whom to have certain meanings taken for granted.
Many life choices are made for the sake of "someone to talk to"
in these senses. The problem, then, is not absence of the
orientation in the person, nor absolute absence of contexts for
an orientation, but a specific network of relations between orientations, contents, and contexts.

This analysis brings us to the way in which problems of
modern society have been interpreted as problems of contrasting
code-orientation by Jurgen Habermas.

Habermas develops a contrast analogous to Bernstein's. His
starting point is not observation of class and family differences
in communication, but analysis of theories of knowledge and communication in science and everyday life. Starting from the neo-
Marxian tradition of the Frankfurt School, with its attention to
the Hegelian roots and cultural problems of Marxist thought,
Habermas has turned to the positive contributions of a psycho-
analytic perspective, and the possibilities of grounding in the
nature of language and communication a theory that is critical
of society and emancipatory in aim. He may be said to give a
reinterpretation of Marxian categories of analysis in communicative and linguistic terms.

Like Bernstein, Habermas contrasts two orientations toward
communication. One is a technical cognitive interest, and has
to do with activity guided by technical rules based on empirical
knowledge; such activity comprises "instrumental action systems"
or, generally, "purposive rational action systems." Scientific,
technological, and to some extent bureaucratic modes of ration-
ality and communication are based on this interest. There is,
however, another equally fundamental and valid orientation, a
practical cognitive interest, which has to do with activity
guided by the symbolic processes of everyday life. It is typically dialogic and narrative in its forms of verification and explanation, and involves interpretive understanding and indeed reflexive self-understanding. It cannot be reduced to the models
and formalizations of instrumental action.

It is Habermas' view that whereas the "free market" concept was the dominant ideological rationalization of the capitalist order in the nineteenth century, the notion of "technological progress" serves that role today, and that a great threat to human life in modern society is the invasion of spheres of practical symbolic interaction by the technological orientation. Value preferences and special interests masquerade in the idiom of instrumental necessity; personal and expressive dimensions of meaning become inadmissible over a greater and greater range of activity. Official social science in its positivistic interpretation of its task actually aids in the maintenance and establishment of technological control, in contrast to those trends in social science concerned with understanding socio-cultural life-worlds and with extending intersubjective understanding (what may loosely be called a family of "interpretive" approaches), and those trends concerned with analyzing received modes of authority in the interest of emancipating people from them.

Whereas the criterion of critical evaluation advanced by Marx stressed material inequality, and the contradiction between production for use and production for profit (use-values vs. exchange-values), Habermas stresses communicative inequality and the conflict between an ideal speech situation and communication distorted and repressed by actual patterns of socialization and interaction. To quote him (from his article, "Summation and Response," *Continuum* (Spring-Summer 1970), p. 131, as cited in Schroyer 1975:161):

> We name a speaking-situation ideal where the communication is not only not hindered by external, contingent influences, but also not hindered by forces which result from the structure of communication itself. Only then does the peculiarly unforced compulsion of a better argument dominate.

This conception has left Marxism and much of social science behind. Habermas' ideal adds an invaluable dimension, necessary to critical analysis of social appearances, but there is no adequate link to ongoing social processes and projected states of affairs. Real situations can be criticized in terms of the ideal. No means of progressing toward the ideal, other than criticism, is given. This is why Schroyer (1975) in a sympathetic account considers Habermas only to complement, not to replace, a Marxian analysis of inequality and change. One can go further and suggest that Habermas' analysis contributes only the generic notion of the ideal communicative situation, as a notion that must be integrated into the foundations of a linguistic theory adequate to social life. He does not contribute a satisfactory formulation of the notion.

Notice that the ideal, as formulated by Habermas, is in the end analogous to the ideal implicit in Bernstein's treatment of the "elaborated code." The need for a complementary orientation is sympathetically recognized by both, and Habermas gives it foundation in a thorough-going critique of narrow conceptions of knowledge. But in the end, the role of the mode of symbolic interaction, for Habermas, is to permit complete explicitness. The explicitness is rooted, not in a "code" as such, but in the dialogic relations of the participants in a communicative situation, and that is a decisive advance. But the possibility of a positive role for "restrictions" within symbolic interaction is forgotten. In the light of the ideal (quoted above), all restrictions fall short.

This, I submit, is "utopian," not in the good sense of an imagined ideal, but in the bad sense of an ideal whose unrealizability distorts evaluation of situations and efforts toward change. The ideal of unrestricted speech is said to be inherent in human communication, and it seems to be assumed that the logic of historical development moves toward its realization. An ethnographically informed analysis of ideals of communication suggests otherwise.

The ideal of unrestricted speech is not the sole ideal inherent in attested ways of speaking. In some societies, indeed, unrestricted speech is viewed as dangerous, and the view is pervasively institutionalized (e.g., traditional Ashanti society (Hogan 1971), Burundi (Albert 1964, 1974), Malagasy (Keenan 1973)). Speech as a source of mischief and evil is a recurrent theme in cultural wisdom. Such cases might be said to represent a stage of human history that is to be transcended, and the particular practices may indeed yield to change (they tend to be associated with a dichtomization of sex roles, for example), but the particulars are expressions of functions that appear to be perennial requisites of social life.

Habermas' unique ideal of unrestricted communication is specifically a cognitive ideal of colloquy. It is an ideal of the right and contribution of every member of a group in the resolution of problems. As such, it is an advance over a purely scientific ideal, for it comprises political decision as well (it resembles the ideal of persuasion long advocated by Kenneth Burke, and taken by many to be regulative for science and democracy). But the ideal does not speak to the perennial requisite of structure. What may appear as restriction is from another point of view simply the existence of structure. And it is not possible to envisage viable social life without structure in the sense at least of shared understandings of rights and duties, norms of interactions, grounds of authority, and the like. Even the most free conversational situation, if there is taking of turns, begins inherently to show elements of restrictive structure. Habermas presumably is concerned simply that no structure prevent a member of a group from having a right to participate in decision. But if one considers the possibility as well of an obligation to contribute what one knows and wants, the lack of right to remain silent or refuse commitment to a consensus--real enough issues--one has raised again the matter of constraint. In general, the universality of *appropriateness* as a meaning and ideal of speech is equivalent to the inherent presence of a principle of structure in human speech situations.

Moreover, not all social life is problem-solving and decision-making in the pertinent sense. There are universally satisfactions in uses of language that embody play, employ unequally shared performance abilities, accept ritual-life repetitions of words accepted as authoritative. One can not envisage a viable life in which every point is open to dialogic determination at every point--in which every one can say everything to everyone in every way at every moment in every place. It can be objected that this last is an unfair *reductio ad absurdum*, but Habermas does not show how to avoid such a reduction. Such a reduction can be avoided only by a theory of communicative competence that is based on more than purely rational reflection, that is built up through patient study and comparison of ideals of communication developed in actual communities.

In sum, every known community embodies alternatives to the unique cognitive ideal, and any community (such as a revolutionary group) that could bring closer approximation to the ideal would have to embody alternatives.[45] But the theory can only criticize communicative structure in the light of its absence; it cannot address real structures and choices among them. Yet there lies the true problem for any community and person, revolutionary or not. The problem can be phrased in terms of Habermas' ideal: What costs in communicative inequality should be accepted in order to gain the benefit of greater equality than now obtains? It would be more adequate to say: What kinds of communicative inequality are acceptable, what unacceptable, in the light of the historical situation and aspirations of a given community? (I say "given community," for if a community wished to maintain certain forms of communicative structure, Habermas' ideal would not condone its being "forced to be free.")

The psychiatrically informed ideal of the ending of repressed communication seems faulty on similar grounds. The cognitive ideal, presumably, is that repression that prevents solution of life-problems should be overcome. From this it does not follow that no repression is permissible, that a life should be lived in the light of an ideal of access to all unconsciously held knowledge. One could not play tennis that way--but to be serious, such a prescription would resemble the Christian ideal of a life without hidden sin, and might entail neurasthenia if rigorously observed. A healthy view of the relation between conscious and unconscious knowledge seems to me to be found in the conjunction of a statement by Sapir and a gloss by Zellig Harris (Sapir 1949(1927): 559, Harris 1951: 330):

Complete analysis and the conscious control that comes
with a complete analysis are at best but the medicine of
society, not its food.

Which means: Don't take it as food; but also: Do take
it as medicine.

Bernstein and Habermas are important, influential, and representative in their pioneering efforts to analyze the problems of
linguistic and communicative inequality. Each falls back in a
crucial respect upon a cognitive ideal to which the absence of
restriction, hence "more is better," is intrinsic. Such an ideal
is essential to certain aspects of social problems, but not sufficient to all. Both scholars are able to criticize cultural situations, but not to articulate alternative situations that answer
the cultural nature of human life, that give a legitimate place to
the practicalities of ordinary life and the full range of needs of
human nature. Both have a sense of the range of needs, to be
sure, and other contemporary theorists of language have hardly
addressed the issues at all. Bernstein and Habermas are representative of this situation particularly in the fact that the analysis of each revolves around a dichotomy. The influence of each
reflects the fact that the dichotomy touches something real in
our experience, and also the fact that the realities involved have
only begun to be analyzed. The dichotomies are symptoms of
initial recognition of an issue, first approximations in addressing
it. Knowledge and successful change require us to be able to
link the insights expressed in such dichotomies to actual situations. Such linkage depends on ethnography, and ethnography
will lead to reconstruction of the initial theories in more articulated, diversified form. Communicative theory, as a foundation
of social theory and practice, will be informed by typologies of
cases, and initial dichotomies will give way to sets of dimensions,
diversely hierarchized and apportioned, in justice to the experience and aspirations of specific communities.
     In sum, the problem of overcoming the function of language
is first of all a problem of discovering the functions language
does have. It is important to imagine ideal states of affairs, but
the process of imagining and, equally, of implementing ideal communicative situations should be, as Habermas implies and Bernstein undoubtedly would agree, an open, dialogic one. If diverse
communities and cultural traditions are counted among the voices,
the outcome of such a process is likely to be a plurality of conceptions of what communicative structure should be. For many
communities, the goals of transformation will be not only to overcome obstacles to openness, but also to overcome threats to patterns interwoven with the meaning of a way of life. If we seek
to evaluate such things critically, a comparative ethnographic
perspective is essential, in order to overcome the obstacle of unwitting ethnocentrism in our efforts to think about principles and

premises of verbal interaction. We are likely to extrapolate and project ideal notions of our own tradition, unwittingly misrepresenting the realities of our own conduct and the ideals of others both. For example, many of us would be likely to link Habermas' speaker-situation ideal of unforced compulsion with the explicitness of Bernstein's ideal-type "elaborated code." We tend to think of explicitness (in public communication at least) as frankness, directness, and as egalitarian and democratic in its implications. In many societies, however, explicitness and directness are experienced as authoritarian, something associated with imposed decisions. Implicitness, allusion, and indirectness are associated with traditional modes of resolving issues in reciprocal colloquy (cf. Rosaldo 1973, both on the Ilongot of the Philippines and on the general issue).

Thinking About Linguistic Inequality

Occasionally linguists have been so carried away by ideological certitude as to state that all languages are equally complex. This is of course not so. It is known that languages differ in sheer number of lexical elements by an order of magnitude of about two to one as between world languages and local languages. They differ in number and in proportion of abstract, superordinate terms. They differ in elaboration of expressive and stylistic devices--lexical, grammatical, and phonological. Languages differ in number of phoneme-like units, in complexity of morphophonemics, in complexity of word-structure (both phonological and morphological), in degree of utilization of morphophonemically permitted morpheme-shapes, etc.

The usual view is that such things are distinctions without a difference, that all languages are equally adapted to the needs of those who use them. Leaving aside that such equality might be an equality of imperfect adaptations, speech communities round the world simply do not find this to be the case. They are found to prefer one language for a purpose as against another, to acquire some languages and give up others because of their suitability for certain purposes. No Third World government can afford to assume the equality of the languages within its domain.

The usual answer to this objection is that all languages are potentially equal. In fact this is so in one vital respect; all languages are indeed capable of adaptive growth, and it is a victory of anthropologically oriented linguistic work, particularly, to have established this point. The difficulty with the usual answer is twofold. First, given that each language constitutes an already formed starting point, it is not at all clear that expansion of resources, however far, would result in languages being interchangeable, let alone identical. Limiting consideration to world languages, we find that many who command more than one prefer one to another for one or more purposes, and that

this is often enough a function of the resources of the languages
themselves. The other difficulty is that the realization of potentiality entails costs. The Chomskyan image of the child ideally
acquiring mastery of language by an immanent unfolding misleads
us here. It has an element of truth to which the world should
hearken, but it omits the costs, and the constitutive role of
social factors. Most of the languages of the world will *not* be
developed, as was Anglo-Saxon, into world languages over the
course of centuries. (It is speculated that Japanese may be the
last language to join that particular club.)

I regret to differ from admired colleagues on this general
issue, but it seems necessary, if linguistic work is to make its
contribution to solution of human problems, not to blink realities.
How could languages be other than different, if languages have
any role at all in human life? To a great extent, languages, as
I have said, are what has been made of them. There is an element of truth in the thesis of potentiality and an element of truth
in the thesis of equivalent adaptation across communities, but
both theses fall short of contemporary reality, where languages
are not in fact found unmolested, as it were, one to a community,
each working out its own destiny in an autonomous community.
Not to take the step to that reality is to fall back on the "Herderian" image, a falling back that is all too common. If that image
were a reality, then the analysis of linguistic inequality would
perhaps be only an academic exercise for scholars who take
pleasure in languages the way one may take pleasure in kinds
of music. Given our world, however, analysis of linguistic inequality is of great practical import.

What, then, are the sources and consequences of linguistic
inequality? The kinds of diversity already discussed contribute,
of course, but the plain fact is that having hardly raised the
question we have no clear notion. A Parsonian set of categories
can serve as an initial guide.

First, languages differ in their makeup as adaptive resources;
the linguistic resources of speech communities differ in what can
be done with them, as has been indicated. A generation ago
some kinds of difference were regarded with a spirit of relativistic tolerance, as the special virtues of the languages that had
them, and so one got at least some account of their lexical and
grammatical strengths. The present temper, however, treats
mention of differences as grounds for suspicion of prejudice, if
not racism, so that poor Whorf, who believed fervently in the
universal grounding of language, and extolled the superiority of
Hopi, has become, like Machiavelli, a perjorative symbol for un-
pleasant facts to which he called attention. Until this temper
changes, we are not likely to learn much about this fundamental
aspect of language.

Second, linguistic resources differ as an aspect of persons
and personalities. In addition to the variability inevitable on

genetic grounds, there is the variability due to social patterning. Conceptions of male and female roles, or of specialized
roles, including that of leadership, may differ markedly among
speech communities so that eloquence or other verbal skills may
be necessary for normal adult roles in one society (commonly for
men, not women), and essential to no important role at all in
another. The requirements of a speaking role may be simple,
or subtle and difficult as they are in the special bind of a traditional Quaker minister who had to speak out of spiritual silence
and, desirably, after periods of doubting his calling.[46] Differences in verbal skills desired, of course, feed back upon the
ways in which the linguistic resources of a community are
elaborated.

Third, linguistic resources differ according to the institutions of a community. So far as I know, comparative analysis of
institutions has not much considered the ways in which they do
and do not require or foster particular developments of verbal
skill and resource, or at least has not phrased its findings as
contributions to the understanding of language. There are indeed some analyses of the development of the verbal style and
resources of particular sciences, of science as a social movement,
and of religious and political movements. My impression is, however, that one finds case studies, but not coordinated efforts
toward a comparative analysis and a theory.

Fourth, linguistic resources differ according to the values and
beliefs of a community. Infants' vocalizations, for example, may
be postulated as a special language, one with serious consequences, such that special interpreters are required, so that a
child's wishes can be known and its soul kept from returning to
whence it came. The shaping of linguistic resources by religious
concerns appears to be attracting a surge of interest.[47] A community's values and beliefs may implicitly identify spontaneous
speech as a danger to the cultural order, as among the traditional Ashanti, or they may treat speaking and especially elaborate speaking, as a badge of inferiority, both between persons
and among the orders of a social hierarchy, as is the case with
the Wolof of Senegal. The normal condition of a community may
be constant chatter on the one hand, or pervasive quiet on the
other, according to how speech is valued.

Such a guide to differences does not in itself go beyond a
"Herderian" perspective of discrete speech communities, each
part of the cultural plenitude of the world. Such description
bears on inequality, however, when speech communities are
viewed in a larger context. Differences by themselves would
constitute inequality only in the sense of lack of equivalence,
not in the sense of inadequacy. But just as the resources of a
speech community must be described as speech styles in relation
to contexts of situation, so must they also be assessed in relation
to their contexts when the perspective is that of human problems.

The essential thing seems to me to be to assess the situation of a
speech community in terms of the relation between its abilities
and its opportunities. Every speech community is to some degree
caught up in a changing relationship with a larger context, in
which opportunities for the meaningful use of traditionally
fostered abilities may be declining, and novel opportunities (or
requirements) for which members have not been traditionally prepared may be impinging. The term *competence* should be employed within just such a perspective. It should not be used as
a synonym for ideal grammatical knowledge as by Chomsky, or
extended to a speech community collectively as by De Camp, or
extended to ideal communicative knowledge as by Habermas, or
done away with as Labov would seem to prefer; rather, *competence* should retain its normal sense of the actual ability of a
person. Just such a term is needed to assess the processes at
work in actual speech communities, and their consequences for
persons. *Competence* as a term for ideal knowledge may overcome inequality conceptually for linguists, but only as a term for
the abilities of persons, assessed in relation to contexts of use,
can it help to overcome inequality practically for the members of
speech communities.

Conclusion

To sum up: from one standpoint the history of human society can
be seen as a history of diversity of language, of diversity as a
problem--both diversity of languages as such, and diversity as
to their media, structures, and functions. From another standpoint, that same diversity has been a resource and an oppor-
tunity--for scholars to understand the potentialities of human
language, and for speakers to develop the potentialities of their
forms of life and of their identities.

From antiquity it has been the mark of a true science of man,
of greatness in a science of man, to attempt to comprehend the
known diversity of cultures and history. Herodotus did so in a
narrative of his age's great conflict between East and West, in-
corporating the ethnology of his world. The Enlightenment,
while recognizing a debt to antiquity, was conscious also of the
superiority and the challenge of a new horizon provided by its
knowledge of manners and customs from the New World, and from
remoter Africa and Asia; the Victorian evolutionists, while recognizing an Enlightenment precedent, were conscious of a superiority and the challenge of a new horizon provided by the recent
recognition of the great prehistoric antiquity of man. In this
century there has been no new horizon of data in space or time
that has vivified the whole (unless one counts primate studies
and finds of fossil man as such), but a principle of methodological relativism has been gradually established that is of equal importance. Now we are a juncture where only the future of

man offers the challenge of a new horizon to a science of man; the choices for its future appear to be irrelevance, the service of domination, or the service of liberation through universalization. That is, the sciences of man have developed in the matrix of a certain relationship between one part of the world and the rest; a relationship defined in terms, not of aspirations, but of activities. Anthropology, for instance, is fairly described as the study of colored people by whites.[48] That matrix has changed irreversibly. A science of man limited to certain societies or interests was always implicitly a contradiction in terms; increasingly, it has become an impossibility or a monstrosity. Knowledge about people is a resource, like control of oil and of armies. Nations cannot accept permanent inferiority in this regard. For the social scientist, the problem is complicated by the relations not only between his own country and others, but by the relations between the governments of other countries and their own peoples; for usually any knowledge that he can gain that is worth the having entails entering into a relationship of mutuality and trust with the people he is studying. Thus universalization of the science of man must mean extension not only to all countries of participation, but to all communities. The proper role of the scientist, and the goal of his efforts, should not be "extractive," but mediative. It should be to help communities be ethnographers of their own situations, to relate their knowledge usefully to general knowledge, not merely to test and document. Such a role could be the safeguard of both the intellectual and the ethical purposes of the science itself.

The study of language has had a checkered career in the history just sketched. It first became a self-conscious activity, and to a great extent has developed since, as an instrument of exclusion and domination. The analysis of Sanskrit in ancient India, of classical songs and writings in ancient China, of Greek and then Latin in the ancient Mediterranean, of nascent national languages in the Renaissance (e.g., Nebrija's grammar of Castilian), were all in the interest of cultural hegemony. It is only in our own century, through the decisive work of Boas, Sapir, and other anthropologically oriented linguists (as components of the general triumph of "methodological relativism" in the human sciences), that every form of human speech has gained the "right," as it were, to contribute on equal footing to the general theory of human language.

The present situation of linguistics in the United States is quite mixed, where it is not obscure. Chomskyan theory holds out the liberation of mankind as an aspiration, but its practice can contribute only conceptually at best, if it does not in fact stand as an obstacle to the kind of work that is actually needed. This paper has argued for the study of speech communities as actual communities of speakers. In this way we can go beyond a liberal humanism which merely recognizes the abstract

potentiality of all languages, to a humanism which can deal with
concrete situations, with the inequalities that actually obtain, and
help to transform them through knowledge of the ways in which
language is actually organized as a human problem and resource.

References

1.   Jean-Jacques Rousseau, *Discourse on the Origin and
Foundations of Inequality Among Men* (1756), trans. Roger D.
and Judith R. Masters, *The First and Second Discourses*, ed.
Roger D. Masters (New York: St. Martin's Press, 1964).
2.   Noam Chomsky, *Problems of Knowledge and Freedom*
(New York: Pantheon Books, 1971).
3.   Edward Sapir, "Psychiatric and Cultural Pitfalls in the
Business of Getting a Living" (1939), *Selected Writings of Edward Sapir*, ed. D. G. Mandelbaum (Berkeley and Los Angeles:
University of California Press, 1949), p. 578.
4.   "Linguistic Theory" ought to refer to a general theory
of language, or at least a general theory of the aspects of language dealt with by linguists, but it has been appropriated recently for just those aspects of language dealt with in transformational generative grammar--another instance of Chomsky's
skill as a polemicist.   Hence the quotation marks.
5.   W. M. Urban, *Language and Reality: The Philosophy of
Language and the Principles of Symbolism* (London: George Allen,
1939), p. 23.
6.   Edward Sapir, "Language," *Encyclopedia of Social
Sciences*, IX (New York: Macmillan, 1933), pp. 155-169, cited
from *Selected Writings of Edward Sapir*, ed. Mandelbaum, p. 11.
7.   G. J. Metcalf, "The Development of Comparative Linguists in the Seventeenth and Eighteenth Centuries: Precursors
to Sir William Jones," and P. Diderichsen, "The Foundation of
Comparative Linguistics: Revolution or Continuation?" *Studies
in the History of Linguistics*, ed. Hymes (Bloomington: Indiana
University Press, forthcoming).
8.   Discussed in Hymes, "Lexicostatistics and Glottochronology
in the Nineteenth Century" (with notes toward a general history),
Proceedings of the Conference on Genetic Lexicostatistics (tenta-
tive title), ed. I. Dyen (The Hague: Mouton, forthcoming).
9.   M. Swadesh, *Origin and Diversification of Languages*
(Chicago: Aldine, 1971).
10.   N. Chomsky, *Cartesian Linguistics* (New York: Harper
and Row, 1966).
11.   F. Boas, "The Classification of American Languages,"
American Anthropologist, XXII (1920), 367-376.
12.   "The Problem of Linguistic Communication in the Modern
World," *La Monda Lingvo-Problemo*, III, No. 9 (1971), 129-176.
13.   G. Steiner, *Extraterritorial* (New York: Atheneum, 1971),
p. 70.

14. Hymes, "Introduction to Part III," *Pidginization and Creolization of Languages*, ed. Hymes (London and New York: Cambridge University Press, 1971), p. 73.

15. There are noble exceptions--Schuchardt in the seventeenth century, for one, and the Prague School and J. R. Frith in the twentieth century, but the main thrust of successive developments has been as described. Transformational grammar is included under structural method here because it shares the same assumptions when contrasted to a functional approach; cf. the contrast drawn in Hymes, "Why Linguistics Needs the Sociologist," *Social Research*, XXXIV, No. 4 (1967), 632-647.

16. L. Bloomfield, *Language* (New York: Holt, Rinehart & Winston, 1933), Ch. 3, and N. Chomsky, *Aspects of the Theory of Syntax* (Cambridge: M.I.T. Press, 1965), p. 3.

17. Assumptions as to the bases of mutual intelligibility, and as to relations among linguistic boundaries, ethnic boundaries, and communication are analyzed in Hymes, "Linguistic Problems in Defining the Concept of 'Tribe,'" *Essays on the Problem of Tribe*, ed. J. Helm (Seattle: University of Washington Press for the American Ethnological Society, 1968).

18. H. Wolff, "Intelligibility and Inter-Ethnic Attitudes," *Anthropological Linguistics*, I, No. 3 (1959), 34-41.

19. This conception is dealt with in more detail in my "Introduction" to *Language in Society*, I, No. 1 (1972), 1-14, and "The Scope of Sociolinguistics," *Report of the 23rd Annual Round Table Meeting on Linguistics and Language Study; Sociolinguistics*, ed. R. W. Shuy (Washington, D.C.: Georgetown University Press).

20. On complex linguistic communities, see C.A. Ferguson, "National Sociolinguistic Profiles," *Sociolinguistics*, ed. W. Bright (The Hague: Mouton, 1966). On comparative study of the role of speaking, see Hymes, "Two Types of Linguistic Relativity," *ibid.*, and "Models of the Interaction of Language and Social Life," *Directions in Sociolinguistics: The Ethnography of Communication*, eds. J. Gumperz and D. Hymes (New York: Holt, Rinehart & Winston, 1972), pp. 35-71. The work of John Gumperz and William Labov has been of special importance to the understanding of the problems dealt with in this and the preceding note.

21. D. Wade, "The Limits of the Electronic Media," *T.L.S. Essays and Reviews*, V (May 1972), 515-516.

22. The following 14 paragraphs are added to the original article. The additional references, in order of occurrence, are: Dwight L. Bolinger, "Visual Morphemes," *Language*, 22 (1946), 333-340; R.A. Hall, Jr., "Review of J. Vachek, *Written Language: General Problems and Problems of English*," *Language*, 51 (1975), 461-5; H. J. Uldall, "Speech and Writing," *Acta Linguistica*, 4 (1944), 11-16; J. Vachek, "Some Remarks on Writing and Phonetic Transcription," *Acta Linguistica*, 5 (1944-49), 86-93; N. Chomsky and M. Halle, *Sound Pattern of English* (New York: Harper and

Row, 1968); Joseph Jaquith, unpublished MS.; Joel F. Sherzer, "Verbal and Nonverbal Deixis in San Blas Cuna," *Language in Society*, 2(1) (1973), 117-132; D. Hymes, *Foundations in Sociolinguistics* (Philadelphia: University of Pennsylvania Press, 1974), p. 102.

23.   The possibility is considered by Joseph Greenberg (*Anthropological Linguistics* (New York: Random House, 1968), p. 133) in the course of a lucid account of approaches to language classification.   He suggests the semantic features of richness in quasi-synonymity as a possible example of a characteristic that would permit one to treat languages that exist in written form as a class from the standpoint of linguistics proper.   Greenberg's requirement is that the linguistically external fact of a functional role go together with internal facts of structure.   In what follows I argue that the fact of written form does not itself uniquely determine functional role; there is need for a typology within the category, "language with a written form."   Greenberg's requirement would still hold for several types within the category, provided the notion of "internal facts of structure: is interpreted in the broad sense of the organization of means of speech (and writing), not in the narrow sense of grammar proper.

24.   Both plenitude and integration are perhaps illustrated by traditional and vernacular styles pointed out by Jaquith.   Each may entail something in speech.   A sign in one spelling may perhaps be read aloud in one way, a sign in the other in another. If so, if "right" et al. go with one spoken style, "rite" et al. with another, the differences cannot be in the sounds the letters are considered to spell.   The spelled sounds are the same.   The differences would be in sub-phonemic detail, tempo, voice quality, intonation, and perhaps other aspects of manner.

25.   See works cited in reference 20 and, on writing, "Toward Ethnographies of Communication," *The Ethnography of Communication*, eds. J. Gumperz and D. Hymes (Washington, D.C.: American Anthropological Association, 1965), pp. 24-25.

26.   K. Basso and N. Anderson, "The Painted Symbols of Silas John: A Western Apache Writing System," *Science*, CLXXIX (forthcoming in 1973).

27.   T. Stern, "Drum and Whistle Languages: An Analysis of Speech Surrogates," *American Anthropologist*, LIX (1957), 487-506.

28.   These observations are from the work of Susan Philips, to be presented in an article in *Foundations of Language Development*, eds. E. and E. Lenneberg, sponsored by UNESCO.

29.   R. Hoggart, *The Uses of Literacy* (London: Chatto and Windus, 1957); note the introduction to the French edition, *Working Papers in Cultural Studies*, trans. J. C. Passeron (Birmingham: Centre for Contemporary Cultural Studies, University of Birmingham, 1971), pp. 120-131.

30.   The ethnography of taking pictures in U.S. society is being studied by Richard Chalfen of Temple University; see Sol Worth, *Through Navaho Eyes* (Bloomington: Indiana University Press, 1972).

31.   I owe this information to Sheila Seitel.

32.   B. L. Whorf, "Language, Mind and Reality," 1942; cited from *Language, Thought, and Reality: Selected Writings of Benjamin Lee Whorf*, ed. J. B. Carroll (Cambridge: The Technology Press, 1956), pp. 246-270.

33.   B. Parain, *Petite Métaphysique de la Parole* (Paris: Gallimard, 1969), translated as *A Metaphysics of Language* (Garden City, N.Y.: Doubleday, Anchor Books, 1971); K. Burke, "Semantic and Poetic Meaning," *The Philosophy of Literary Form* (Baton Rouge: Louisiana State University Press, 1941); E. L. Mascall, *Words and Images* (London: Darton, Longman and Todd, 1968); I. T. Ramsey, *Religious Language* (New York: Macmillan, 1957).

34.   From a comment by G. E. von Grunebaum, in *Language in Culture*, ed. H. Hoijer (Chicago: University of Chicago Press, 1954), pp. 228-229.

35.   R. F. Jones, *The Triumph of the English Language* (Stanford: Stanford University Press, 1953); cf. F. Brunot, "La Propagation du français en France jusqu'à la fin de l'Ancien Régime," *Histoire de la Langue Française des Origines à 1900*, VII, 2nd ed. (Paris: Colin, 1947), and E. A. Blackall, *The Emergence of German as a Literary Language* (Cambridge: Cambridge University Press, 1959).

36.   E. Sapir, *Wishram Texts* (Leiden: E. J. Brill, 1909), p. 48, lines 1-2.

37.   E.g., Eliot's "one has only learnt to get the better of words/For the thing one no longer has to say, or the way in which/One is no longer disposed to say it." *Four Quartets* (New York: Harcourt Brace, 1943), p. 16.   The general question of the "Herderian" standpoint and of the mixed standing of linguistic resources as determinants is reviewed in Hymes, "Linguistic Aspects of Comparative Political Research," *The Methodology of Comparative Research*, eds. R. T. Holt and J. E. Turner (New York: The Free Press, 1970), pp. 295-341.

38.   E. Cassirer, *The Logic of the Humanities* (New Haven: Yale University Press, 1961), pp. 24-25.

39.   B. L. Whorf, *The Relation of Language to Habitual Thought and Behavior* (1941), cited from Carroll, *Selected Writings of B. L. Whorf*, pp. 158-159.

40.   E. Sapir, *The Grammarian and His Language* (1924), cited from *Selected Writings of E. Sapir*, ed. Mandelbaum, pp. 153, 157.

41.   From work of David French.   On the general issue, see my papers cited in reference 20.

42. H. M. Hogan, "An Ethnography of Communication among the Ashanti," *Penn-Texas Working Papers in Sociolinguistics*, I (Austin: University of Texas, Department of Anthropology, 1971); R. Darnell, "Prolegomena to Typologies of Speech Use," *Texas Working Papers in Sociolinguistics* (Austin: University of Texas, Department of Anthropology, 1972), and papers by J. T. Irvine, E. O. Keenan, and J. F. Sherzer in *The Ethnography of Speaking*, eds. R. Bauman and J. F. Sherzer (London and New York: Cambridge University Press, forthcoming).

43. M. Cole, J. Gay, J. A. Glick, D. W. Sharp, *The Cultural Context of Learning and Thinking* (New York: Basic Books, 1971) is an excellent demonstration of the necessity of ethnography for assessment of linguistic and cognitive abilities, even though, unfortunately, the authors do not disclose the linguistic characteristics of the material on which their work rests.

44. The following 34 paragraphs are added to the original article. The references in this section, in order of occurrence, are: D. Hymes, *Foundations in Sociolinguistics* (Philadelphia: University of Pennsylvania Press, 1974); B. Bernstein, "A Critique of the Concept 'Compensatory Education,'" *Functions of Language in the Classroom*, eds. C. Cazden, V. John-Steiner, and D. Hymes (New York: Teachers College Press, 1972); M. Rosaldo, "I have Nothing to Hide: The Language of Ilongot Oratory," *Language in Society*, 2 (1973), 193-223; Hymes, "Introduction, Part III," *Pidginization and Creolization of Languages* (London and New York: Cambridge University Press, 1971); B. Bernstein, *Class, Codes, and Control, II* (London: Routledge, Kegan Paul, 1973); Martin Joos, "Linguistic Prospects in the United States," *Trends in European and American Linguistics 1930-1960*, eds. C. Mohrmann, A. Sommerfelt, and J. Whatmough (Utrecht and Antwerp: Spectrum, 1961); J. Habermas, *Knowledge and Human Interests* (Boston: Beacon Press, 1971); T. Schroyer, "A Reconceptualization of Critical Theory," *Radical Sociology*, eds. J. D. Colfax and J. L. Roach (New York: Basic Books, 1971); Schroyer, "Toward a Critical Theory for Advanced Industrial Society," *Recent Sociology No. 2*, ed. H. P. Dreitzel (New York: Macmillan, 1970); Habermas, "Toward a Theory of Communicative Competence," in Dreitzel, op. cit.; J. B. Neustupny, "The Modernization of the Japanese System of Communication," *Language in Society*, 3 (1974), 33-48; T. Schroyer, "The Critique of Domination," *The Origins and Development of Critical Theory* (Boston: Beacon Press, 1975); Helen M. Hogan, "An Ethnography of Communication Among the Ashanti," *Penn-Texas Working Papers in Sociolinguistics, I* (Austin: University of Texas, Department of Anthropology, 1971); Ethel Albert, "'Rhetoric,' 'Logic,' and 'Poetics' in Burundi: Cultural Patterning of Speech Behavior," *Directions in Sociolinguistics*, eds. J. Gumperz and D. Hymes (New York: Holt, Rinehart and Winston, 1972); Elinor Ochs Keenan, "A Sliding Sense of Obligatoriness: The Poly-Structure of Malagasy Oratory," *Language in Society*, 2 (1973),

225-243; E. Sapir, "The Unconscious Patterning of Behavior in Society," *The Unconscious: A Symposium*, ed. E. S. Dummer (New York: Knopf, 1927), reprinted in *Selected Writings of Edward Sapir*, ed. D. G. Mandelbaum (Berkeley and Los Angeles: University of California Press, 1949), 544-559; Zellig S. Harris, "Review of *Selected Writings of Edward Sapir*," *Language*, 27 (1951), 288-333.

45. Cf. these lines from a poem from a conscientious-objector camp in Oregon in World War II:

> The pacifist speaks, / Face to face with his own kind, / And seeks to fashion a common course / That all may mark. / But whatever he offers, / Finds already framed in another's thought / A divergent approach. / The binding belief that each allows / Is cruxed on rejection: / *Thou shalt not kill.* [stanza] But for all the rest, / What Voice shall speak from the burning bush, / In the work-site noons, / When the loaf is broken, / And brief and rebuttal countercross, / And no one wins? (William Everson).

46. R. Bauman, "Speaking in the Light: The Role of the Quaker Minister," *The Ethnography of Speaking*, eds. Bauman and Sherzer.

47. Papers on language and religion from a working group at the 1972 Georgetown Round Table Conference; it is expected that these papers will be published under the editorship of W. Samarin.

48. W. S. Willis, Jr., "Skeletons in the Anthropological Closet," *Reinventing Anthropology*, ed. D. Hymes (New York: Pantheon, 1973). This discussion draws on my introduction to the book.

qualitative/quantitative research methodologies in education: a linguistic perspective[1]

The study of language has a special role to play when one seeks to come to terms with the relation between quantitative and qualitative methods. The rise of linguistics in this century as an autonomous discipline is based on the discovery of a qualitative methodology. The success of linguists in discovering relationships that are capable of rigorous formulation, of patent reliability and validity, without recourse to numbers, has stood as an object lesson. It is an object lesson that has been heeded most of all in anthropology, where it is familiar in writings of Sapir, Kluckhohn, Lévi-Strauss, Goodenough, Lounsbury, Frake, and others, and has spawned a series of special approaches and debates. (One can mention componential analysis, ethnoscience, structural analysis of myth, paralinguistics and kinesics, and various forms of semiotics.) For whatever reason, this import of linguistics has not been particularly discussed in educational anthropology. I should like to sketch its history and present standing, so as to indicate both the value and the limitations of the perspective it brings. Linguistics is increasingly being extended today through attention to social context and use. Such attention entails ethnography, and I will end by trying to say how the linguistics and the ethnography fit.

I

A few dates and historical reference points are needed. Most people may not realize that there were no departments of linguistics in this country before the Second World War. The professional association of linguists, the Linguistic Society of America, is only 51 years old, roughly half the age of the major social science associations founded in the latter part of the preceding century. Fifty years ago what we consider the study of language was mostly the study of individual languages and language families, Indo-European having pride of place. Study of general linguistics, and study of Indo-Euorpean languages, as its foundation, were often considered equivalent. In the 1930s the introductory courses at the first Linguistic Institutes sponsored by the new Linguistic Society focused on Indo-European languages.

There were of course students of language in general. But if one sought a career in the study of language, one pretty much

had to choose between becoming a specialist in the languages and
literatures of some major language group of European fount, or
becoming an anthropologist who could write down languages mostly
unwritten. All this changed and changed dramatically. It
changed in connection with the exploitation of a little-noticed gap
in the existing academic citadel: the sounds of language. The
study of speech sounds was hithergo either taken up within individual languages, language families (Romance, Germanic, Slavic),
or taken up as an aspect of psychophysics, of phonetics as a
distinct physical science. For the former purpose, the analysis
was specific to the languages in question. For the latter purpose, one sought exactness of measurement. For many students
of language, the two activities were wholly separate categories.
To study languages was a human (or "moral" or "mental") science:
a *Geisteswissenschaft*. To study speech sounds, those physical
phenomena, was something altogether different: a *Naturwissen-
schaft*.

What happened in the 1920s and 1930s was that the men we
now revere as founders of the discipline of linguistics--men such
as Edward Sapir and Leonard Bloomfield in the United States--
created a methodology, a qualitative methodology, which on the
one hand generalized the insights into particular patterns of
speech sound from the study of particular languages, and on the
other hand transcended the phonetics of pure physical measurement. What they accomplished is loosely called the discovery of
the concept of the phoneme and the creation of phonology as an
entirely general science of the systematic properties of the dimension of language having to do with sounds. What they did, in
effect, was to integrate the study of sounds in general into a
Geisteswissenschaft of language study by replacing one conception
of rigor with another. Rigor of measurement was replaced by
rigor of functional contrast.

The classical locus of this discovery in American linguistics is
the 1925 paper by Sapir, "Sound patterns of language." From
that paper has flowed not only much of the development of methodology in linguistics, but also much of the effect that linguistics
has had on conceptions of methodology for the study of behavior
more generally (see Hymes 1970).

Sapir's essential point was the distinction between a physical
event and an element in a system of signs. The distinction was
dramatized by consideration of cases in which one and the same
physical feature could have entirely different significance, depending first of all on whether or not it was an element in a system of
signs, and, if it was, then on the relations into which it entered
in the particular system of signs to which it belonged. As to the
first, Sapir considered the difference between a breath through
pursed lips to extinguish a candle, and such a breath as the beginning of an English word such as "when" (when pronounced in
the standard form with the aspiration (hwen)). [2] The initial
breath of the English word can distinguish forms within the

language (hwen : wen (of the skin)), can be an object of attention as a difference (sometimes stigmatized) between styles of
speech with regard to the adverb "when" itself, and makes possible exact or approximate puns (as in commenting on someone's
reiterated "When?" with "This must be W(h)ensday."). More
strikingly for the subsequent development of phonology, linguistics, and anthropology, Sapir compared hypothetical inventories
of sounds for whole languages. Two languages might have identical inventories of sounds, according to observations of physical
properties; yet when the functional relations among the sounds
within the system of the language were considered, the two languages might be found to have quite different patterns, configurations, or structures of elements. In each, for example,
one might hear both "p" and "b," "t" and "d," "k" and "g."
In the one, such a minimal difference might be functional, serving to distinguish words by itself. A word beginning with (p)
would be a different word from one otherwise the same but beginning with (b), and so on. In the second language, the difference between the two types of sound might not be functionally
relevant. It might be a predictable alternation ((b) perhaps
occurring always between vowels, and (p) never). In the second
language there would be, from the standpoint of functional relevance, just one series of stops that could best be written /p t k/
(since it is the "voiced" sounds, b, d, g, that are predictable
from their environment). In the first language, there would be
two series, /p t k/ and /b d g/. To repeat, the difference between the languages would lie, not in the presence or absence of
observed sounds, but in the status of the observed sounds within
the system of the language. And the principle that determines
the status is qualitative, an all-or-nothing principle that leads to
invariant, fixed reference points. From this perspective, there
is not such a thing as more or less of such a unit. There is
rigor in the work, and a branch of formal scientific inquiry to
which to appeal, but it is qualitative and discrete mathematics,
not statistics or experimental measurement.

Sapir went on to complete the picture by considering two inventories that were different as observed sets of sounds but
identical, once analyzed in terms of functional relevance, as elements within a system of mutually contrasting points in a pattern.
A brief illustration: one language might have (p t k) as stops,
all functionally relevant. A second language might have (p t k)
and (b d g) as well, but, like the second language in the previous example, no relevant distinction between the two series.
In sum, there would be three observed stops in the one language,
six in the other, but just three systemically relevant units in
each.

Some linguists resisted the development of phonology, feeling
that it began to leave behind the concrete realities of the sounds
of language. For to the principle of contrastive relevance (often
called the principle of communication), was added concern with

symmetry and simplicity of the systems disclosed, and concern with elegant solutions to the sometimes complex consequences of tension between the phonological and the other sectors of a language. Sound patterns of languages are subject to the strains of historical change and communicative specialization, to the sometimes contrary pushes and pulls of external adequacy + internal economy, with grammatical and lexical considerations sometimes taking priority. Logical models invite a conception of a language as a monolithic system, with the meaning at one end and sounds or letters at the other, but history and comparative perspective quickly show that a more adequate conception is one of languages as composed of interconnected major sectors, somewhat like interconnected continental shelves whose occasional displacements can create untidy interfaces. The interrelation between phonology and the rest of a language is often one such untidy interface. In some languages the interrelation can be specified with few detours and only occasional mounds and valleys, whereas in others it is rather as if a mountain range had been thrown up.

II

The point of this extended analogy is that language is not as neat as linguists sometimes make it out to be. Herein lies the limitation of the lesson from linguistics. Any consideration of qualitative methodology in the study of human life must take into account the success of linguistics in establishing a domain of study, central to human life, that has a methodology that is at once qualitative and rigorous. But our consideration cannot leave matters there. The student armed with qualitative methodology can be just as a priori in assumption, just as prone to overlook disquieting empirical facts, just as heavy-handed in the service of his methodological god as can the quantitative researcher of fabled evil. In short, the success of linguistics is often appealed to, and rightly so, as evidence that quantitative methodologies are not sufficient, not the only model of rigorous science, in the human sphere. That lesson is a crucial lesson. There is a tendency perhaps for the sophisticated statistician or sensitive experimentalist to believe that all methodologies ultimately reduce to his. Qualitative insight and observation may be given great scope, mindless counting depored, but still the belief is that the final test comes with the quantitative or experimental design. This belief is unfounded, and linguistics shows it to be so. At the same time it is essential not to fall into the trap of believing that the foundations of linguistics as presently practiced are adequate and secure, such that quantitative measurement and experimental design can only complement and come after findings obtained by other means. This belief is the inverse of the other, and it is prevalent in American linguistics. It is equally unfounded.

The history of psycholinguistic research since the early 1940s shows the truth of the matter. At first in the study of the acquisition of language it was necessary to learn what in fact was acquired. Gradually psychologists interested in child development and language acquisition became knowledgeable about phonological and morphological units. The work of Roger Brown and numerous associates is noteworthy here. Once the rule-governed nature of language was utilized in planning research, one could investigate the presence or absence, and the stages of acquisition, of the specific rules. One could go beyond gross measures of length of utterance and the like to specific properties of the system concerned. It is rather like being able to go beyond comparisons of motors in terms of external properties such as size or color, to analyses of engines in terms of internal properties such as combustion pressure or piston rate.

When the course of modern linguistics reached syntax (having started out, as we have seen, with a focus on phonology), and when controversy over models of syntax was resolved effectively in favor of transformational-generative grammar, begot by Chomsky out of Harris, it seemed to some psycholinguists that almost a millenium was at hand. George Miller, who had been prominently associated with the development of information theory, became a convert--a nice example of a conversion from a quantitative to a qualitative "paradigm" (although not with loss of experimental design). Experiments based on the Chomskian model gave initially exciting results. It seemed that the grammatical model and psychological reality were twins, and the job of psychology was to devise ingenious experiments on the basis of the linguistic model. A few years later the bloom was off that particular rose. The relation between psychological reality (the mechanisms of the mind) and grammatical theory (the mechanisms of a model of grammar) came to seem increasingly remote. Indeed, a number of psychologists have come to the conclusion that experimental analysis of relations between linguistic elements is itself a primary source of knowledge. A certain command of linguistics is required in order to deal with the units of language, but where relationships among the units is in question in terms of alternative models, experimental study need not wait upon the linguist. To be sure, Chomsky has consistently maintained that other kinds of study concerned with language must wait upon the outcome of his. But that contention is increasingly ignored. We see some of the productive outcome of such independence in studies discussed by Cazden (1977) and Shuy (1977), and the use of such terms as "ecology of language," "functional linguistics," and "communicative competence."

In this history, there is a second methodological lesson from linguistics. It has to do with validity as much as does the first. The first lesson has to do with validity in the sense of structure. the second has to do with validity in the sense of function. The two are indeed interrelated. What Sapir showed with regard to phonology was that recognition of structure depended upon

recognition of functional relevance. The acutest ear, the most
careful design, could not take the fundamental first step in the
analysis of sound patterns in language, so long as the presence
of pattern was not understood to depend upon the linguist's version of experimental control, the test of commutation.[3]

The fundamental elements of a system were determined in
terms, not of the relationship of sound to sound alone, but in
terms of the relationship of sound to sound in the service of distinguishing units of another level (words, sentences). And internal analysis of the relationships among such elements might
result in patterns that were rather different than observable
patterns.

Linguists both learned and neglected this lesson in subsequent stages of their discipline. They learned it for phonology,
as against phonetics, and for morphology, but many resisted it
for a time when it became an issue with regard to syntax. The
structure of sentences was studied in terms of similarities in the
distribution of elements within sentences of the same type. Sentences such as "John is easy to please" and "John is eager to
please" would be seen as sentences of the same type, and "easy"
and "eager" as words of the same type. They contrasted as
words, of course (another instance of form/meaning covariation),
but not in terms of grammatical function. Chomsky's view,
crudely put, was that fundamental syntactic structure depended
upon recognition of functional relevance at a further level. This
level was discernible when sentences of a different type and different in overt pattern were seen to be related, sharing invariant
sets of grammatical functions and derivable from one another, or
from a common base, by regular rules, and seemingly similar sentences and words to be different by the same token. "John is
easy to please," "It is easy to please John," "Pleasing John is
easy," show a common core of meaning and functional relationship
among the elements "John," "please," and "easy." And "John is
easy to please" no longer appears the simple analogue of "John is
eager to please," when the same commutation test across that set
of sentence types yields unacceptable sequences, *"It is eager to
please John," *"Pleasing John is eager." (The asterisk marks the
unacceptable sequences.)

It is fair to see here a parallel to the lesson Sapir taught in
"Sound Patterns of Language." A major characteristic of the syntactic work inspired by Chomsky was that seeming diversities
among sentences were found to have an underlying unity, and
seeming likenesses an underlying difference.

Having established this lesson in syntax, Chomsky was to be
confronted by students who insisted on applying it again in semantics. Syntactic relationships that were clear and distinct
according to his model came to seem not so to them, when viewed
from the standpoint of semantic relationships. The dispute between those insisting on the primacy of syntactic relationships and
those insisting on the primacy of semantic relations continues.

And Chomsky, having established syntax to his own satisfaction
as the core of language, insisted that studies of use, of styles
and such, was as dependent on the results of syntax, as any
other study of language. But this is a partial truth. To be
sure, as Cazden points out (quoting Crystal), one must attend
to the specific units of language or one will not see any relationships at all (just as ignorance of the speech sounds of a foreign
language will yield a sense of noise, not of phonology). But the
relationships that are there will not all come into view if one stays
at a given level. Each functional sector or level of language
organizes units in a way not given by the units themselves. To
use an old example of mine, the functional category of greetings
may range from single morphemes to complex sentences, from "Hi"
to "Well, I'll be a son of a gun, if it isn't Sid Mintz" (Hymes
1964). Nothing in syntactic analysis itself would bring these two
together. One has to start with the category of greeting itself,
and discover what elements and relationships among elements may
serve it. Shuy's studies of functional language illustrate this
principle in their examples of alternative ways to accomplish requests, directions, instructions, and the like.

We are almost to ethnography now, but not quite. In their
recent papers on assessing language development both Cazden
(1977) and Shuy (1977) point out the need for ethnography, implicitly at least. Cazden asks, how does one decide what communication functions are of the most worth, and where does the
list of communicative competencies end? If an answer is not to
be imposed a priori, ethnographic inquiry into the communicative
repertoire of a community is essential. Again, Shuy, using extended observation and videotaping in a school setting, can recognize functions and probe them experimentally because of conso-
nance with his own cultural knowledge. I shall try to indicate
the character of a fully ethnographic approach below, but first
let me finish the path begun with linguistics.

The path so far described for the course of linguistic methodology is step-wise. A level of functional relevance is recognized,
the step of structure dependent upon it analyzed; then something
of a kick and a leap must occur to move the field as a whole to
the next step, so easily does the student of language become im-
mersed in familiar form. The leap now before the field, though
continuous with the rest, produces in many a sense of falling outside linguistics itself. It is the leap to the study of the relationships among linguistic elements in the service of speech styles.[4]

From the standpoint of a speech style, one has to do not with
an additional level of language, possessing an additional set of
units, parallel to phonemes, morphemes, syntactic constructions,
semantic features. True, the term "styleme" has been used, but
it can really only refer to units (or co-occurring units) already
identified and seen, from the standpoint of style, to be characteristic or expressive. With styles, one has to do with a novel
organization of units at perhaps all the standard levels. What

distinguishes a formal style, say, from an informal style, may have to do with pronunciation, choice of words, choice of syntactic construction, and preferred and inadmissible meanings. A style is more a configuration than a level. And the elements of a style may differ in scope from those of levels such as phonology and syntax. It is possible to give a sense of an "archaic" or "archaicizing" style (seriously or humorously) by occasional use of a few salient features--say, a "thee" and a "thou," a "natheless" and a "howbeit," a syntactic inversion or two. The rest of what occurs may be indifferent.

In sum, the difference of a style, as a configuration, from a structural level of language is this. In phonology one has to do with elements and relationships that are exhaustive of sentences in one of their aspects. All of a sentence (or a discourse) can be represented as a sequence of phonological units, mapped in terms of phonological units. The same is true for morphological units, syntactic units, and semantic units. Indeed, when linguists speak of their subject matter as having to do with the relation between sound and meaning, with the mapping of the intervening structures, it is the exhaustive kind of level that is thought of as intervening. There is "total accountability," so to speak, for the linguistically relevant features at each level. Styles need not be like that. To be sure, they can be. In the Yana language spoken by Ishi, of whom Theodora Kroeber has written so well, men's speech and women's speech were distinguished in the phonological ending of every word. But the differences between men's and women's speech styles generally in American society are not evident in every word. Such gender-linked styles are indeed superb evidence of the need for a functional starting point. They entail differences that appear only when one sets out to discover them, starting from men and women, rather than from grammar.

We have, then, to do with language in which traits may constitute the relevant difference. And while some differences among styles may depend upon presence or absence, be all or nothing contrasts, others depend upon proportions and frequencies. (Shuy (1977) discusses some of these cases.) We recognize such phenomena when we speak loosely of someone having a "touch" of an accent or of someone having a "thick" accent, or of a high proportion of features at one end of the scale as "deep."

We have also to do with language in a respect in which it is inescapably sensitive to situation. Progress in linguistics has mainly been independent of social context, becuase it could be assumed that the features being analyzed were common to all users and uses of a language. That assumption is never wholly correct, and the relation between what is analyzed by a linguist as "English" and what you or I can say and understand may be very problematic. The fundamental point here is that when we reach consideration of style, we inevitably reach consideration of styles. Even when a speaker of a language can be thought of as

having a single grammar, he or she cannot be thought of as having a single style. When we reach consideration of styles, we
must consider speakers as having, not a grammar, but a *verbal
repertoire.* In some cases that repertoire may comprise more than
one language. In every case the consistent continuation of the
principle of functional relevance leads to the questions--What are
the differences by which the styles in a speaker's repertoire can
be described as contrasting? What are the dimensions underlying
those differences? (What are the relations between the styles and
their occasions of use?)

We have reached, in effect, a study of language that is inseparable from a study of social life, and in which quantitative
differences are inseparable from qualitative effects.

III

Many linguists may say that such a study of language is not
linguistics, but some other field, perhaps anthropology, psychology, sociology. Whatever its label, it is beginning to emerge
into prominence, and it is the sort of study of language that is
fundamental to education. From one standpoint, such a study of
language may be "applied" linguistics, especially if it is concerned
with language use in schools. But "applied" taken alone is a mis-
nomer. Linguists do not now know enough about these phenomena for others to come to them to ask simply for application
of knowledge already in hand. Research into these questions is
not applied, but is foundational and at the frontiers of linguistics.
Its practical relevance is obvious, but it is no less concerned with
issues of theory for that. The plain fact is that practical needs
and theoretical challenges coincide here, as they do in so many
other places. And there are not enough who are taking them up.

In this regard we pay a price for the isolation of linguistic
and educational research from each other, for polarization between
qualitative and quantitative methodologies, for the lack of a sufficient cadre of linguistic ethnographers. Perhaps we must always
pay this price. Perhaps the values that are institutionalized in
our academic disciplines, our institutions and government, and our
culture, are such as to prevent the growth of the work that is
needed. It is so easy for modes of work to become frozen in
doctrinaire niches. Language is a subject beset by prejudice
and preformed opinion. In attempting to change the way in which
it is studied and understood, one may unwittingly be challenging
deep-set assumptions of the society. Perhaps language development is assessed as it is today, for the most part, because to do
so supports the present order of things. Perhaps the vested
interest of an elite in the notion that change and the masses cor-
rupt language, and the vested interest of a highly stratified,
bureaucratized social order with a democratic frosting, such that
individuals must be considered to have ended up where they do

as a result of their own doing, converge. Just as we would not know what to do if schools failed to keep millions of young people out of the job market, so we would not know what to do if schools succeeded in producing millions of young people with the language competence they take as an ideal. Or rather, perhaps we would indeed know what to do. If accents and dialects and vernaculars were to disappear and no longer be available as ways of discriminating, if everyone spoke standard English, we might simply substitute a finer lens in the microscope of correctness. No more "he do" for "he does?" But plenty of "transpire" for "occur," confusion of "infer" and "imply," jarring plain "impact" as a verb instead of "have an impact on." After all, a great many of the distinctions upon which we now insist came into existence only as a result of the rise of the middle classes in the eighteenth and nineteenth centuries. If new ones are needed, or more weight need be given to old ones in order to maintain the desired level of linguistic insecurity in the populace, the necessary sense that most people do not deserve better because of linguistic inadequacy, it could surely be done (cf. pp. 104–118 in this volume).

All this is speculative, of course. If it is too dramatic, my excuse must be that there seems to me an issue here that constantly eludes us, and must somehow be forced into attention. Before we can make satisfactory contributions to the assessment of language development, we must know far more than we do about the role of the assessment of language development in the history of American schooling and American society. Fortunately, a few scholars are beginning to pioneer in research in the history of our language attitudes and policies (e.g., Shirley Brice Heath, Glendon Drake). The histories I have seen give little attention to it. A broad picture is clear enough: wipe out the Indian languages, erase linguistic differences due to immigrant origin, disvalue or stereotype dialect, insist on a single standard as a badge of intellectual and personal virtue. Little seems to be known about the formation of these views in schools of education, their implementation in schools and school districts, the tensions, interactions, and adjustments in specific regions, where specific configurations of linguistic difference and verbal repertoire prevailed. One senses a pervasive difference in attitude today between groups differently situated in the class structure, a pattern of difference perhaps between the Eastern seaboard and the West, but without adequate documentation.

Perhaps we need to step back, imaginatively, in a way analogous to "zero-budgeting." What if there were no assessment of language development at all? Would anything be lost? Most of mankind in time and space, after all, has not had explicit assessment of language development of the sort with which we are concerned. Why do we? Why do we have to? How did it start? What functions, latent as well as manifest, does it serve? Is it possible that language development of children in our schools would improve if it were *not* assessed? To what extent are the functions and effects of assessment different for different children, according to region, class, sex, program?

Some essential light can be shed by knowledge of assessment of language development as it occurs outside the classroom. Insofar as parents and communities have not come to accept the figures of formal tests as the only criterion of achievement, there must remain at least residues of informal assessment according to the norms of local cultures. One would want to know what kinds of use of language are valued, which users of language are valued, how these values are exhibited, experienced, and acquired. One would want to know how the relationship between language use in school and language use outside of school is viewed, where there is continuity, where conflict, where compartmentalization.

Research outside schools could discover evidence of abilities in community situations that might put the display of abilities in schools and test situations into perspective. It is well known that display of abilities may be tied to situations. Sometimes it is a matter of appropriate content, sometimes a matter of appropriate norms of interaction. In their study of Kpelle children, Cole and Gay found that children who had difficulty in school with lessons in mathematics that dealt with certain principles could be seen to employ these same principles in certain work situations. Susan Philips has documented the cultural pattern that underlies the "shyness" of Indian children from Warm Springs reservation, when directly questioned by teachers. The teachers perceive the children often simply as "shy," not talking. Observation of the children in play and home situations shows that they can be very talkative indeed.

Here may be an opportunity to unite research with effective change. One might start with what the teachers and the school personnel perceived as the problems associated with language development of a group of children. Given this definition of the problem, as perceived in the school situation, one could undertake a study of the language activity of the children in the full round of their lives, putting the phenomena of the classroom into perspective as part of that round. One could involve the teachers as participants in the ethnographic study to a certain extent, or at least as participants in an on-going seminar in which the ethnographic inquiry was regularly reviewed and discussed. The results of the study, of course, might confirm the teachers' initial perception. If the results indicated a different interpretation of the children's language activity in school, the teachers would not be confronted with it cold. They would have participated in its development, and understand the process by which it was reached. Such involvement in the process might make acceptance of the product more likely.

IV

Let me now take up a conception of ethnography, in order to make clear what the term implies for me, as method and discipline that can be vital for educational research in language.

One hears the word "ethnography" more often these days in educational and linguistic circles, and one also begins to hear the question, "What is ethnography?" There is no single answer. Almost anything that involves direct contact with people as a source of information may find itself included under the label, especially if the contact is made by an anthropologist. The conception I sketch here is shared by some but not by all. It is intimately connected with the sketch of the development of linguistic methodology given above.

It is important to distinguish between *"ethnography"* and *"field work."* There are two related reasons for this. First, "field work" is a suitable general term for any contact with people as sources of information; second, and most important, not all "field work" in this sense is "ethnography" in the sense I intend. There are again two reasons.

First, contact, having been there, is not enough. Sometimes the claims of anthropologists to a distinct and even superior methodology embody an element of "I was there." This ought to give us pause when we reflect on how many people we met there whose views of the people we studied we would not trust. Those of us who work with Native American communities often enough meet the local resident who "knows all about the Indians" from having lived there. We often discover that what is known is limited to what Indians were willing to disclose in certain, partial contexts, or is colored and constrained by an economic or social relationship that closes off certain kinds of knowledge as uncomfortable.

If the anthropological methodology in field work is effective, it is based on more than being there, however romantic some of us may make the field work experience sound. It may, to be sure, be based on insights and intuitions, but these are nourished and controlled by a certain kind of training. It is this training that is often missed by those who have not had it, giving rise to an equation of ethnography with sheer presence in the field. Indeed, a focus on field work may easily miss the training, because the training commonly occurs apart from the field. It has to do with the systematic, comparative knowledge of phenomena and systems like those under study which the ethnographer brings to the description and interpretation of the particular case. It has to do with the knowledge that enables him or her to recognize in a funny use of words for "aunt" and "uncle" a kinship system of an Omaha, or Crow, or other type; in a problem of attendance at schools or jobs the persistence of a seasonal round; in a consistent failure to say "Thank you," not ingratitude, but a pattern of reciprocity that avoids closure in single situations.

Such inferences presuppose the skills to obtain the information from which they are inferred, and these too entail more than presence and observation. These skills involve the questions asked in the mind, if not in speech, that guide presence and observation. This brings us to the second way in which I should like to restrict the term "ethnography." I should like to give "ethnography" the connotation of inquiry that is open to questions and answers not foreseen, for which possible observations need not be precoded, and for which the test of validity need not fit within a prestructured model. When anthropologists limit their inquiry to observations and questions for which the set of alternative answers is already fixed, I should like to say that that may be field work, but not ethnography.

These two poles of validation through field work, then--"I was there" contact, precoded content--represent a Scylla and Charybdis between which true ethnography steers. The steering is not reducible to a routine; that is what makes it hard, and seemingly ineffable at times. Sensitive awareness, empathy, and intuition are not ruled out, far from it, but merely not enough. Pre-existing models and frameworks are inseparable from the requisite training, but one must be able to get beyond them. It all comes down, unfortunately, to being attentive and smart. Being there won't allow one to sop it up; methodology won't allow one to grind it out. The steering is indeed cybernetic, a matter of feedback, of dialectical interplay, if you will. It has to be so, because of the kinds of situations in which one works and the kinds of knowledge one seeks. One works in situations which require the trust of others, accommodation to their activities, participation in ways that often preclude writing or recording at the time. One sacrifices certain kinds of reliability for the validity that one hopes and often finds to come with depth. In a sense, one is half in the position of a child or newcomer learning the ways of the community. One has not the time and full immersion of the child or newcomer, but a measure of orientation through training that compensates. Just so in acquiring a local language: the limited opportunity to hear and use it is compensated for by a training in what to listen for and what to do with what one hears.

In a word, ethnography is inquiry that begins with recognition that one is at work in situations that are, indeed, massively prestructured, but prestructured by the history and ways of those among whom one inquires. At the heart of it is a process of which linguistic inquiry is indeed a model, if we set aside any particular model of grammar, and think of linguistic inquiry in the generic sense as *the interpretation of codes*.

For the ethnographer in this sense, the world of inquiry is neither merely a source of raw data for general schemes, nor a gallery of essences that can only be intuited and expressively

expressed. It is a world of many codes, of many structures.
Not a single natural world, indeed, but a plurality of worlds
(*Lebenswelt*); worlds that are *constituted* in the lives and experience of participants in a group or activity, in important part
through selecting and grouping and reinterpreting received traditions, traditions which from the point of view of other traditions may seem unintelligible or irrational. From the standpoint
of a merely universalizing or generalizing science, such traditions
and worlds may seem arbitrary and parochial. Yet even a science
that wishes to rise from human worlds to something called "Man,"
if it wishes to effect change, must reach into these worlds, be
mediated by them, if change is to be consonant with intention.
From the standpoint of a science dedicated to generalization and
universals, the specifics of each world may seem simply boundary
conditions, specific constants and ranges to which the parameters
of general theory must be adjusted. From the standpoint of a
science imbued strongly with a historical sensitivity, the specifics
may contain qualities of emergence. To the one view, qualities
that are rare or unique may seem something that can be set aside
because of their infrequency. To the other view they may seem
opportunities for insight, configurations that disclose hitherto un-
realized and unsuspected potentialities. To take an example from
language: a general theory of language can regard a specific language as an exemplification, and perhaps a test, of features of
the design of language in general. Some would hold that only
universal considerations are important. Others would regard a
specific language from a typological point of view--remaining concerned with universal language design, but concerned as well
with the recurrence of major types of structure, themselves seeming to reveal potentialities of language structure that recur independently of history, and that are not easily reducible to a single
model, if the model is at all rich in content. Still others, myself
included, accepting and valuing the preceding interests, would
want to keep in view a third concern. Navajo is what it is because it is an instance of human language; it is an instance of
certain types of language structure that have great interest; it
is also what it is because it is the language of the Navajo. To a
great extent its structures are what they are because of possibilities and impossibilities inherent in language structures mediated
by the mind. Its flesh and blood, as it were, the meanings it has
for those who use it, the texture that it takes and gives in their
speech and reflection, are what they are because of the specific
experience of those who have spoken and continue to speak it.
What role the language can play in the modern world, in schools,
is to be understood in terms of that history, valuation, and outlook. Linguists long ago, in what must seem the ancient time of
Boas and Sapir, established that there is nothing intrinsic to the
structure of any language that precludes its adaptation and
elaboration to serve new needs of whatever kind. If there are
limitations and disabilities, when a language is confronted with new

circumstances, these reflect nothing about its potentiality; they reflect the fact that its vocabulary and idiom, its conventional speech acts, routines, and genres, the assumptions as to etiquette of speech, have evolved and been embedded in a certain way of life. (As is true, of course, of any language, even those which become world languages through their adaptation to the needs of commerce and science, and their association with world powers. Their near universal currency is a demographic, political, and cultural fact, not one due to any unique structural property.)

It follows that there can be field work with a language, even field work devoted to applied goals, educational goals, that falls short of ethnography. One can devise an orthography to permit the use of a language in primers and bilingual education, but knowledge of the role of writing and reading, of language in visual form, is needed, if the written material is to be used. Indeed, knowledge of the meanings associated with the alphabets and letters known to the people is necessary, if the alphabet itself is to be successful. One cannot make general assumptions about the role of literacy. One has to find out through ethnography what it means in the case in hand. In general, it is not enough to decipher the code of the language itself; one has to decipher the codes associated with the use of the language, as an element in the verbal repertoire of the community.

A brief citation from Lévi-Strauss on this role of ethnography. He once observed that if an object of art came to Paris, and the code was known, it would go to the Louvre, but if the code was not known, it would go to the Musée de l'Homme (the ethnological museum).

A further part of this view of ethnography as inquiry into worlds is a view of these worlds as inherently adapting and changing, recreated and reinterpreted by individuals in their own lives and in relation to the experience of the group as a whole. From this standpoint, one taken initially in American anthropology, so far as I know, by Sapir in his writings of the 1930s, a cultural world has not been accounted for if treated in terms of its conditions alone.[5] One such condition, a major concern in the development of anthropology, is of course historical provenience and transmission, cultures as interesting and distinctive wholes that persons acquire, manifest, transmit, but as their *locus* rather than their source. From this point of view, what is cultural tends to be equated with what is in fact common or shared. From Sapir's point of view, the fundamental nature of the cultural is that it is *capable* of being shared, that is, of being communicated. A sharable symbolic trait, something capable of becoming more generally part of a group's repertoire of codes, is already within the sphere of the cultural. Such a point of view is necessary to cope anthropologically with the modern world, where the overt signs and diacritics of cultural traditions float, jostle, and merge as if each city were an eddy, left behind by a flood that swept all detachable bits of culture about the world. Sometimes anthropologists have been able to see an object of study only in cultural worlds like those sketched in their textbooks, saliently distinct. Indians driving new cars, buying cases of pop, watching color television --where's the cultural world there? There is one, and one not so wholly like the non-Indian as appears, but it may go unwitnessed, if we shake our heads and mourn that the god of cultures has long ago finished his task of creation. When it comes to cultural worlds, the seventh day will never come. (This theme is developed in Hymes 1973; see esp. p. 34.)

Such a view, restricting anthropology to the "other" cultures that historically fell to its lot in the great handing out of subject matters a century ago, seems to rest on the assumption that isolation, or at least strong barrier, is necessary for the flow of culture to acquire distinctive form, and that this requisite is increasingly absent. There is truth in the assumption, but so to interpret it involves an inadequate conception of the nature of boundaries. On the one hand, the salient boundaries, marked by a language, a geographical barrier, a political line, have proven very permeable. On the other hand, the sense of a distinct cultural world depends ultimately upon taking something as a boundary. It is a function of self-definition, identification, of meaning given to whatever differences may obtain. The differences may be few in number, may be less in physical and observable traits than in configuration, or simply in shared experience and what Raymond Williams has called "structure of feeling." Such a basis for boundary may have been more important than usually realized in the cultures traditionally studied by anthropologists.[6] Such a basis may be prevalent within a conglomerate social structure such as our own. Perhaps each of us moves too much in a round of activities and people that matches our own conception of a world to appreciate the diversity about us. We can share a city such as San Francisco or Philadelphia with hundreds of thousands, and meet only professional colleagues. But if the paths of each were traced, and the meanings glinting on either side gleaned and understood, a multitude of distinct worlds might become evident. Beyond our own rounds, and the spheres defined as public problems by media, perhaps lie a great many worlds unmentioned and out of sight.

If this is so, then there is plenty of work for ethnography, and work that only ethnographers do (though the assistance of novelists is to be welcomed). The existence and character of these worlds, their bearing on schools and education, can become known only through participation.

Let me give an example. The Warm Springs Reservation, where my wife and I work with speakers of two Indian languages, has been a distinct political entity for more than a century. Although three different peoples were brought together on it, and a lively awareness of the original tribal affiliations persists, reinforced by financial considerations in treaty settlements, much

intermarriage and interaction has resulted in a common sense of
membership in the "Confederated Tribes." A certain amount has
been learned and recorded about the aboriginal culture of the
people, and about its persistent elements, some of which--one of
the languages, certain rituals, certain patterns of activity, etc.--
remain today. A certain amount of attention has been focused on
the Reservation as an example of Indian people seeking economic
self-determination and self-sufficiency. The policies adopted in
this regard, the various activities, the consequences, can be
known. Various other aspects of life, such as housing and health,
attract attention because of the involvement of governmental
agencies. So far as I know, no one has addressed the question,
what is it like to grow up and live at Warm Springs Reservation?
How does the world appear? What is that world like? It is a
world with color television, suburban-style housing developments,
a resort hotel catering to whites, a golf course, an organized historical society, a new administration building, etc. It is also a
world in which a good many of the brightest people become alco-
holics, or so it seems to us; in which bright and motivated children often leave or are forced from high school, marry, get preg-
nant, go to work, whatever; a world in which some young people
die every year in auto accidents; in which a major bulwark of the
social fabric continues to be a number of responsive, responsible
grandmothers; in which the security of assured shares of tribal
income interacts somehow with severely limited opportunities for
work and hopes for responsibility or authority; it is a world
whose every member must at some point decide for himself or herself what it means to be an Indian, because there is no way to
avoid or deny the identity.

One anthropologist appears to feel that there is not much more
than tidbits to be gleaned there--the old people who "knew the
culture" are almost all gone. Whether or not there is still at Warm
Springs a "culture" in some of the older ethnological uses of the
term, there is a cultural world. It is a world not wholly or
analytically understood by its members, who have as categories
of understanding mostly only either traditional ones or ones sup-
plied by external institutions and the surrounding rural white
society. What happens to children in schools appears to depend
on how the children interpret their world, given such categories
as they have available. To find out what they see and do, to
convey that knowledge in a way that permitted some of the texture
of their lives and world to come through, would be what I mean by
ethnography.

The level of cultural worlds completes the chain of levels
within which structure is to be discerned through functional
relevance.

Let me try to show how this is so, and in so doing link the
discussion of linguistic methodology with the discussion of ethnography.

V

The methodology at the basis of modern linguistics, as has been said, depends upon the notion of commutation, of demonstration of functional relevance through contrast (as against repetition), showing that a particular change or substitution or choice counts as a difference within a larger frame of reference. This methodological principle should be taken into account in any general discussion of qualitative methodology, and it is capable of extension beyond what has been made of it in linguistics proper. There are indeed two important kinds of extension to be encouraged by those concerned with language as part of social life. One has to do with the basis of linguistic structure, the other with the building of it.

Our modern edifice of language structure has employed the principle of contrastive relevance primarily in the service of cognitive functions, what can be rather simplistically called "reference." The correlative notions of contrast and repetition have been used to establish features that enter into the kinds of meaning involved in naming, statement, logical claims, and that illuminate relations of grammatical structure in the service of such kinds of meaning. To be sure, there has always been some attention to features and meanings that can be called "stylistic" or "expressive," but their domain has seemed marginal or secondary. In point of fact, the principle of contrastive relevance applies to both kinds of meanings, and if it is a fundamental goal of linguistic theory to explain what counts as repetition, what counts as contrast, then expressive, or (as I prefer) "stylistic" functions are equally fundamental to linguistic structure.

There is not space to deal with the ramifications of this fact, but an illustration may show what is involved. The first, and common, kind of contrastive relevance is illustrated by contrast between /p/ and /b/ in English, such that "prattle" is something a baby may do, and "Brattle" a nonhomonymous street in Cambridge. The second kind is illustrated by contrast between a heavily aspirated and a weakly aspirated /p/. In the first case a difference in referential structure is conveyed, in the second a difference in attitudinal structure: emphasis perhaps to make the word clear, to express disgust or elation, whatever. Heavy aspiration of a stop such as /p/, precisely because it does not serve referential function, can serve stylistic function. It does so as a conventional device available to speakers of English, a part of their linguistic competence. Like the referential contrast between /p/ and /b/, the stylistic contrast between heavily and lightly aspirated /p/ is diacritic. That is, it distinguishes meanings, it does not embody them. The meaning conveyed depends upon further features of the utterance. For this reason, I would refer to the two, complementary bases of contrastive relevance as establishing two "elementary diacritic functions." (This point is elaborated in Hymes 1974a, ch. 8 and 1974b, and taken up in Hymes 1972.)

The presence of the second, complementary function is implicit in the difference between paradigmatic sets of sentences, chosen to illustrate points of grammatical structure in the narrow sense, and paradigmatic sets of sentences, chosen to illustrate actual choices in the use of sentences in social life. An example of the first comes from Postal (1974:3):

    a. I think that he is rich (*that* clause)
    b. That he is rich is thought by me (?) (1st passive)
    c. He is thought to be rich by me. (2nd passive)
    d. But not: *I think him to be rich. (complement)

Leave aside the fact that Postal finds (d) unacceptable, whereas it seems perfectly natural to me, a slightly elegant or literary mode of expression. Leave aside the fact that (c), which Postal finds acceptable, and which illustrates his grammatical argument, seems odd to me, and that the only way I can make it acceptable is to introduce stylistic function in support, so that one would be saying (or hearing) a response: "He is thought to be rich by *me*," following, perhaps, "No one ever thought him to be rich" (in my speech, not apparently in Postal's; cf. (d) above). The main point is that when one asks, what are the alternative ways by which one would express the notion (a) in conversation, people do not ring changes on the grammatical paradigm exhibited above, keeping other things constant, but change their utterances in a variety of ways. They make use of choices in other sectors of language, lexicon, intonation, other types of construction. Lexical options come readily to mind (rich, wealthy, loaded). What people appear to be doing is to consider the reasons (functions) for saying the thing differently, that is, they invoke possible differences of situation, both verbal and social, and consequent options of style.

One might refer to the kind of relations disclosed by the first kind of contrastive relevance as having to do with *resource grammar*. The bare bones of grammatical possibilities, preserving reference and neglecting style, are examined and collated. The second kind of contrastive relevance brings to light paradigms of a sort that might be called "natural conversational paradigms" (as opposed to "analytical grammatical paradigms").

This kind of contrastive relevance has to do with what can be called *discourse grammar*. It employs the recognition of stylistic functions to extend linguistic inquiry beyond the usual levels of language to the styles and choices involved in use of language. Even in studies of literary style, the question of contrastive relevance, of whether or not an observed feature represents a choice (for the author, or for the reader), is fundamental. (Vendler 1975 uses this principle nicely, e.g., pp. 13-6, 22-3).

The theoretical approach of Michael Halliday makes use of such
an approach in a particularly stimulating way, envisaging grammatical means (the discoveries of resource grammar) as organized
according to four generic types of function, ideational, interpersonal, textual, and logical (see Halliday 1973). The conception
remains to be tested fully in English and across a variety of languages (I do not think, for example, that pronouns would be
found to occupy quite the same place in all languages). Much
current work by linguists and others, studying texts, conversation, speech acts, and associated properties of coherence and
conduct, does a great deal to explore language from essentially
this standpoint, the standpoint of alternatives in actual uses of
language. Extension at the base and extension at the top, as it
were, are not always integrated, unfortunately. Speech acts,
such as promises and threats, may be analyzed without regard for
the role of stylistic (and communicative) features that enter into
their meaning (cf. Hymes 1974a, ch. 9). Current studies of discourse, texts, conversion, speech acts, are doing a great deal
to explore these areas. Social interactional meanings are beginning
to receive their due.

We cannot adequately evaluate language development and the
uses of language that enter into education without attention to
both these extensions of the principle of contrastive relevance.
Properly pursued, they entail a general conception of language
development and use as a matter of meaningful *devices*. The
still common use of mean length of utterance as a measure of development is not in keeping with this principle. The measure
may helpfully correlate with other things, but it can shed no
light on what is happening, what is being acquired and used.
Again, it is like comparing motors by their size instead of by
their structure. Language, from sound to style, is a complex of
form-meaning covariation. That is another way of putting the
point of contrastive relevance. To discover what is there, what
is happening, one seeks to discover which changes of form have
consequences for meaning, what choices of meaning lead to
changes of form. One works back and forth between form and
meaning in practice to discover the individual devices and the
codes of which they are part.

The limitation of linguistics proper has been that, despite the
potentiality of its methodological principle, it tends to stop short
of the full range of form-meaning covariation, and to stop short
of ethnography.

This is an old story. Modern linguistics advanced decisively
over the popular notion that one could tell something about the
character of a people by the presence or absence of individual
words ("They have no word for 'thank you'," "the Germans have
a word *Schadenfreud*," as if the absence of the word meant a
posture of ingratitude, the presence of the word a special delight
in the misfortunes of others). Franz Boas made central to his
linguistic work the question of the categories that were not

merely present in a language, but obligatory, that is, unavoidably involved in verbal expression. (Tense is such a category in English when verbs are used, number when nouns.) Benjamin Lee Whorf proposed to go beyond registering the obligatory categories to a study of their articulation with other features in actively employed "fashions of speaking," but the study of "fashions of speaking," which would entail ethnographic inquiry into styles, was not taken up. (This point is discussed in chapter 8 of Hymes 1974.)

We see the same story today in studies that are called "pragmatics" or "discourse" in linguistics. From a strictly linguistic point of view, it is interesting to investigate how it is that a question may be the answer to a question in certain types of encounter--how to the query, "Do you have any coffee left?", the answer may be, "Do you want cream?", presupposing a positive but unspoken answer to the initial question. These elliptical sequences are characteristic of exchanges in stores where the dimensions of the encounter are limited and mutually well known. An examination of such encounters must necessarily involve field work, that is, observation of actual cases, to obtain its data. But if the analysis is limited to the consequences of such sequences for a theory of language organization, it is not ethnography, but field work. A larger frame of reference of contrastive choice would be required. When are service encounters of this type appropriate, when not? When are people insulted by the restriction of an encounter to such an exchange? What does it mean to an old store-owner in an ethnic neighborhood that the new young sales representatives limit their interaction with him to truncated exchanges of this type? What genre of verbal exchange has been replaced? What is the nature of the verbal ability that now has no occasion? More generally, what is the range of the truncated service encounter in the society in relation to the full set of alternative types? And what are the common styles? One has the impression that the American style is found brusque to the point of insult in England, the English style overly polite to the point of archness of effeminacy in the United States. In sum, the full pursuit of form-meaning covariation would not stop with consequences for linguistic structure. It would discover something of the *resonance and consequence* of this instance of a genre within cultural worlds.

This reasoning of course holds for speech acts and small genres of all kinds, requests, commands, greetings, teasings, etc. Since such study unavoidably engages phenomena in change, as well as choices across a range of settings, quantitative information and analysis is essential. One expects to find proportions and trends as much as or more than categorical rules of appropriateness.

The principle of the linguistic ethnography that is needed can be put in terms of complementary perspectives. If one starts from social life in one's study, then the *linguistic* aspect of the ethnography requires one to ask what are the communicative means,

verbal and other, by which this bit of social life is conducted
and interpreted? What is their mode of organization, from the
standpoint of repertoires of codes? Can one speak of appropriate and inappropriate, better and worse uses of these means?
How are the skills entailed by the means acquired, and to whom
are they accessible? These questions lead one into the territory
of the other starting point. If one starts from language in one's
study, then the *ethnography* of the linguistic work requires one
to ask, who employs these verbal means, to what ends, when and
where and how? What organization do they have from the standpoint of the patterns of social life?

VI

In a critique stressing the use of language and ethnographic
inquiry one should consider one's own uses of language as scholars
and scientists. The discussion has concentrated on qualitative
structures, with recognition of the relevance of quantitative
methods. In mentioning resonance, and using a word like "texture," one raises the question of narrative reporting as well. To
the best of my knowledge, some of what we learn and know and
should convey can only be expressed through skillful prose. It
is a commonplace in anthropology to admit, or enjoy, the fact that
novels about a country may be a valuable source of understanding.
In recent years a growing number of anthropologists have felt im-
pelled to write a narrative about their field work. Having published the scholarly analysis, they write a second book to try to
say what it was really like. This seems to me a healthy impulse.
It has roots in the increasing concern with the reflexive nature
of social science inquiry, but is not to be reduced to that. Much
of what we know, in anthropology and in personal life, is known
by means of narratives, anecdotes, first-hand reports, telling observations. In the vital decisions and directions of our lives we
willy-nilly rely on what we know by such means. In our scholarly
chairs we find it difficult to acknowledge their validity, though we
may admire their artfulness. There are many purposes and kinds
of verbal art, but some of it, I believe, is a way of getting at the
truth. One can read poems for fun, sanctity, duty, or a liveli-
hood, but some poems one can read for what they enable one to
experience and know. If we are to extend our understanding of
language to the full, so that we can fully comprehend its role in
schooling, in education, in social life, in our own lives, we have
to find a way to come to terms with the validity of uses of languages that are aesthetic. Some people are brilliant at numbers
and research design, some excel in discovering and articulating
qualitative structure and pattern, and some are masters of the art
of conveying events and experience and insights in words. To
admit this is not to give way to rampant subjectivity. We can and
must discriminate, establish canons of judgment, make explicit our
criteria for trusting one set of words, taking another under

advisement, and distrusting a third. It is a job of verbal criticism and inquiry that has a great deal to contribute to the legitimation of much that anthropologists believe they know through ethnography.

These considerations bear on the final point to be made about the role of ethnography. Ethnography can of course be used for many purposes, serve different interests. In my conception, its validity is dependent in part on the knowledge already had of their ways of life by those whose ways of life one seeks to study. Behind every classic ethnography, I suspect, stands one or more members of the culture who were themselves ethnographers without portfolio. Wherever meaning in the third sense discussed above, having to do with resonance and consequence, is successfully conveyed, one suspects a process of inquiry that was collaborative. Such a process is one to which the members of the cultural world bring knowledge of its codes and experiences, and to which the ethnographer (who may be a member) brings methodological skills and comparative perspective. A good part of the knowledge held by members of the culture is necessarily tacit. Their languages, their expressions and styles, are indispensable sources of insight, but never in themselves a complete and adequate metalanguage for their own world. One of the fundamental questions of anthropology, indeed, or at least of linguistic ethnography, has to do with the degree to which a given language is an adequate metalanguage for the way of life of which it is part. What concepts and meanings have found explicit linguistic shape for reporting, discussion, reflection, and which not? And what is the role of language as such, as a means of communication more or perhaps less employed, enjoyed? Some cultural worlds are permeated with language, others not.

A consequence of this fact for ethnography is that native documents and testimony, while indispensable, as Boas insisted, are never sufficient. To a fair extent, subject to ethical choice and judgment, the process of ethnography can be an exchange of knowledge. Many linguistic informants have become fair analysts of their own languages in the course of contributing indispensable knowledge about it. The same can be true in ethnography generally. In this possibility lies a possibility for a mode of ethnography that is not exploitative and that contributes as well as takes in the world in which it works. Obviously this possibility is surrounded by many complications, not to be gone into here. But it is important to note it, especially when we are concerned with ethnography in institutions of our own society, such as schools. An ethnography that served only higher levels of government, national institutions, and theory is hardly possible in any case, as superintendents and principals are quick to tell us. In the exploration of ways in which ethnographic inquiry in education can be founded on mutuality, questions of language themselves, of the sort considered just above, have a part to play. I would like to think that some of what one learns and knows and has to report is inseparable from uses of language that are continuous with those of ordinary life. These are the narrative uses, the uses into which an aesthetic consideration of apt expression enters. Cultivation and analysis of such uses may contribute to mutuality between ethnographer and school. And it may be a healthy thing for the democratic quality of our society if such uses can be given the justification and legitimacy they deserve. Indeed, such uses do play a vital part in decisions and perceptions, so that we handicap our understanding of educational institutions and the forces that affect them if we do not make them explicit objects of attention. Our own language development is in need of assessment.

ENDNOTES

1. This paper was stimulated by participation in the Workshop Exploring Qualitative/Quantitative Research Methodologies in Education, held in Monterey, California, July, 1976, and sponsored by the Far West Laboratory for Educational Research and Development, in cooperation with the National Institute of Education and the Council on Anthropology and Education. An abstract of the paper, prepared by members of the Laboratory, appears under the title "Critique" on pp. 91-3 of this *Quarterly* (vol. VIII, no. 2). I am grateful to the editor of the *Quarterly* for finding space for the paper, which proved too long for the issue devoted to the Workshop as such. I should also like to thank the reviewers of the paper for the *Quarterly*, not all of whose cogent comments I have been able to act upon, since the result might well have been another whole issue. I hope that various references may help fill out what may be too cursorily treated here.

2. John Dewey used the example of the expulsion of lip-rounded breath to blow out a candle or to begin an English word, before Sapir, but I have forgotten the reference. Sapir does not mention Dewey. Perhaps he had forgotten too.

3. The logic is really much the same as in the discovery of significant relationships through the assignment of subjects to experimental conditions. It is just that in the core of language, viewed as a referential mechanism, the conditions sort out answers of a "yes" : "no", all or nothing sort, rather than of a "more" : "less" sort. A typical hypothesis, in terms of the simplified illustration previously given, would be that a given sound is (or is not) independently relevant. Consider (b) occurring between vowels. The hypothesis is tested by substitution (commutation). If (b) cannot be replaced by (p), then in this position it cannot contrast with (p); the difference between them cannot distinguish words in the language in question, and the similarity would lead one to group the two together as members of the same systemic unit. The difference would be readily explainable in terms of local conditions and general theory. Voiceless sounds, such as (p), often become voiced (as is b), when occurring between

voiced sounds (such as vowels). The same inference and explanation would hold if (b) could be replaced by (p) between vowels, but the replacement had no concomitant (correlated) difference in meaning. (The commutation test is an application of the general principle of form/meaning covariation.) Of course if replacement by (p) resulted in a different word, the two sounds would belong to different units. The concomitant change would demonstrate that one had to do with not one, but two, elements of the minimal arbitrary code of the language.

4. On this conception of a development, see Hymes 1974, ch. 8. Of course stylistics has been cultivated for a long time, and sometimes even seen as fundamental to linguistics, but for most linguists "style" has been a marginal category, and most investigations have been of specialized genres. I am arguing that the heritage of findings and insights into style becomes relevant now to the central challenge facing linguistics, that the study of speech styles can be seen, not as additional, but as fundamental.

5. This is a poor place to try to open issues of social theory, but what I mean by "conditions" can be briefly sketched. The historically given traditions are one such condition, one means out of which cultural worlds are constituted. The forms, constraints, and possibilities of recurrent types of structure, ecological or economic structure, say, or social structure as a whole, can be distinguished as another set of conditions. The experiences, motives, minds of persons are another. There is a recurrent tendency to take some one of these as the object of study and theory. In Sapir's day, an impersonal objective "culture" in the sense of a historical set of traditions was often so taken, and his writings of the 1930s are in critique of that, for the sake of the role of third condition, the personal. What we call "social anthropology" often seems to fix upon the second, as if the first and third were secondary or epiphenomenal; Marxism that derives "superstructure" from "base" is akin. The fine insights of the ethnomethodological movement in sociology run the danger of reducing the whole to the third, as if the fact that cultural worlds are constituted by participants could be enlarged to the proposition that they are solely or wholly so constituted, or that only their constitution was worthy of study. All these things--received traditions, environmental and social structures, personal constitutive activity--seem to me conditions, origins, of cultural worlds, jointly, and even all together, not exhaustively. By occasional use of the word "configuration" I mean to suggest that cultural worlds, like lives and works of art, come out contingently and have to be experienced to be known.

6. Ethnological studies of the distribution and diffusion of traits have shown how permeable mapped boundaries may be. I recall a Berkeley-trained ethnologist exclaiming that the Tübatulabal differed from a neighboring tribe in only two traits. One, to be sure, was their language. I suspect a specific structure of feeling would have been found also.

REFERENCES

Cazden, Courtney, et al. 1977. "Language Assessment: Where, What and How." *Anthropology and Education Quarterly* 8(2): 83-91.

Cole, Michael, et al. 1971. *The Cultural Context of Learning and Thinking: An Exploration in Experimental Anthropology.* New York: Basic Books.

Halliday, M. A. K. 1973. *Explorations in the Functions of Language.* London: Edward Arnold.

Hymes, Dell. 1964. "A Perspective for Linguistic Anthropology." In *Horizons of Anthropology*, Sol Tax, ed., pp. 92-107. Chicago: Aldine.

_____. 1970. "Linguistic Method of Ethnography." In *Method and Theory in Linguistics*, Paul Garvin, ed., pp. 249-325. The Hague: Mouton.

_____. 1972. "Introduction." In *Functions of Language in the Classroom*, C. Cazden, V. John, and D. Hymes, eds., pp. xi, lvii. New York: Teachers College Press.

_____. 1973. "Introduction." In *Reinventing Anthropology*, Dell Hymes, ed., pp. 3-58. New York: Random House.

_____. 1974a. *Foundations in Sociolinguistics.* Philadelphia: University of Pennsylvania Press.

_____. 1974b. "Ways of Speaking." In *Explorations in the Ethnography of Speaking*, R. Bauman and J. F. Sherzer, eds., pp. 433-451. New York: Cambridge University Press.

_____. 1976. *Toward Educational Linguistics.* (Horace Mann Lecture, University of Pittsburgh School of Education, May 1976). Philadelphia: Graduate School of Education, Working Paper #1.

Kroeber, Theodora. 1961. *Ishi, Last of a People.* Berkeley: University of California Press.

Philips, Susan. 1972. "Participation Structures and Communicative Competence: Warm Springs Children in Community and Classroom." In *Functions of Language in the Classroom*, Cazden, John, and Hymes, eds., pp. 370-394. New York: Teachers College Press.

Postal, Paul M. 1974. *On Raising: One Rule of English Grammar and its Theoretical Implications.* Cambridge: The MIT Press.

Sapir, E. 1949. "Sound Patterns in Language." *Language* 1:37-51, 1925. Reprinted in D. Mandelbaum, ed., *Selected Writings of Edward Sapir*, pp. 33-45. Berkeley and Los Angeles: University of California Press.

Shuy, Roger W. 1977. "Quantitative Language Data: A Case For and Some Warnings Against." *Anthropology and Education Quarterly* 8(2):73-82.

Vendler, Helen. 1975. *The Poetry of George Herbert.* Cambridge: Harvard University Press.

Williams, Raymond. 1965. *The Long Revolution.* London: Pelican Books.

what is ethnography?[1]

"Ethnography" is coming to be much discussed in education. Often enough one hears some form of the question, "What is ethnography?" The National Institute of Education has commissioned a report to answer the question. All this might be puzzling to an anthropologist, especially to one with an interest in the history of the subject. If one traces the history of ethnography where it leads, one goes back centuries, indeed, to the ancient Mediterranean world, and the temporary rise and fall of ethnographic inquiry there, Herodotus being its most famous, but not only, exemplar. With regard just to the Americas, one can trace a fairly continuous history of the ethnographic reports, interacting with the posing of ethnological questions, from the first discovery of the New World. There is a considerable modern literature on the practice of field work, both in general and with regard to specific techniques, and more recently, ethics. A recent book addressed to ethnography in our own society (Spradley and McCurdy 1972) is being used, I understand, by teachers of composition to stimulate topics for their students. If ethnography is new to some in education, certainly it is not new to the world. When asked "What is ethnography?", would it not be enough to provide a short reading list, or to point to the discussion in some text of what research proposals often refer to as "standard ethnographic method?"

I fear not. Anthropologists do not themselves have a unified conception of ethnography. In particular they do not have a unified conception of ethnography in relation to the study of institutions of our own society, such as education. And anthropologists are far from accepting or perfecting an integration of the mode of research they would consider ethnography with other modes of research into a society such as our own. And the changing intellectual context of the human sciences as a whole introduces new questions and sources of diversity.

Educational research has been dominated by quantitative and experimental conceptions of research. It is easy for anthropologists of a variety of persuasions to criticize such methods. It is often harder for them to state concisely the alternatives. "Ethnography" cannot be assumed to be something already complete, ready to be inserted as a packaged unit in the practices and purposes of institutions whose conceptions of knowledge and research have long been different. If there is not careful thinking through of underlying conceptions, and explicit attention to differences in

them, "ethnography" may be a brief-lived fad in educational research. Or worse, partial or superficial conceptions may be
taken up.

The true opportunity of the current interest in ethnography
is to enter into a mutual relation of interaction and adaptation between ethnographers and sponsors of educational research, a relation that will change both. Because of my conception of ethnography, I see in this prospect a gain for a democratic way of life.
The following sketch is offered because I do not know of a similar attempt to consider the issues raised here in brief compass.
Many others must contribute from their own experience and outlook.

II

One difficulty with the notion of "ethnography" is that it may
seem a residual category. It is associated with the study of
people not ourselves, and with the use of methods other than
those of experimental design and quantitative measurement.

Clearly not everything that is not those two things should be
considered "ethnography," but a positive definition is not easy
to provide. A major reason for the difficulty is that good ethnography has been produced under a great variety of persons, some
of it before there was a profession to train such people, and professional training has been very much a matter of the transmission
of a craft and of learning by doing, by personal experience.

It has not helped that some people talk as if the key to
ethnography were a personal psychological experience, rather
than the discovery of knowledge.

It is clear that ethnography involves participation and observation. What should count as ethnography, what kinds of ethnography there are, may be more easily seen if we consider what
makes participation and observation *systematic*--what, in short,
counts as systematic ethnography.

The earliest work that we recognize as important ethnography
has generally the quality of being systematic in the sense of being
comprehensive. To be sure, any and all early accounts of travel-
lers, missionaries, government officials, and the like, that may
contribute information and insight about the culture of the peoples
of the world, has been welcomed and gleaned for what it could
provide. But when Ibn Khaldun or Father Sahagun are singled
out, it is because they are both early and comprehensive. Their
curiosity was not limited to curiosities; they had an interest in
documenting and interpreting a wide range of a way of life.

Much of the early attempts to make ethnographic inquiry an
explicit procedure reflect the desire to be comprehensive. These
attempts are guides to inquiry, lists of questions, of observations
to make. They bespeak a stage of history when much of the non-
Western world was little known to Europe, and when a variety of
reasons, scientific, religious, practical, motivated some to seek

more adequate knowledge. These guides to inquiry have in common a concern with all of a way of life (although their coverage may be unequal). What are the people of such and such a place like?

It was not long before there were explicit procedures that can be distinguished as *topic-oriented*. (Indeed, the Domesday Book and the inquiries of Sir William Petty (1623-87) share in this lineage.)[2] The great American example is Lewis Henry Morgan's questionnaires for recording kinship terminologies in the middle of the nineteenth century. It is worth pausing to consider the several aspects of Morgan's great work. First, he had a contrastive, or comparative insight: from his experience with the Iroquois Indians, together with his knowledge of classical Greece, he realized that there was a principle of kinship organization sharply contrasting with that familiar to contemporary Americans and Europeans. He sought then to determine the main types of kinship systems and their locations throughout the world. Second, he needed systematic information, information not available except as he sought it himself. Hence his own travels in the Western United States and his relentless correspondence with those who could help. Third, he made use of his findings to formulate first a historical (*Systems of Consanguinity and Affinity*, 1870) and then evolutionary interpretation (*Ancient Society*, 1877) of the most general sort, of human development as a whole.

These three aspects of inquiry seem the essential ingredients of anthropological research proper, as distinct from inquiry that contributes to anthropology. Each aspect may exist independently --a contrastive insight, a seeking of specific information, a general interpretation. Anthropology proper exists insofar as the three are united in a common enterprise. Ethnography is more than a residual technique, but the name of an essential method, when all three are united.

With time there has come to be a certain body of ethnographic inquiry that can be said to be *hypothesis-oriented*. To be sure, Morgan had a general hypothesis. But it seems reasonable to distinguish the kind of ethnography organized and guided by John and Bea Whiting, for example, to inquiry into socialization in several contrasting societies. The Whitings had attempted to come to general conclusions, testing hypothesis on a theoretical base, from the ethnographic literature that existed at the time. They found, as so many find, that their questions were more specific than the literature could answer. The sources were not detailed enough for their purpose, and not comparable enough. Therefore they organized a project to provide the detailed, comparable information they needed. Ethnographic teams (generally, couples) were trained in terms of a guide to the field study of socialization, sent into the field in several different societies for an extended period of time, kept in touch with through correspondence throughout the field study, and brought back to write up their

results. (*Six Cultures*, by Bea Whiting, is a principal outcome.)
Like Morgan, the Whitings had insight into contrasting types of
society, a need for specific information, and a general theoretical
frame (in this case, psychodynamic) to which contrast and specifics were relevant.

All three types of ethnographic inquiry continue to coexist in
anthropology today. There are still occasional discoveries of unknown peoples (as in the Philippines a few years ago), for whom
comprehensive information has to be provided from scratch.
There are still many peoples, knowledge about whom has never
been adequately systematized, for knowledge about whom has
serious gaps. Fresh ethnography may be undertaken for first-
hand knowledge as a basis from which to integrate all that is
known, or to fill a gap in what is already known.

There are still discoveries of aspects of culture, or of perspectives on culture, such that the existing literature fails to
provide much information. The "ethnography of speaking" is a
case in point. The Human Relations Area Files, although rich in
ethnographic data, simply did not contain much information on
cultural patterning of speech, let alone information at all on the
fundamental theoretical question, the functions of speech in the
society. (Anthropological theory had taken for granted that the
functions of speech were everywhere the same.) When such a
discovery or perspective comes to the fore, topic-oriented ethnography may be undertaken. One needs to find out something of
the range of cultural patterning, once cultures are investigated
from the new point of view.

Both comprehensive ethnography, and topic-oriented ethnography, lead to hypothesis-oriented ethnography. Given a substantial general knowledge of a culture, precise investigations can
be planned. Indeed, hypothesis-oriented research depends on the
existence of comprehensive ethnography, and can be fruitfully
pursued only where the latter exists. Again, once something of
the range of patterns for an aspect of culture is known, one begins to formulate more precise questions. Research may show the
recurrence of a contrast in styles of speaking that can be called
"direct" vs. "indirect"--but are the attributes of the two styles
the same in each case? Are the functions the same? In the
ethnography of speaking right now, one is aware of broad contrasts, usually presented as dichotomies (cf. Bernstein's "elaborated" and "restricted" codes). This fact is a sure sign, I think,
of the topic-oriented stage and of the need to proceed to the
hypothesis-oriented stage.

III

What might the subject of schooling in America be like in this
context? Clearly there is a great deal of information already in
hand. It is not so clear that the information is obtained and

analyzed in ways that permit all the insight possible into schooling. If schools were considered from the same standpoint as kinship systems or languages, the first question might be: what
kinds of schools are there? It would not seem informative enough
to know that test scores were up or down in general across all
American schools, if in fact the country contains schools of many
different types. The point would apply even within a single city
or district. Are the schools of District 1 in Philadelphia all
alike? If they are different, how many different kinds are there?
Probably at any level of consideration, one would not want to say
that all were alike, nor that all were incomparably unique. In
sum, one would recognize a question of typology, as central to
analysis.

A useful typology has to be designed in terms of a particular
purpose. Kinship is important to social life, and central to many
societies, but even so, a classification and analysis of societies
according to kinship is not the same as a classification and analysis according to religion. There are strong connections, but not
invariant bonds, among the various sectors of a way of life, and
so also, among the various sectors of schools. A typology of
schools in District 1 in terms of verbal skills, questions having to
do with literacy, would not necessarily be the right typology for
some other purpose. Conversely, and here is an essential point,
a typology for some other purpose is not necessarily right for a
concern with verbal skills.

This essential point is an example of a general consideration
that divides many ethnographers from an experimental model, at
least as that model is understood by them. For many ethnographers, it is of the essence of the method that it is a dialectical, or feed-back (or interactive-adaptive) method. It is of the
essence of the method that initial questions may change during
the course of inquiry. One may begin with the assumption that
every community must have a pattern for the residence of newly-
married couples that can be of only one of four types, yet discover that the community one is studying actually determines the
residence of newly-married couples on the basis of principles one
had not foreseen. (The illustration is an actual one. See
W. Goodenough, "Residence rules," 1956.)

The history of anthropology is replete with experiences of
this sort. The general mission of anthropology in part can be
said to be to help overcome the limitations of the categories and
understandings of human life that are part of a single civilization's partial view. For many ethnographers, an essential characteristic of ethnography is that it is open-ended, subject to self-
correction during the process of inquiry itself.

All this is not to say that ethnography is open-minded to the
extent of being empty-minded, that ignorance and naiveté are
wanted. The more the ethnographer knows on entering the field,
the better the result is likely to be. Training for ethnography is
only partly a matter of training for getting information and getting

along. It is also a matter of providing a systematic knowledge of
what is known so far about the subject. The more adequate this
knowledge, the more likely the ethnographer will be able to avoid
blind alleys and pursue fruitful directions, having a ground sense
of what kinds of things are likely to go together, what kinds of
phenomena need minimal verification, what most.

One conception of this process is that of Kenneth Pike. Pike
generalized the experience of linguistic inquiry. In order to discover the system of sounds of a language one had to be trained
to record the phenomena in question, and one had to know what
types of sound were in general found in languages. Accurate
observation and recording of the sounds, however, would not disclose the system. One had to test the relations among sounds for
their functional relevance within the system in question. The result of this analysis of the system might in turn modify the
general framework for such inquiry, disclosing a new type of
sound or relation. Pike generalized the endings of the linguistic
terms "phonetic" and "phonemic" to obtain names for these three
moments of inquiry. The general framework with which one begins analysis of a given case he called "$etic_1$." The analysis of
the actual system he called "emic." The reconsideration of the
general framework in the light of the analysis he called "$etic_2$."

When ethnographic and linguistic inquiry are described in
such terms, it may be easy to see the connection with general
scientific method, and the exemplification of such method in the
experimental sciences. For many ethnographers and linguists the
spirit of inquiry is indeed the same. The scale and conditions of
inquiry in ethnography, nevertheless, impose essential differences
in tactics. Perhaps the key to these differences is *meaning.*

For ethnographic inquiry, *validity* is commonly dependent
upon accurate knowledge of the meanings of behaviors and institutions to those who participate in them. To say this is not to
reduce the subject matter of ethnography to meaning, let alone to
native views of meaning. It is simply to say that accurate knowledge of meaning is a *sine qua non.* The problem is obvious
enough in the case of a language and culture we do not know.
It is less obvious in the case of communities around us. Yet
even though one may live nearby, speak the same language, and
be of the same ethnic background, a difference in experience may
lead to misunderstanding the meanings, the terms, and the world
of another community. In Philadelphia, for example, a questionnaire was prepared by a person generally qualified by training
and background. The purpose of the questionnaire was to find
out what parents thought of a community-relations policy and person. The questionnaire was duly administered. The student
administering the questionnaire discovered, by informal conversations with parents, that they interpreted the questions differently than the designer and the school. They distinguished between a playground (having equipment designed for children to
use) and a playyard, but the questionnaire did not. When asked

if they had had a chance to meet their School-Community Coordi-
nator, they answered "no," because to them to "meet" would require having *talked*, and knowing by name, even first-name, not
just having been introduced, but in terms of the questionnaire
their "no's" were interpreted as "not having met." The student
administering the questionnaire was distressed, but there was no
way in the procedure of inquiry for him to take account of what
he had learned or to have what he had learned affect the pre-
sumed results (Abbott 1968).

Experiences of this kind make ethnographers distrust questionnaires, and quantitative results derived from them, if the meanings of the questions to those asked to answer are taken for
granted in advance. Many ethnographers do use questionnaires,
but questionnaires devised after sufficient participation and observation to ensure their validity.

The validity of knowledge about persons, families, neighbor-
hoods, schools, communities in our country depends upon accurate and adequate knowledge of the meanings they find and impute
to terms, events, persons, institutions. To an important extent,
such meanings cannot be taken for granted as uniform, even
within a single city or school district, nor as known in advance.
The overt forms may be familiar--the words, the attire, the
buildings--but the interpretation given to them is subject to
shift, to deepening, to fresh connecting up. (It has been found
that within a single small factory in Pennsylvania, those who
worked in different parts had different terms for the same things
[see Tway (1975)].)

It is in the nature of meanings to be subject to change, reinterpretation, re-creation. One has to think of people, not as
the intersection of vectors of age, sex, race, class, income, and
occupation alone, but also as beings making sense out of disparate
experiences, using reason to maintain a sphere to integrity in an
immediate world.

All this is not to say that ethnography indulges in an infinite
regress of personal subjectivity and idiosyncratic worlds. It has
to be open to that dimension of social life, because that dimension
affects the reality of social life, and the success or failure of
social programs. The point is to stress the necessity of knowledge that comes from participation and observation, if what one
thinks one knows is to be valid. And all this is not to say that
members of a community themselves have an adequate model of it,
much less an articulated adequate model. All of us are only partly
able to articulate analyses of our lives and their contexts. The
meanings which the ethnographer seeks to discover may be implicit, not explicit. They may not lie in individual items (words,
objects, persons) that can be talked about, but in connections
that can only gradually be discerned. The deepest meanings and
patterns may not be talked about at all, because so fully taken
for granted.

Here again the need to discover and validate in the given case is paramount. Our familiar categories of institutions, modes of communication, or the like, are an indispensable starting point (Pike's "etic$_1$"), but are never to be equated with an analysis of the organization of a local way of life. We necessarily distinguish speech and song, and as polar opposites, there may be speech with no musical quality, and singing without words. In our own musical traditions and in the cultures of the world, the inter-connections and conceptions of these relationships of speaking and singing (and music generally) are various and diverse. Modern serious music includes such categories as *Sprechstimme*. The Maori of New Zealand consider the playing of the flute a form of speaking. It is especially these local nodes of connec-tion, these community-specific ways of putting the encyclopedia of culture together, that cannot be assumed in advance of in-quiry, and that can only be discovered through participation and observation over time.

We know that Philadelphia has newspapers, radio stations, television stations, libraries, books, comic books, magazines, in-scriptions and plaques, narrators and joke-tellers. Without eth-nography we can collect statistics as to production and distri-bution. Only with ethnography can we discover the connections among these things in the lives of particular kinds of people. Even self-report cannot be relied upon--people are notoriously unable or unwilling to give accurate accounts of the amount of time, say, they spend on various things. And a key to the sig-nificance of a type of television program may not be in the amount of time the family set is on, but in the family pattern of speaking around it. Is the set on, but ignored? Does someone insist on and get silence? Is the program essentially a resource for continuing conversation?

All that I have said is compatible with a generous view of scientific method. The subject-matter of ethnography--people and their worlds--imposes conditions such that validity and re-search design have a complexity and openness at the other end of the scale from experimental design in many fields. Even so, there is a similarity to the problems of fields such as astronomy and geology in their observational aspects. In principle, a sufficient accumulation of valid knowledge about a particular society would make possible rather efficient, precise inquiries of an experimental or quasi-experimental sort. Indeed, there are some cases of this sort. My own experience is with lan-guages. Given the accumulated knowledge of the Native Ameri-can language I have studied, it is possible to address many par-ticular questions rapidly, systematically, precisely. If a new word is in question, it is a matter of minutes to establish its grammatical place in the system. One does know already just what questions must be asked, to establish that the word is a noun or verb, say, and just what kind. If a newly discovered recording of a familiar word is in question, one knows exactly

what the possibilities of interpretation are, how the facts of the
language constrain the sounds that the letters may represent.
(All of this presupposes a native speaker who has become accus-
tomed to collaboration in work of this kind.) A social anthropologist can look at a newly collected schedule of kinship terms
and place the system approximately quite quickly.

IV

These examples illustrate two points made previously--that
ethnographic training involves training in the accumulated comparative knowledge of the subject, and that the existence of comprehensive knowledge about a community makes more precise
hypothesis-testing possible.

To leave matters here, however, might suggest that ethnography can become almost equivalent to laboratory work. The theoretical foundations on which it rests, however, have yet to prove
as certain as that. The social knowledge that ethnography serves
is in the paradoxical position of becoming increasingly certain of
more and more, and yet at the same time vulnerable to dispute
about its very foundation. Our last example, that kind of kinship
terms, is an excellent case in point. No one could deny the striking progress in our ability to recognize and describe the terms
and behaviors relevant to kinship in the hundred years or so
since Morgan's pioneering work. Descriptive technique, comparative typology, even mathematical modelling are well advanced.
Yet it is possible to dispute the correct interpretation of particular findings (cf. Blu 1967) and even the correct definition of the
domain of "kinship" itself (cf. Schneider 1972; Geertz and Geertz
1975). Differences in analytic point of view can take different
vantage points within a shared body of data (e.g., Blu), and
even prescribe different definitional constructs for master-
concepts such as the "cultural" and "social," such as to require
different placements of findings.

Notice that such disputes presuppose the success of ethnography. Ethnography has provided what there is to dispute. To be
sure, new theory can bring out new aspects of old data, or point
up its limitations, or require new kinds of data to develop adequately. Still, such disputes presuppose a great deal of valid
first-order data. And they tacitly assume that valid first-order
data is largely a matter of competence and talent, requiring per-
ceptiveness and imaginative projection, to be sure, but not miracles
of rapport and identification. The native's point of view can be
grasped by someone who does not always like it or them (cf.
Geertz 1976).

In sum, ethnographers have available in many areas a first-
order language of description that permits them to do work that
can be judged for its competence, validity, richness, and the like.
At the same time they work in a discipline whose second-order
language of analysis is contested. A set of native terms may be

accepted, but analysts argue as to the priority of one or another part of the data, or as to the scope of the data to be considered, or as to whether the case does or does not fit a certain concept or type. Some of these disputes can be resolved with increasing attention and precision. Others depend on conscious or unconscious commitments to what it means to be a scholar or scientist, and to what the world is or should be, such that resolution is unlikely.

One can look at a schedule of kinship terms, then, and place it approximately quite quickly. But "approximately" is a crucial term. Others may agree, that is a Crow system, and add, "But ...". The ethnography of schooling and education no doubt will have the same experience. We can hope to reach the point at which anyone can look at a body of data and say quite quickly, "Ah, that is a Henry Lea type of school," or the equivalent, or say, that community or that family has a Hopi type of educational process. We can probably not hope to reach the point at which no one will object, but you analyzed the school in isolation from X, or started the analysis from Y instead of Z.

There is a second question of language which may differentiate ethnography from the ideal conception of an experimental science. Some of what we believe we know about cultural patterns and worlds is interpretable in terms of structure, whether the ingredients of the structure be lines, graphs, numbers, letters, or abstract terms. Some of what we believe we know resists interpretation in terms of structure. It seems to require, instead, *presentation*.

The need for *presentation* seems to cause no comment when the presentation is visual. "A picture is worth a thousand words" and all that. Especially when the object of analysis is material culture, visual presentation is accepted as indeed essential. Even with social life, there is an increasing recognition of the value of visual presentation, through photographs and films. A telling account of necessity here was made by Frederick Barth, the Norwegian anthropologist, when he reported that in order to make good sense of a deceased colleague's field notes, he had to go to the place in question. He had worked ethnographically in the region (which is why he was asked to interpret the notes for publication), but still needed to *see* the land, the distances between dwelling and well, the heights and contours of the place-- so much of the spatial configuration of life was taken for granted in the notes on behavior.

The difficulty with *presentation* seems to arise when the presentation is verbal. What is one to make, for example, of the relation between the two parts of Clifford Geertz' "The Balinese cockfight"--one part narrative, one part analytic (1972). Geertz thinks that both parts are important.[3] I do also. Through his narrative skill, he is able to convey a sense (mediated by his personal involvement) of the quality and texture of Balinese fascination with cockfighting. Evidence of the fascination is important. It supports taking the activity as a key to something essential about the Balinese; it helps us understand the analytic statements. A film might help too, but it would need something verbal from Geertz to teach us what we should learn from it. The narrative part of Geertz' article in effect points, as the narrator of a film might do, and, also, in the absence of a film, shows. It does so through texture and proportion.

Many anthropologists agree that something of value can be learned from novels of certain sorts, and even recommend certain novels. Clearly there is a sense in which narrative can be a source of knowledge. For some scientists and philosophers of science, it is a source of knowledge secondary to others, if not in principle reducible to others. Some ethnographers and philosophers of science hold the contrary. Narrative does not seem to them in principle entirely reducible to other forms of knowledge, but fundamental in its own right. Indeed, they may suspect that narrative accounts play a role in what scientists and administrators believe themselves to know, even though some of these may not acknowledge that role. It may be the case that structural forms of knowledge about social life are usually interpreted, even if covertly, in terms of images of kinds of person and situation, implicit or remembered narratives. If so (and I think it is so), the general problem of social knowledge is two-edged: both to increase the accumulated structural knowledge of social life, moving from narrative to structurally precise accounts, as we have commonly understood the progress of science, and to bring to light the ineradicable role of narrative accounts. Instead of thinking of narrative accounts as an early stage that in principle will be replaced, we may need to think of them as a permanent stage, whose principles are little understood, and whose role may increase. How often, one wonders, are decisions reached on the basis not only of numbers and experiments, but also on the basis of privileged personal accounts, fleshing out the data to make it intelligible? Sometimes these accounts may be provided by the investigator, sometimes by the audience ("I knew a case once...".) Sometimes they may not be articulated, yet influential nevertheless.

If narrative accounts have an ineradicable role, this need not be considered a flaw. The problem is not to try to eliminate them, but to discover how to assess them. What criteria can we provide equivalent to the criteria for assessing the significance and validity and reliability of statistical tests, and experimental designs?

The question of narrative brings us to another aspect of ethnography. It is continuous with ordinary life. Much of what we seek to find out in ethnography is knowledge that others already have. Our ability to learn ethnographically is an extension of what every human being must do, that is, learn the meanings, norms, patterns of a way of life. From a narrow view of science, this fact may be thought unfortunate. True objectivity may be

thought to be undermined. But there is no way to avoid the
fact that the ethnographer himself or herself is a factor in the
inquiry. Without the general human capacity to learn culture,
the inquiry would be impossible. The particular characteristics
of the ethnographer are themselves an instrument of the inquiry,
for both good and bad. For good, it is important to stress, because the age, sex, race, talents of the ethnographer may make
some knowledge accessible that would be difficult of access to
another. For bad, as we all recognize, because of partiality.
Since partiality cannot be avoided, the only solution is to face up
to it, to compensate for it as much as possible, to allow for it in
interpretation. The conditions of trust and confidence that good
ethnography requires (if it is to gain access to valid knowledge
of meanings) make it impossible to take as a goal the role of impartial observer. The normal people from whom one has to learn
will not put up with that. In principle, the answer lies in the
view taken by Russell Ackoff, that scientific objectivity resides,
not in the individual scientist, but in the community of scientists.
That community has provided methods which to some degree, often
a great degree, discipline the investigator and overcome partiality;
the rest is a responsibility of critical analysis within the community.

The fact that good ethnography entails trust and confidence,
that it requires some narrative accounting, and that it is an extension of a universal form of personal knowledge, make me think
that ethnography is peculiarly appropriate to a democratic society.
It could of course be reduced to a technique for the manipulation
of masses by an elite. As envisioned here, ethnography has the
potentiality for helping to overcome division of society into those
who know and those who are known.

Such a vision of a democratic society would see ethnography
as a general possession, although differentially cultivated. At
one pole would be a certain number of persons trained in ethnography as a profession. At the other pole would be the general
population, respected (on this view of ethnography) as having a
knowledge of their worlds, intricate and subtle in many ways
(consider the intricacy and subtlety of any normal person's knowledge of language), and as having necessarily come to this knowledge by a process ethnographic in character. In between--and
one would seek to make this middle group as nearly coextensive
with the whole as possible--would be those able to combine some
disciplined understanding of ethnographic inquiry with the pursuit
of their vocation whatever that might be. From the standpoint of
education, obviously one wants to consider the possibility of adding ethnographic inquiry to the competencies of principals, teachers, and others involved with schools. But on the one hand,
there is no reason not to seek to extend a knowledge of ethnographic inquiry to everyone. And, on the other hand, there is
no reason to think professional ethnographers privileged. In
their own lives they are in the same situation as the rest--needing

to make sense out of a family situation, a departmental situation,
a community situation, as best they can.

If this account sounds a little like a form of conscious-raising,
perhaps it is, but it is not the ordinary sort. In this sketch I
have not brought out the sociocultural substantiality of ethnographic inquiry. It is a mode of inquiry that carries with it a
substantial content. Whatever one's focus of inquiry, as a matter
of course one takes into account the local form of general properties of social life—patterns of role and status, rights and duties,
differential command of resources, transmitted values, environmental constraints. It locates the local situation in space, time,
and kind, and discovers its particular forms and center of gravity,
as it were, for the maintenance of social order and the satisfaction of expressive impulse.

It is for this reason that much observational analysis of classrooms does not seem to me to merit the term "ethnography." On
the one hand, there is a kind of work which consists essentially
of recurrent observations according to a pre-established system of
coding. Such work violates the principle of being open to discovering meanings and patterns of behavior not foreseen. There
is no provision for meanings, and patterns are excluded, since
integral stretches of behavior are not observed. A superior kind
of work analyzes intensively integral sequences of behavior. It
contributes greatly to analytic control and to penetration to underlying meanings and connections. The limitation of the work is
the lack of a comparative perspective. Thus, Ray McDermott
(1977) interprets the difficulties, and projected failure, of one
group of first-grade readers, in terms of the mode of interaction
among them and the teacher (in contrast to the mode of interaction of another group with the teacher). Since his data is
limited to the classroom, he is not able to consider differences in
mode of interaction that the children may have brought with them
to the classroom. A comprehensive ethnography would consider
all the types of scenes in which the children (and teacher) participate, in order to assess validly the meaning of the behavior in
one scene. From a larger point of view, the lack of a comparative ethnological perspective weakens the contribution the research
might make. Suppose it is the case that what happens in the
first-grade classroom is going to determine the success or failure
of the children as readers, and ultimately, as adults. (This is
McDermott's view.) We have to ask whether or not such a circum-
stance is inevitable. Some Third World societies have had great
success with literacy programs, through mobilization of the society
to accomplish it. Is it impossible for the United States to give
that kind of priority to universal literacy among its citizens, and
mobilize to accomplish it? Is the fundamental question not this:
how does it come about that one society, and not another, lets
literacy depend on patterns of interaction in first-grade classrooms?

Such an interdependence between general and particular inquiry is essential to ethnography as a mode of inquiry--at least
it is essential in my reading of the history of anthropology, and
to what I would see as the contribution ethnography ought to
make to education.

FOOTNOTES

1.   I want to thank Peggy Sanday for stimulus to write this
paper, Richard Bauman and Joel Sherzer for including it in the
series of Working Papers in Sociolinguistics, and Perry Gilmore
for inviting its inclusion in the conference on education and ethnography that she has coordinated for Research for Better
Schools and the Graduate School of Education of the University
of Pennsylvania.
2.   Petty outlined "A method of enquiring into the state of
any country" and in 1686 a series of questions concerning "The
nature of the Indians of Pennsylvania" (Hodgen 1964:190; Slotkin
1965:481, n. 363, where the title is given as "Quaeries concerning
the nature of the natives of Pennsylvania").   Petty's questions
were part demography--he has been called "the greatest exponent
of social statistics in the seventeenth century" (Slotkin:139), part
ethnology.   He was a man who both recommended that the Royal
Society admit only words that mark number, weight, or measure,
and who was concerned with clearer definitions of ethnological
entities.   Altogether a worthy forefather for any effort to integrate quantitative and qualitative methods today.   His program of
ethnological investigation was similar to what Roger Williams (1643)
had actually done some 40 years earlier among Indians, but still
quite unusual for its time.   By the eighteenth century serious
frames of reference for the collection and interpretation of cultural
facts ("manners and customs") were to become part of an established tradition, as in the Scottish work of Adam Ferguson, Lord
Kanes, James Millar, and William Robertson.
3.   Geertz (1976) expresses superbly the dialectic between the
two orders of analysis, the descriptive and the generalizing, that
requires concern with adequacy of "presentation."   Thus, he
writes (p. 223):

Confinement to experience-near concepts leaves an ethnographer awash in immediacies, as well as entangled in
vernacular.   Confinement to experience-distant ones
leaves him stranded in abstractions and smothered in
jargon.   The real question...is...how, in each case,
ought one to deploy [the two sorts of concepts]...so as
to produce an interpretation of the way a people lives
which is neither imprisoned within their mental horizons
...nor systematically deaf to the distinctive tonalities of
their existence.

REFERENCES

Abbott, Lloyd M., Jr. 1968. "Considerations of language and culture for a social survey." *Paper for Anthropology* 528, University of Pennsylvania.

Blu, Karen I. 1967. "Kinship and culture: Affinity and the role of the father in the Trobriands." *Southwestern Journal of Anthropology* 23:90-109. [Reprinted in *Symbolic anthropology*, ed. by J. L. Dolgin, D. S. Kemnitzer, pp. 47-62. New York: Columbia University Press, 1977.]

Geertz, Clifford. 1972. "Deep play: Notes on the Balinese cockfight." *Daedalus* 101:1-37.

_____. 1976. "'From the native's point of view': On the nature of anthropological understanding." In *Meaning in anthropology*, ed. by K. H. Basso and H. A. Selby, pp. 221-237. Albuquerque: University of New Mexico Press.

Geertz, Hildred and Clifford Geertz. 1975. *Kinship in Bali*. Chicago: University of Chicago Press.

Goodenough, W. H. 1956. "Residence rules." *Southwestern Journal of Anthropology* 12:22-37.

Hodgen, Margaret T. 1964. *Early anthropology in the sixteenth and seventeenth centuries*. Philadelphia: University of Pennsylvania Press.

McDermott, R. 1977. "The cultural context of learning to read." In *Issues in evaluating reading*, ed. by S. F. Wanat, pp. 10-18. (Linguistics and Reading Series, 1). Arlington, Va.: Center for Applied Linguistics.

Morgan, L. H. 1870. *Systems of consanquinity and affinity of the human family*. Washington, D.C.: Smithsonian Institution.

_____. 1877. "Ancient society." *Researches in the lines of human progress from savagery through barbarism to civilization*. New York: Henry Holt.

Petty, Sir William. [1686] "Queries concerning the nature of the natives of Pennsylvania." In *The Petty papers: Some unpublished writings of Sir William Petty*, ed. from the Bowood Papers by the Marquis of Lansdowne. London: Constable, 1927. Vol. II, pp. 115-9.

Pike, Kenneth L. 1965. *Language in relation to a unified theory of the structure of human behavior*. The Hague: Mouton.

Schneider, David M. 1972. "What is kinship all about?" In *Kinship studies in the Morgan centennial year*, ed. by Priscilla Reining, pp. 32-63. Washington, D.C.: Anthropological Society of Washington.

Slotkin, J. S. 1965. *Readings in early anthropology*. (Viking Fund Publications in Anthropology, 40). Chicago: Aldine.

Spradley, James P. and David W. McCurdy, eds. 1972. *The cultural experience: Ethnography in complex society*. Chicago: Science Research Associates.

Tway, Patricia. 1975. "Workplace isoglosses: Lexical variation and change in a factory setting." *Language in Society* 4(2):171-183.

Whiting, Beatrice B., ed.   1963.   *Six cultures: Studies of child
    rearing.*   New York: John Wiley.

ethnographic monitoring

I want to consider the contribution of ethnography to bilingual
education, and to argue, indeed, that ethnography is essential
to the success of bilingual education.

One contribution of ethnography has to do with the planning
of programs and the need for knowledge of the initial state of
affairs. This contribution of ethnography (initial knowledge) is
perhaps familiar, though neglected. There are two other kinds
of contributions as well. One has to do with the conduct of programs, the need to recognize and understand patterns and meanings that may emerge during the course of a program, perhaps
outside the classroom. The other has to do with the evaluation
and justification of programs, and ultimately, the evaluation and
justification of bilingual education itself. The second and third
contributions can be thought of as *ethnographic monitoring,* the
one of an ongoing operation, the other of effects and consequences. Attention should be paid to both.

Ethnography might be thought of as something purely descriptive and objective, done by someone who comes from outside.
This is not the view I hold. Ethnography must be descriptive
and objective, yes, but not only that. It must be conscious of
values and goals; it must relate description to analysis and objectivity to critical evaluation. Bilingual education involves social
change in the light of certain goals. As a matter of law, it is
defined in terms of the goal of equality of educational opportunity.
As a matter of social change, it involves much more--personal
goals and commitments, what people consider their life chances
and identities to be, what they want them to become. Not everyone may agree on the goals of change, or how much and what
kind of change is desirable. An ethnographer must come to
understand the values involved and the validity of those values
to those who hold them, as well as come to understand his/her
own attitudes (perhaps attitudes that emerge in the course of his
or her work) and the reasons for them. Only explicit concern
with values, in short, will allow ethnography to overcome hidden
sources of bias. To be truly useful, ethnography must relate
what is described to goals. It may be that certain goals and certain situations are not compatible, or that certain goals and certain means are not, or that an unwitting inconsistency exists
among goals or means. Ethnography is an essential way of discovering what the case is, and social programs that ignore it are
blind, but ethnography that ignores values and goals is sterile.

Ethnography might be thought of as something done by some-one from without, a hired professional. It does require training and talent; not just anyone can do it. But of all forms of scien-tific knowledge, ethnography is the most open, the most compati-ble with a democratic way of life, the least likely to produce a world in which experts control knowledge at the expense of those who are studied. The skills of ethnography consist of the en-hancement of skills all normal persons employ in everyday life; its discoveries can usually be conveyed in forms of language that non-specialists can read. It comes to know more of a way of life than those that live it are consciously aware of, but must take crucial account of what they consciously, and unconsciously, know. A crucial ingredient of ethnography is what in a sense is already known to members of a community, what they must know, consci-ously and unconsciously, in order to be normal members of the community. As a discipline, ethnography adds a body of concepts and techniques that directs attention and relates observations more systematically than community members would normally have occasion to do, that provides for making explicit relationships and patterns that members leave implicit, and that provides for inter-preting patterns in the light of a comparative knowledge of other ways of life to which a community member would not usually have access. Ethnography, in short, is a disciplined way of looking, asking, recording, reflecting, comparing, and reporting. It mediates between an understanding of what members of a given community know and do, and an accumulated comparative under-standing of what members of communities generally have known and done.

A member of a given community, then, need not be merely a source of data, an object at the other end of a scientific instru-ment. He/she already possesses some of the local knowledge and has access to knowledge that is essential to successful ethnogra-phy; he/she may have a talent for sifting and synthesizing it, a special insight into some part of it. What the member needs is the other part of disciplined ethnography, the comparative insight distilled over the decades. This can come in a variety of idioms and does not require a graduate degree. Indeed, one might argue that an educational system devoted to a democratic way of life would provide this other part to every student, as a right and as a basis for citizenship. Not to do so is to withhold from citizens the best that we have to offer for the understanding of social experience and for coming to terms with it or changing it.

When I refer to ethnography, then, I assume that the person doing the ethnography may be from the community in question. Indeed, I think it is highly desirable that this be the case in a large proportion of cases (Hymes, 1974a; Hymes, 1972).

The contribution of ethnography to initial knowledge may be familiar. Still, when I suggested ethnography to the director of a language program in a large city, the response was, "What would you want to know?" The only elaboration of the answer

was that the people in the community would not want it to be
known that so many of them were illiterate.

Such a response suggests that the idea of sociolinguistic description, of ethnography of speaking, has not gone very far beyond academic halls. Indeed, it has not gone very far within
them, so far as educational settings are concerned. One repeat-
edly cites Philips' study (1972, 1974) of the relation between
Madras, Oregon classrooms and the Warm Springs Indian reservation culture, not only because it is good but also because it remains unique.

Most educators would agree with the principle that teaching
should start where the child is. Few appear to recognize that to
do so requires knowledge of the community from which the child
comes. Many teachers would agree with the Office for Civil Rights
that formal tests do not adequately show the abilities and needs of
children. These teachers may not recognize that their own observations may be skewed, confounding impressions of intellectual
ability with impressions of voice and visual appearance. Observation needs to be systematic across a range of settings and activities: in class, on the playground, and at home. The interdependence between specific settings and a display of abilities and
skills is coming to be recognized as a crucial focus for research.

To start where the child is, then, one needs systematic
knowledge of the *verbal repertoire* of the child in relation to that
of his/her community: the range of varieties of language, the
circumstances, purposes, and meanings of their use. These can
differ from one community or district to another, and local knowledge is needed. One needs to know the role of speaking, hearing, writing, and reading, in a given language variety and what
it means to do each of these activities. These can differ from
one place to another, too, and local knowledge again is needed.
One needs to know, in short, the locally relevant *ways of speaking* (using "speaking" as a shorthand expression for all modes of
language use). The organization of language use in a classroom
is but part of a systematic whole, from the vantage point of the
student, and from that vantage point, classroom norms may take
on a meaning not intended or comprehended by school personnel
(Hymes, 1974b).

It is common to think of a choice of one language or another,
one variety or style or another, one genre or another, a mode or
occasion of use of language, as appropriate or inappropriate,
right or wrong. Certainly teachers in classrooms often seem to
think in this way. An essential ethnographic point is to remember that a choice may have to do with elements in a system of
signs. The language used has to do with more than right and
wrong. It is not only the elements within a language that are to
be understood as signs, as uniting form and meaning or as showing their status by contrast with other signs. Every choice
within a way of speaking--of language, variety, style, genre,
mode, occasion--conveys meaning through contrast with other

choices not made quite in addition to the meaning conveyed by
what is written or said. The same is true for the use of language; Goffman (1956) has called it deference (what one conveys
about one's attitude toward oneself). Too often one thinks that
one particular choice represents order, anything else, a lack of
order. This assumption can keep one from discovering the true
order that is present, the system of sociolinguistic signs implicit
in students' communicative conduct. One may wish to change
that conduct--to change that system. One has to recognize it,
be able to interpret accurately what is communicated, in order to
know what one wishes to change. (This is an example of the
relation between the descriptive and critical aspects of ethnography.)

The point applies both to rules of language and to rules of
the use of language. Let me say a little more about the latter
first in order to highlight their importance.

A teacher or curriculum may make an assumption--about the
role of language in learning, about the etiquette of speaking,
listening, writing, reading, about getting and giving information,
getting and giving attention in talk--that is at variance with what
students experience elsewhere. Variance in itself of course is
simply a fact. Whether or not it is a problem depends on the
situation. If a classroom pattern is accepted and respected by
all concerned, it may succeed, at least as success is defined by
those concerned. (Their goals of course may not include equality
or social change.) The pattern may also stamp what is learned in
the classroom as appropriate only in similar settings.

Schools have long been aware of cultural differences, and in
recent years have attempted to address them, rather than punish
them. Too often the differences of which the school is aware, of
which even the community is aware, are only the most visible,
"high" culture symbols and the most stereotyped conventions.
What may be slighted is the "invisible" culture (to use Philips'
title), the culture of everyday etiquette and interaction, and its
expression of rights and duties, values and aspirations, through
norms of communication. Classrooms may respect religious belief
and national custom, yet profane an implicit ceremonial order having to do with relations between persons. One can honor cultural
pride on the walls of a room yet inhibit learning within them.

One may find children fitting classroom expectations, but in a
way that defeats the purpose of their being there. Some Anglo
teachers in Philadelphia schools have been delighted to have
Spanish-speaking children in their classes because the children
are so well behaved--that is, quiet. The reason for the quietness
is that the children do not understand what is being said. When
they do understand (after being placed in a bilingual classroom,
for example), they participate actively. The equation of being
good with being quiet implies a further equation with being dumb
(both senses of the word). Communities, of course, may differ

in the meanings and normal occasions of silence, something that
needs to be known in an individual case.

Knowledge of the local repertoire of varieties of language is
obviously essential. In terms of the descriptive contribution of
ethnography, a salient concern is the local meaning and interpretation of the joint use of both Spanish and English forms. Of
course, instances of the occurrence of elements of one language
in the context of another may be quite *ad hoc*, due to the familiarity or the forgetting of particular words. But some may
consider mixing of any sort reprehensible, and especially if it is
extensive. Others may recognize in extensive mixing a special
style of speech, appropriate to certain people and situations.
They may find not a failure to keep languages apart but rather a
skill in mingling them, one that has to be learned. Someone who
knows Spanish and knows English may not know how to mingle
them in the special style. From one standpoint, then, error and
confusion are something to be stamped out; from another, a skill
with social meaning to be enjoyed.

The significance of mixing cannot be judged without knowledge of the community and individual norms, but the knowledge
is not an end to the matter. The temptation of descriptive ethnography is to let understanding imply acceptance, but ethnography can be used critically. In a given case, a community may
not have been conscious of some aspects of its pattern of language
use, and it might wish to reject some part when brought to its
attention. Or a community may decide that a change of pattern
is desirable, even necessary. Or it may decide to accept and
value a pattern previously little noted. Whatever the case, the
goals of bilingual education should be informed by ethnography
but set by those affected. The most difficult issue may be to
analyze and assess information bearing on choice of *linguistic
norm* and on its implementation.

It is clear that there is an issue. There have been classrooms in which the native speakers of Spanish were seated in the
back of the Spanish class and the Anglo students in front. There
is a school in West Chester, Pennsylvania, whose Spanish-speaking
Colombian teachers are certain that their Spanish-speaking Puerto
Rican students need to be taught correct (Colombian-flavored)
Spanish, ignoring a demonstration that the students are able to
read newspapers published in Madrid. In both cases, a different
classroom norm would yield different results.

There well may be a genuine problem of inadequacy of competence in certain cases. Puerto Rican children raised in New York
City may be disadvantaged in schools in Puerto Rico. Children
growing up in a particular community may not acquire the full
range of varieties and levels of Spanish, especially if Spanish has
been part of a stable multilingual situation as a language of the
home rather than of education. Ethnography can help discover
the facts of local situations in this regard. Whatever the facts,

difficult matters of analysis and assessment remain. At this point the critical, comparative use of ethnographic knowledge becomes essential.

Let me address the issue of linguistic norms--of which to use, accept, and reject. Some leaders in bilingual education have been heard to say there might be a danger of perpetuating through Spanish the failures of schools conducted in English. We are indeed familiar with the kinds of misperception and misconception of ability that can be fostered by prejudicial attitudes towards varieties of English different from the variety assumed in the classroom. Is the problem of attaining equality then simply one of such differences? Could the problem be solved by eliminating the differences, either by stamping out all but the preferred norm, or by substituting or adding one common norm in the repertoires of everyone?

I think that such an approach fails, and fails necessarily, in the United States, if the problem is indeed defined as one of eliminating linguistically-defined inequality. If every user of English in the United States used certifiably standard English, in recognizably middle-class ways, little would change except for the cultural impoverishment, the loss of diversity, and interest in American ways of life. Fault would continue to be found. People who do not use double negatives may be found redundant in their adjectives. People who do not misuse tenses can be faulted for their use of adverbs and conjunctions.

Variability and evaluation of usage are indeed universal in human life, but the issue here is not one of individual differences --of the variation in personal ability inevitable in any group. If such were the case, it would be a matter of talent; as it stands, it is a matter of shibboleths. If linguistic discrimination is a culturally deep-seated way of maintaining social distinctions, then discrimination is likely to continue. If not through English against other languages, then through one dialect of English against others, or one style of standard English against others. What Barth (1969) has shown for ethnic boundaries holds for class boundaries as well: even slight and infrequent features will serve as boundary markers, if there must be boundaries.

One can further suggest that the United States is culturally organized to produce continually the appearance of a "falling rate of correctness," of a "law of increasing illiteracy." There is not only the constant reproduction of linguistic inferiority, but also the constant renewal of markers of it. There is also the constant projection of decline. This last one draws on a disposition to interpret change in language (itself inevitable) as inevitably for the worse. From this standpoint, necessary distinctions are always being lost, never gained; etymology condemns vitality. Intelligibility is so often found wanting that one must infer that for the vast majority of people, talk is nothing more than a verbal blind man's bluff.

It is a curious thing that a country whose civic ideology has been so committed to "progress" should so despair of language.

I suspect two complementary attitudes and interests to be at work: a widespread popular distrust of verbal skill and an elite's definition of verbal skill as something only it can have and so control. It is perhaps an interaction between these two forces that produces a phenomenon such as a President careful to explain to an audience that he did not know a word he used and had to look it up in a dictionary, while expecting to be trusted to manage a vast bureaucracy that lives and breathes with the manufacture and manipulation of esoteric discourse.

The role of language in the maintenance of cultural hegemony in the United States has been little explored. The main point-- and this brings us back to the role of schools--is that the United States would seem to have a culture in which discrimination on the basis of language is endemic. To achieve equality within a given language, it would never be enough to change the way people speak. One would have to change what the way people speak is taken to mean.

In this regard, one can hardly avoid the thought that a latent function of schools has been to define a certain proportion of people as inferior, even to convince them that they are so, and to do this *on the seemingly neutral ground of language*. Language seems a neutral ground, so long as one can maintain that there is just one proper norm, and that the schools do their duty if they provide everyone access to that norm. The language of the norm is necessary, and everyone has a chance to acquire it (so one can imagine the reasoning). Any inequality of outcome cannot be the fault of the school or system, but must be fair and reflect differences in ability, effort, or desire on the part of students. If it is pointed out that some students begin unequally, relative to the norm assumed in the school, the responsibility is assigned to the student or student's community, for lack of proper language or even a virtual lack of language at all.

Centers to stimulate verbal communication in infants in disadvantaged homes are even now being newly established. From what I have said, you can see that questions about such centers would arise. What are the norms of communication, including use of language, in such families? What is the evidence that they are inadequate? Are they judged to be inadequate intrinsically, or inadequate in relation to the assumptions made in local schools as to the role of language? Is the set of assumptions made in local schools the only possible set? Is the difference between schools and homes a difference between normalcy and impoverishment, or a difference between two ways of doing things, two ways of speaking, each normal in its own setting? Is the program of such a center to change the culture of the home something we would call cultural imperialism if it were reported from the Soviet Union? Is change of the culture of the homes the only option? Could the differences be tolerated, or the schools change? These questions are not rhetorical. Reasonable people might arrive at different answers, given different situations. The essential thing is that such questions be asked. Given the many differences among societies in the role of language in child-raising, yet the unfailing success of children in acquiring language, together with the norms of use appropriate to their society, it is doubtful that any viable community needs a program of verbal stimulation for its children for its own successful continuation. A program, of course, may be a way of changing the community or of diverting the children from it.

Bilingual education challenges the very fabric of schooling insofar as it adheres to the goal of overcoming linguistic inequality, by changing what happens in schools themselves. But if linguistic discrimination is a culturally deep-seated way of maintaining social distinctions deeply embedded in educational institutions, is bilingual education likely to escape its influence? I have suggested that the form of attention to language in schools serves to maintain social stratification, and as long as the society requires such stratification, it is likely to find ways to reproduce it linguistically. The society is defined as one of opportunity, yet the relative distribution of wealth and class position hardly changes year after year, decade after decade; language plays some part in accomplishing and legitimizing that result. Is success for bilingual education then to mean that the accusation, "That's not Spanish," will be heard as widely as the accusation, "That's not English?" Or that children who know varieties of Spanish other than the norm adopted for a classroom will bear the stigma of not knowing *two* languages? (One hears of teachers saying to a child, "I thought your problem was that your language was Spanish instead of English; now I find out that you have no language at all.")

The issue of linguistic norms is inescapable within the level of an established standard itself, because of the distinctness of Cuban, Puerto Rican, Mexican, and other national standards represented in the United States. It is inescapable as well with regard to the relation between national and regional standards, on the one hand, and the other components of the verbal repertoires of Spanish speakers in this country. The issue of norms involves the verbal repertoire as a whole. What is the desired role of each component of the repertoire, and what is the attitude toward each? As I have indicated, ethnography can assist in obtaining the initial knowledge needed to determine the present state of affairs. Clearly, ethnography is needed instead of questionnaires and surveys. What to make of the knowledge provided by ethnography is a matter for the bilingual community to decide. Perhaps in a given case it may be decided that an insistence on standard Spanish is necessary in order to maintain the language. It is also entirely possible that some may decide to reject bilingual education and Spanish as necessary ingredients of, say, Puerto Rican identity, spurred in their decision perhaps by elitist decisions as to the norm within Spanish (see Language Policy Task Force, 1978).

Let me make clear that I do not mean to imply that all evaluation of language and usage is merely social bias. The point is that social bias infects evaluation. It is not the case that "anything goes," but it is also not the case that there is a single, homogeneous, unquestionable norm. The existence of a norm is a social fact, but not a fact beyond critical analysis in the light of knowledge of other norms, of the effects of the norm in question as it is implemented, of alternative relations between linguistic norms and ways of life.

There are normative criteria that apply to languages and their use, e.g., criteria of clarity, elegance, pithiness, musicality, simplicity, and vigor. The difficulty is that people differ in the criteria to which they give most weight, even within the same community, let alone between communities. People may differ in what they count as satisfying a norm on whose importance they agree. Much of the history of language policy and attitude, much of the history of linguistic research itself, can be related to alternate attitudes towards the existence and character of two broad classes of norm, "standard" and "vernacular." In general, social bias affects willingness to recognize the presence and legitimacy of a norm in the first place and the interpretation placed upon meeting or failing to meet it. Is adherence to a "standard" elegance or pretentiousness? Is it logical regularity or empty form? Is adherence to a "vernacular" revitalizing or corrupting? Natural or uncouth? Is it an expression of the spirit of the folk or of the spawn of the uneducated?

Differences in pronunciation are stigmatized as stupidity the world over; absence of features of grammar is taken as absence of logic; propriety of diction identified with virtue. Such interpretations of the speech of others are frequently arbitrary. The association between a feature of language and a feature of intelligence or character is generally not inherent and universal, but local, secondary, and projected.

Within one's own linguistic tradition, one may be on surer ground in assessing the speech of those who share it, but it is ground that cannot be made more secure than the tradition itself. One can judge others (and oneself) in relation to known norms but not withhold the norms themselves from scrutiny, if their consequences cause them to come into question. Despite their pervasiveness and familiarity, the norms may be secondary and projective. We may honor them because through them we have experienced so much that is inseparable from our own naming and knowing of life: satisfactions and illuminations even that mastery of a norm may sometimes permit. Even so, we have to accept that similar experiences may occur in relation to norms we can hardly recognize as such. There must be norms, if there is to be mastery, whether of interactional wit or composed art. But the norms themselves are not fundamental, I think. What is fundamental is that which the norms make possible, the functions served in creative, resourceful, adaptive, and expressive uses of language. Many norms can serve those functions, and a given norm can be made into an enemy of them.

We want to ask, then, not if the norm is observed but what is accomplished through observance of the norm? Is it desirable to spend a term insisting that a child be perfect in a minor grammatical feature, if the result is to teach that child that the norm of which the feature is a part is a torture chamber? Or if the child is inhibited from ever attempting to use that norm resourcefully?

We recognize that there are universal capacities for the structures and functions of language shared by all normal human beings; that a degree of individual variation in ability is inescapable; that a degree of normative stability is essential to the possibility of reliable communication and expressive mastery; that mastery of features may facilitate their resourceful use, but that the same features, treated as shibboleths, may inhibit resourceful use of language. The functions of language are fundamental, the forms instrumental. Quite literally, the letter killeth, but the spirit giveth life.

The goals of a community of course may not be to encourage creative and resourceful use of language. The goals may be to ensure that persons can be placed by the way they speak and write. Or to ensure that persons can perform useful work, can read instructions, newspapers, and other communications from those who direct things. (It is perhaps instructive that our society defines reading, a receptive ability, as its main concern, not the productive ability to write.) Insofar as a community both says and means that resourceful, creative use of language is a goal for all its citizens, then questions of norms, and questions of pedagogy too, must be decided in favor of an emphasis on function as primary, form as instrumental. This is not to ignore the one in favor of the other but to recognize which of the two will bring the other in its train.

If this view is accepted, then the task of ethnography is both indispensable and difficult. It is not enough to discover what varieties of language are in use, when and where and by whom, what features of language vary according to what parameters. One has to discover what varieties of language, features of language, are being used *for*, and to what effect. Is the choice of one norm over another the choice as well of certain functional possibilities as against others? Let me cite the circumstances of many Native American communities, which have acquired English but not the literary glories that English departments like to cite, while having lost rich literary traditions of their own. These communities have English instead of some Native American language, insofar as it is a question of language alone. They have been impoverished insofar as it is a question of the functions of language.

The issues and choices are difficult. I only hope to have shown that the knowledge one needs in order to deal with them

is ethnographic in nature. This is true, not only with regard
to initial knowledge, but with regard to the monitoring of ongoing
programs and of outcomes.

Whatever the strategy of a program, those who direct it obviously benefit from feedback during its course. Test scores and
other classroom results may give some indication of the progress
of students. Even with regard to what is learned alone, observation is desirable as well. Students may show abilities in peer-
group interaction and other settings that do not appear on tests.
Insofar as the program is concerned with the general development
of the students, and with the success of bilingualism itself, ethnographic observation is essential. A central question will be:
what does it come to mean to succeed, or to fail, in the program?
What does it come to mean to do well or poorly?

Perhaps some of the meaning will have been clarified through
the assignment of students to locations in the classroom or to
other groupings. Studies by Rist (1970), McDermott (1974), and
others have shown the importance for success and failure, and
for social meaning of success and failure, of teacher-assigned
groupings.

Some of the meaning of the program to its students, and to
the community from which they come to school, will emerge in
interaction outside of school. Peer-group discussions and judgments, family discussions and judgments, community perception
of the purposes and consequences of the program, need to be
known and taken into account. While the program is teaching
language, it will also be creating social definitions and judgments.
These definitions and judgments may be as important to success
for bilingualism in the country as formal instruction.

A great deal can be accomplished by establishing regular
community participation in the guidance of the program. Still,
no one is a perfect or even adequate ethnographer of him/herself,
if engaged in observation, comparison, and inference only *ad hoc*.
It would be a valuable element of the monitoring of a program
during its operation to have one or more persons formally responsible for ethnographic observation and inquiry. What groupings emerge in classrooms, playgrounds, or elsewhere? Does use
of language change outside of class during the course of the program, and if so, in what ways? Does conversation about language
change? What is said about the program, about those who succeed better than others, about those who do less well? Even more
meaningful is discovery of what is *presupposed* in what is said--
what comes to be taken as shared assumption in terms of which
specific remarks are to be understood, e.g., that a student who
does well is a teacher's pet, that a student who does poorly is
stupid, that only students from a certain class or neighborhood
or kind of family do well, or do poorly.

Ethnographic monitoring need not be conceived as an isolated
task. The staff of the program and representatives of the community could participate valuably, if one or a few people were

responsible for coordinating information, for providing initial
orientation as to the kinds of observation needed, and, indeed,
for listening to learn the kinds of observation that might not have
been initially thought of. A much higher degree of validity might
be possible through cooperation. Since the purpose of the ethnography is to aid the program, its result must be communicated
to the participants in the program in any case. It is far better
to have the communication as an ongoing process throughout the
program. An additional benefit may be to share ethnographic
skills that participants in the program will be able to use in other
circumstances.

The greatest value of cooperative ethnographic monitoring is
that the participants in the program will have the firmest grasp
possible of the working of the program, of its successes and
failures, strengths and weaknesses, in relation to their hopes for
it. They will not be in the position of being confronted by an
outside evaluator's charts and tables, and told a rating for their
program, with nothing to say, or nothing, at least, that such an
evaluator feels required to heed. The participants will not have
been bystanders. They will have concrete knowledge of the process of the program, and be able to address the processes that
have produced whatever statistics and graphs a formal evaluation
process may yield. An evaluation in terms of gross numbers can
only guess at what produced the numbers, and indeed, can only
guess as to whether its numbers were obtained with measures
appropriate to what is being evaluated. The participants in cooperative ethnography may benefit from having their cumulative
observations and interpretations compared with independently obtained measures. Both kinds of information could be combined to
provide a deeper understanding. But if measures are to mean
anything, especially in relation to bilingual education as a process
of social change, the ethnography is essential.

All this is the more important, if we look ahead, and think of
the monitoring and assessment of individual programs as contributing to judgments likely to be made a few years from now as to the
success or failure of bilingual education as a national policy.

A few years from now the charge is likely to be made that
bilingual education has failed. Money was spent, little was accom-
plished--it is easy enough to predict what will be said if bilingual
classrooms join busing and poverty programs as targets of resent-
ment.

The political strength of those who support bilingual education
may be great enough to offset the pressure of those who will make
such charges, once the first wave of support and funding has
crested. And much can be said to deflate the prejudice that may
lie behind such charges. From the standpoint of what is known
about languages and their uses, it is clear that bilingualism can
be an entirely taken-for-granted aspect of a society, something
entirely within the normal capacity of individuals. The list of
flourishing bilingual, even multilingual, situations throughout the

world is long indeed. The evidence that human beings can readily acquire a range of varieties of language is so clear that the question must be, not, is it possible, but where it does not happen, what prevents it?

Arguments from suspicion of bilingualism in general, then, can be won. Arguments from the situation of bilingualism in the United States may be more difficult. Arguments will likely raise two issues: educational success, and political consequences. As to educational success, it can be pointed out that a few years is hardly enough to overcome the consequences of generations of effort to impose monolingualism in schools. And insofar as successful programs require research, there has been little accumulated knowledge on which to build. Most linguists have been as blind to the importance of the linguistic diversity of the country as anyone. They too have proceeded as if knowledge of English alone would be sufficient. Far too few scholars of other disciplines have been helpful. Only in recent years has any substantial number of anthropologists thought ethnographic research in their own country legitimate. As we know, bilingualism has been made a vital issue through social, political, and legal processes. These have led the way. Research, by and large, has only begun to follow. Insofar as successful programs require accurate initial knowledge of the situations in which they operate, and appropriate methods for assessing the communicative competence of students, they have had little on which to draw. Bilingual education may be accused of having failed before it has been fairly tried, if to be fairly tried means to have the support of the kinds of knowledge and methods indicated.

In this regard, the ethnographic monitoring of programs can be of great importance. The circumstances and characteristics of successful results can be documented in ways that carry conviction. Unsuccessful efforts can be interpreted in the light of the conditions found with success. Attempts to argue that bilingual education as a whole has been a failure in the United States can be countered by getting down to cases and knowing well what the cases are. To do this requires confidence in the kind of knowledge that ethnography provides, a willingness to accept the legitimacy of the conclusions arrived at by cooperative ethnographic observations and analysis, if such conclusions differ from formal tests and measurements. I think we frequently accept the legitimacy of understandings of our own that are ethnographic in nature, as against statistics that run counter to our personal knowledge. I think we should do so; to do so is essential to a democratic way of life. But it is necessary to admit that we do; only by admitting that we do can we proceed to go beyond impressions and attain the validity of which an ethnographic approach is capable.

Some will argue against the political consequences of bilingual education, claiming that it is divisive. There is a general answer to this, of course; the social meaning of languages is not inherent

in them, but a consequence of the uses to which they are put.
Where languages are symbols of division, it is because of social
forces that divide and pit people against each other along lines
that coincide with language boundaries. Difference of languages
is hardly necessary; a single sound will suffice, as the Biblical
example of the killing of those who said *shibboleth* instead of
sibboleth indicates. The greatest internal conflict in the history
of the United States, the Civil War, was not fought in terms of
language boundaries. On the other hand, there are many areas
in which multiplicity of language is in no way a part of social
mobilization and conflict. In sum, small differences can become
symbols of hostility and large differences can be accepted and
ignored. The causes are outside of language.

To be sure, a given language policy may favor some interests
as against others. Bilingualism may be experienced as a burden
by people who have been able to assume that theirs was the only
language that counted, that their convenience and the public interest were the same. But to argue that bilingualism is divisive is
really to argue that it makes visible what one had preferred to
ignore, an unequal distribution of rights and benefits. It is
common to call "political" and "divisive" the raising of an issue
that one had been able to ignore, and to ignore the political and
oppressive implications of ignoring it. In this regard, the ethnographic monitoring of programs can also be of great importance.
The ethnographic approach can go beyond tests and surveys to
document and interpret the social meaning of success and failure
to bilingual education.

It may be that some years from now those who work for bilingual education will not themselves be of one mind about its
role. One view of the relation between such movements and
general social processes is that they represent a phase of the
interdependence between an expanding world economy and locally
exploited groups. It may not be presently clear to what extent
the movement for bilingual education is a recognition of sheer educational necessity, an expression of a phase in the relation between a minority group and forces dominant in the society, an
expression of a growing commitment to the ideal of a multilingual/
multicultural society. It may be that some sectors of the Spanish-
speaking community will argue for intensive English training as a
preferable route to economic opportunity while others argue for
Spanish maintenance programs on the grounds of cultural identity.
Class differences may appear in this regard.

My own belief is that a multilingual society is something to be
desired and maintained, but it is for others to decide their own
interests. Whatever the ultimate policies decided upon, the wisdom of those choices will be greatly enhanced if ethnographic
monitoring has been an integral part of bilingual education.

REFERENCES

Barth, Frederick. "Ethnic Groups and Boundaries." *The Social Organization of Culture Difference*, ed. Frederick Barth. Boston: Little, Brown & Co., 1969.

Goffman, Erving. "The Nature of Deference and Demeanor." *American Anthropologist* LVIII (June, 1956), 473-502.

Hymes, Dell. "Introduction." *Functions of Language in the Classroom*, eds. Courtney B. Cazden, Vera P. John, and Dell Hymes. New York: Teachers College Press, 1972, pp. xi-lvii.

_____, ed. *Reinventing Anthropology*. New York: Vintage Press, 1974a.

_____. "Ways of Speaking." *Explorations in the Ethnography of Speaking*, eds. Richard Bauman and Joel Sherzer. New York: Cambridge University Press, 1974b, pp. 433-451.

Language Policy Task Force. "Language Policy and the Puerto Rican Community." *Bilingual Review* (February, 1978). (An earlier version was circulated as "Toward a Language Policy for Puerto Ricans in the United States," by E. Gonzalez Atiles, P. Pedraza, and A.C. Zentella.)

McDermott, Ray P. "Achieving School Failure: An Anthropological Approach to Literary and Social Stratification." *Education and Cultural Process: Toward an Anthropology of Education*, ed. George D. Spindler. New York: Holt, Rinehart and Winston, 1974, pp. 82-118.

Philips, Susan U. "Participant Structures and Communicative Competence: Warm Springs Children in Community and Classroom." *Functions of Language in the Classroom*, eds. Courtney B. Cazden, Vera P. John, and Dell Hymes. New York: Teachers College Press, 1972, pp. 370-394.

_____. "The Invisible Culture." Unpublished PhD dissertation, University of Pennsylvania, 1974.

Rist, Ray C. "Student Social Class and Teacher Expectations: The Self-Fulfilling Prophecy in Ghetto Education." *Harvard Educational Review* XL (August, 1970), 411-451.

educational ethnology[1]

One hears a good deal about "ethnography" in education today, but not about "ethnology." I use "ethnology" in my title to call attention to issues that the use of "ethnography" alone might leave obscure. These issues have in common the theme: What would knowledge of schooling in the United States be like, if anthropologists regarded it more like knowledge of kinship, chieftainship, religion, technology, and the like, in areas of the world in which anthropologists have worked long and intensively?

Two caveats: I do not wish to idealize anthropological study of Native American kinship, African chieftainship, South Asian religion, Oceanic economic life, and the like. In focusing on schooling, I do not wish to forget that an anthropological perspective on education is broader than schooling, and necessarily seeks to understand schooling as one mode of learning and institutionalization among others.

It remains that educational research in the United States does focus on schooling, and that it would be different were an anthropological perspective to be thoroughly established. The difference would be a benefit, I think, to schools, to anthropology, and potentially, to democratization of knowledge and to the relations between academic centers of research and the communities of which they are part. The difference to research can be summarized in three words: *cumulative, comparative, cooperative.*

Understanding of individual schools is not now cumulative, but for the most part a matter of in and out. An individual school does not seem to count as a legitimate object of long-term study.[2] Boas is known for life-long study of the Kwakiutl, others are associated with other groups, but anthropologists do not seem to be associated with long-term involvement with particular schools or school systems. That makes the anthropology of schooling seem odd. One way to describe anthropology is to say that it has divided the world into names--names of peoples, languages, cultures--that it has made legitimate objects of knowledge. There are bibliographies of such knowledge, organized in terms of such names. If I discover an additional fact about such a unit, I can publish it as a legitimate addition to knowledge. My first publication, indeed, resulting from a first summer of field experience as a graduate student, was such: "Two Wasco motifs." I had been able to record incidents missing from the texts collected a half-century earlier by Sapir, and a helpful professor encouraged me to write them up and send them off.

It is hard to imagine publishing "Two Longstreth classrooms" on the grounds that an earlier study had overlooked the two. (For "Longstreth," the name of a school in West Philadelphia, substitute the name of any school near where you live.) Schools do not seem to be thought of as objects that it might take a long time, many hands, and even more than one generation, to come to understand. Individual schools do not seem to be thought of as individual in character. They are thought of, perhaps, as "urban," "inner-city," or the like, but mostly they seem to be thought of as equivalent settings for the interaction of certain recurrent variables--principals, teachers, pupils, curricula, and methods of instruction. Comparative perspective seems to be a matter of differences on such variables, together with demographic data, test scores, and the like. There does not seem to be a comparative perspective in terms of any, say, of the integrative approaches to the little community that Redfield sketched years ago, or in terms of any other dimensions found in the anthropology of other areas.[3] Such comparative perspective, of course, would depend on knowledge of sociocultural context.

I do not claim to know educational research well, and apologize to those of you who do, but it is my impression, so far not corrected by any to whom it has been mentioned, that educational research does focus on the testing of relation among variables without much regard to sociocultural context. Specialists in educational research have been heard to lament its inconclusiveness on various points: ten studies, say, show a positive relationship between two variables, and 17 studies show a negative relationship. The obvious implication, it would seem, is that there may be two types of school, and that the variables under study were interacting in two different types of systematic contexts. That is a familiar anthropological point, from speech sounds to avoidance behavior and presence of belief in a supreme being. But, I am told, it is usually difficult to recover from educational studies the information about context that would enable one to characterize it.

If this impression is correct, then knowledge of schools in the United States is about one hundred years behind knowledge of American Indian kinship. The pioneer work of Lewis Henry Morgan brought together systematic information and proposed a broad typological dichotomy in 1871. Since that time, a galaxy of names --Kroeber, Lowie, Leslie Spier, George Peter Murdock, Driver, Lounsbury--have contributed to the more precise identification of relevant features, dimensions, processes, and types. We seem nowhere near the identification of what would correspond to Omaha, Crow, Dakota, Iroquois, etc. types of school. Note that such types are not pigeon-holes, but bases for systematic analysis of particular structures and processes of change.

We do not have such bases for analysis of structure and change in American schools. Yet it cannot be the case that all schools in the United States, or even in a single city, are the same. Nor, on the other hand, can it be the case that each is entirely unique. In a city, or the country, it seems a reasonable able, fundamental question: What kinds of schools are there?

I suggest that we do not know because there has not been enough anthropology in educational research, and because educational anthropology has understandably been concerned with establishing its ethnographic mode of work. In education by and large, "anthropology" has come to mean "ethnography," and "ethnography" has come to mean field work: participant observation, narrative description, and the like. I believe strongly in this mode of work, and will take it up briefly at the end. Here I want to stress the danger of letting the anthropological perspective on education become equated in other minds with just a mode of field work. The result will be dozens of people called "ethnographers" because they have observed, although with little or no training in cultural analysis; attempts to insert "ethnographic components" in helter-skelter research designs; a brief vogue for the name "ethnography"; and at the end a heightened immunity to the true challenge of an ethnographic, anthropological mode of thought.

Ethnography, as we know, is in fact an interface between specific inquiry and comparative generalization. It will serve us well, I think, to make prominent the term, "ethnology," that explicitly invokes comparative generalization. And it will serve schooling in America well. An emphasis on the ethnological dimension takes one away from immediate problems and from attempts to offer immediate remedies, but it serves constructive change better in the long run. Emphasis on the ethnological dimension links anthropology of education with social history, through the ways in which larger forces for socialization, institutionalization, reproduction of an existing order, are expressed and interpreted in specific settings. The longer view seems a surer footing.

Let me come at the matter in terms of a map. If Harold Driver had tried to map North America in terms of what is known about its schools, would not most of the map be empty? If so vacant a map dealt with kinship, would there not be a demand for studies, an unwillingness to talk about "Indians" in the abstract until more were known in the concrete? The need for cumulative, comparative research would be obvious, as it is obvious today in a less explored region such as New Guinea.

Some may object that such a call for an ethnological approach is based on a mistaken analogy. Schools and cultures, say, Longstreth in West Philadelphia, and Wasco in Oregon, are not alike. Schools are less autonomous and more subject to change, even manipulation, by external forces. An Indian community and an elementary school are not comparable units. I think the analogy holds, despite the differences. First, our sense of each named Indian community as a distinct entity is partly an artifact of our own profession. The academic requirement of contribution to knowledge through research, and the need to have a contribution of one's own, contributes to a tendency to differentiate the anthropological world into named entities that anthropologists can claim. Second, the similarities among differently named Indian communities may be great; their contemporary circumstances on a reservation may be greatly shaped by external forces. Common ecological base, diffusion, pan-tribal movements, retention of elements of ancient tradition, and orientation common to many, all make the autonomy and distinctiveness of named Indian groups an empirical question, just as is the case with named schools. If one school has changed drastically in a decade, through change in the population served, another a mile or two away may have not. An essential dimension of comparative research might be the continuities that schools have, and are felt to have. Third, the issue of access to the research site may be very much the same today. With both schools and reservations one has to address suspicion rooted in past experience; concern about exposure and embarrassment; demands that research and the researcher be useful to those studied.

In regard to access, anthropology encounters the same problems with American schools that it encounters throughout the world, and has, perhaps, a better chance of solving them. Sustained cooperation can serve both parties, academics, and schools. To say this is not to overlook the conflicts of interest that are latent; not everyone wants everything known, or even to know certain things at all. But the problems seem intrinsic to research, not to schools.

A leading element of sustained cooperation is the involvement of others in the research. Here a major anthropological tradition can be an essential asset. In the study of a language, a kinship system, or the like, one is to a great extent seeking to make explicit in a comparable framework what others, in a certain sense, already know. Speakers of a language, participants in a network of kinship, are not merely objects, but, as sources of information, partners in inquiry as well. This tradition suggests that the appropriate strategy for school personnel who seek advanced degrees is to capitalize on what they know where they are. Often enough they have been made to believe that a legitimate contribution to knowledge, and advanced degree, requires methodology and subject-matter disconnected from their experience. Anthropological tradition suggests that they can capitalize on their experience, and make a far more valuable contribution to knowledge by doing so.

If the map of American schooling is to be made less empty, after all, it will require more than the anthropologists and anthropological funding available. Just so, knowledge of Native American traditions would be far less rich, given the small number of anthropological investigators, were it not for members of those cultures--George Hunt, William Beynon, and others--who became contributors of knowledge themselves.

At the Graduate School of Education at the University of
Pennsylvania we have such a program, now in its third year,
involving a group of principals mainly, together with a few other
school personnel. It is still too early to judge the research outcome, but indications are encouraging. It is clear that the program could not have begun, let alone prospered, had the nature
of degree requirements not been rethought in terms of principles
of cooperation, indeed, partnership. Past experience, distrust,
uncertainty of mutual benefit had to be overcome gradually. The
anthropological principles were heard but only gradually believed.
Had there been insistence on the model previously familiar to the
principals, the isolated researcher carrying out an experimental
design, the program would never have been possible. One essential aspect of the program has been training in observation and
narrative reporting, concerned with better perceiving and expressing the process of implementing a reading program in each person's
school. Another essential aspect has been grouping researchers in
teams. The grouping provides moral support among people who
are pursuing a degree above and beyond a full-time job. Ideally,
rather than "cheapening" the degree, it provides for deeper insight. The grouping builds controlled comparison into the process. Finer perception of similarities and differences among
schools results.

These principals, and members of other school districts in the
region, perceive this approach as taking their circumstances and
needs into account. They see such a program as evidence that
an "Ivy League" university, reputedly disinterested in less than
elite affairs, is in fact responsive. We in the faculty see such a
program as a golden opportunity. There is little chance that we
could find funding to study fifteen or thirty schools simultaneously. Even given funding, there is little chance that the schools
would let researchers in just because they knocked. The principle of cooperative ethnographic research leads to the schools and
the University having investments in each other.

This short account highlights the positive, ignoring the
tremors, misunderstandings, partial understandings; it ignores
the fragile dependence of the effort in the University itself on
adjunct faculty. Yet it is fair to say that the effort has led to
an atmosphere in which an anthropological approach is welcomed,
indeed so welcome that interest outruns supply, an atmosphere
in which the long-term questions of the role of anthropology in
educational research can be addressed.

Two long-term questions seem to me of especial importance:
What will be the structure of knowledge of schooling? What will
be its form? The importance of the questions lies in their implications for a democratic way of life. A mode of research that
focuses on experimental design, quantitative techniques, and the
impersonality of the investigator has its place, but, carried to its
perfection, as the exclusive mode, it would tend to divide society
into those who know and those who are known. The

anthropological recognition of the contribution of the practitioner as one who also knows counteracts that tendency. So does the legitimacy, indeed necessity, in ethnographic research of narrative. Good narrative accounting is not easy, and may be harder sometimes than quantitative analysis, but it is more accessible to the citizens of society. Moreover, it can be argued that even quantitative analysis invokes narrative models of social life at some point, and that institutional decision making certainly does. Explicit attention to narrative accounts and models can make an essential contribution. It can legitimate the form in which the knowledge of most citizens as to their circumstances is cast, and it can make apparent a hidden form of cultural hegemony. Of all the disciplines interested in schools, anthropology is best equipped to make that contribution.[4]

To sum up: I have argued that Native America and School America pose anthropological problems of the same kind. The question, "What kinds of schools are there?", is naive, yet natural to an anthropological perspective. An answer draws on those aspects of anthropological tradition that regard research as cumulative, comparative, cooperative. A strategy that draws on such an answer, while looking to the long run, can hope to serve change and even immediate advantage.

FOOTNOTES

1. This is the text of my address as outgoing presidential officer of the Council on Anthropology and Education, during the business meeting of the Council, at the annual meetings of the American Anthropological Association, December 1, 1979, in Cincinnati.
2. An exception is the ten-year involvement in three State of New York high schools on the part of Francis Ianni and others.
3. Gastil (1975) calls attention to regional cultural differences insofar as statistical indications permit, but notes the lack of explanatory power in such a preliminary approach. See his discussion of "The relationship of regional cultures to educational performance," pp. 116-127.
4. See discussion of narrative in Hymes (1977) and in Cazden and Hymes (1978). On cognitive analysis of norms of interaction, embodied in an expressive genre, see Hymes (1979) and the book to which it is a foreword.

REFERENCES

Cazden, Courtney and Dell Hymes. 1978. "Narrative thinking and story-telling rights: A folklorist's clue to a critique of education." *Keystone Folklore* 22(1-2):21-35.
Gastil, Raymond D. 1975. *Cultural Regions of the United States.* Seattle: University of Washington Press.

Hymes, Dell. 1977. "Qualitative/quantitative research methodologies in education: A linguistic perspective." *Anthropology and Education Quarterly* 8(3):165-176.

_____. 1978. "What is Ethnography?" *Working Papers in
Sociolinguistics* 45. Austin: Southwest Educational Development Laboratory. To appear in a volume edited by Perry
Gilmore and Allan Glatthorn, and published by the University
of Pennsylvania Press.

_____. 1979. "Foreword." *In Portraits of "The Whiteman,"*
by Keith H. Basso. New York: Cambridge University
Press.

narrative thinking and story-telling rights: a folklorist's clue to a critique of education

INTRODUCTION: Dell Hymes

This article has its origin in instances of its own subject—use of narratives to explore and convey knowledge. In the course of a conversation with Courtney Cazden, I mentioned material recorded by Joanne Bromberg-Ross. She had recorded consciousness-raising sessions of a women's group, and presented a portion to my seminar. One session in particular contained a marvelous demonstration of interdependence between two different modes of clarifying meaning. The topic was what was meant by "strength" in men and women. Discussion began with discussion of terms. An unresolved back and forth about terms was followed by a series of personal narratives. Suddenly definitional discussion returned, stated in a way that made it clear that there had been no break in metalinguistic focus. Narrative had solved the problem of differentiating two kinds of "strength" (one good, one bad), when direct definition had floundered. The second mode of language use continued the purpose of the first, coming successfully to its rescue.

These two foci, terms and stories, often appear to contrast, rather than to complement each other, as here. My telling of the example from Bromberg-Ross reminded Cazden of instances of contrast from her experience at Harvard, which she recounted. I urged her to write them up, for they highlighted the possibility that one form of inequality of opportunity in our society has to do with rights to use narrative, with whose narratives are admitted to have a cognitive function. Cazden's written account follows next. After it, I will cite other observations and suggest some general implications. The most pertinent and obvious implication for folklore can be stated right off. If differential treatment of narrative experience plays an important role in present educational practice, then folklore can claim a special place in the study and change of education in this regard.

WAYS OF SPEAKING IN A UNIVERSITY: Courtney Cazden

We who work in universities may find contrasts in ways of speaking in our own classrooms. Two personal reports from graduate students and one case study of changes in language use over an undergraduate's four college years point to a particular contrast between narrative and non-narrative ways of clarifying meaning (exemplified, I realize, in the following account).

One fall recently I gave my class in "Child Language" to two different student groups: two mornings a week to a class of graduate students (master's and doctoral level) at Harvard Graduate School of Education, and one evening later in the week as a double lecture to a class in Harvard University Extension. The latter is a low-tuition, adult education program whose older than college-age students are either working for a college degree through part-time evening study or taking single courses for personal or professional interest. My Extension class had a mixture of the two groups--degree candidates like the tuna fisherman from San Diego who works as a bartender while progressing slowly toward a BA and then law school, and teachers in local day care centers, bilingual programs, and Perkins Institute of Helen Keller fame. Each class knows of the other's existence, and students have been encouraged to switch when convenient--as an evening make-up for the morning class, or the chance to experience "real" Harvard atmosphere for the Extension students.

One evening, I noted two Black students from the Graduate School in the Extension class. Instead of sitting in a far corner, they were near the front. Instead of remaining silent, they participated frequently in the evening's discussion. Finally, the man spoke publicly about his perceptions of the difference in the two classes. I paraphrase his unrecorded comments:

> In the morning class, people who raise their hand talk
> about some article that the rest of us haven't read.
> That shuts us out. Here people talk from their per-
> sonal experience. It's a more human environment. [1]

I remember a similar contrast described to me two years ago by a Tlingit woman graduate student from a small village in Alaska. She spoke about discussion in another course during her first semester at Harvard. Here the contrast was not only between ways of speaking, but how these ways were differentially acknowledged by the professor. Again I paraphrase:

> When someone, even an undergraduate, raises a question
> that is based on what some authority says, Prof. X says
> "That's a great question!", expands on it, and incor-
> porates it into her following comments. But when people
> like me talk from our personal experience, our ideas are
> not acknowledged. The professor may say, "Hm-hm,"
> and then proceed as if we hadn't been heard.

In Philips' (1974) sense, contributions to class discussion based on narratives of personal experience did not "get the floor."

"Michael Koff" came to Harvard College from a working-class community in Boston. Yearly interviews with him had been conducted at the Bureau of Study Council as part of a study of the impact of college experience. Some years later, for a Graduate School term paper, Bissex (1968) analyzed the transcripts for linguistic indicators of what she called "the Harvardization of Michael." She found a cluster of co-occurring shifts between Michael's sophomore and junior years, including one from *for instance* to *I mean*.

In Michael's sophomore interview, there are twenty-five occurrences of *for instance* and other words used to introduce examples, compared with ten, three, and four in his freshman, junior, and senior years. His language as a sophomore is, as he says, "concrete": every page of the transcript includes at least one illustrative incident, and the last half of the interview is almost entirely anecdotal. These incidents always function to clarify points. Michael does not trust the "big, vague general words that do not mean anything"; he trusts the meaning that resides in concrete experience (Bissex 1968:11-12).

> *One of the things that I developed an interest in over this past year is some young high school people who live in a housing project.... Somehow if I wanted to talk about life in the project, I either said, "Life is terrible!" or "Life is not too bad." It didn't mean anything. It's easier to, I mean, for instance, just talking here, it would be easier if I could think of some, something—some specific instance. (pause) For example, this family in Larchwood Heights...*
> *Michael Koff, sophomore*

Michael's junior interview is marked, in contrast, by twenty-four occurrences of *I mean* compared with nine, seven, and four in his freshman, sophomore, and senior years. "*I mean* has replaced *for instance* in its function of introducing an intended clarification of a previous statement. The interesting difference is in the nature of the clarification during his sophomore and junior years; the shift from concrete illustration to restatement, generally on the same level of abstraction as the original statement" (Bissex 1968:16).

> *I mean, you just look at things differently. I—ah—it's hard to say what. It's hard, I mean, because you can only put your finger on some of them. You feel you're growing up. I mean, certain things become less important, certain things become more important.... I mean, the things that you think are important drop out and new things take their place.*
> *Michael Koff, junior*

Although narratives have an honorable history as "the temporizing of essence" (Burke 1945:430), they are often denigrated, particularly by social scientists, as "mere anecdotes." Evidently there is a press in at least some speech situations in this university to substitute other modes of explanation and justification.

A NARRATIVE VIEW OF THE WORLD: Dell Hymes

Let me try to generalize, or at least extend, Cazden's observations. We tend to depreciate narrative as a form of knowledge, and personal narrative particularly, in contrast to other forms of discourse considered scholarly, scientific, technical, or the like. This seems to me part of a general predisposition in our culture to dichotomize forms and functions of language use, and to treat one side of the dichotomy as superior, the other side as something to be disdained, discouraged, diagnosed as evidence or cause of subordinate status. Different dichotomies tend to be conflated, so that standard:non-standard, written:spoken, abstract:concrete, context-independent:context-free, technical/ formal:narrative, tend to be equated.

When we think of differences in verbal ability, for example, many of us think in terms of command of standard varieties of English, command of the vocabulary, syntax, and written genres associated with standard varieties. We tend to group standard norms and verbal acuity together. William Labov's widely reprinted essay, "The logic of non-standard English," has done something to change that situation, by contrasting two examples of discourse, the cogent flow of one with the stumbling of the other--the cogent discourse being in a non-standard variety, the stumbling in a standard. Still, it is probably hard for narrative to get a hearing or approval in our schools, however apt its inner form of idea, if its outer form of pronunciation, or spelling, word-form and sentence-form, is not approved.

There is a connection here with Bernstein's well known contrast between "elaborated" and "restricted" codes. (More recently Bernstein speaks of contrasting coding orientations, each with its "elaborated" and "restricted" variants.) The orientation that Bernstein calls "elaborated" is associated with such things as independence of context, objectivication of experience, analysis of experience, a kind of metalinguistic potentiality. The orientation called "restricted" is associated, among other things, with dependence on context and a taking of pre-established meanings and values for granted. One suspects that the contrast is in some respects a version of the older contrast between "abstract" ("elaborated") and "concrete" ("restricted") modes of thought. Certainly it is Bernstein's view that an "elaborated" orientation is necessary in order to go beyond the socially given. This is part of his defense against charges of favoring the middle-class and putting down the working-class: an elaborated orientation is necessary for the kind of analysis that could lead to a transformation of the condition of the working class. Other sociologists have taken up the notion of a link between an "elaborated" code or orientation, and a radical social perspective, taking the one to be a condition of the other (Mueller 1973 and Gouldner 1975-6).

Now, if one applies Bernstein's contrast to everyday genres, then one is likely to take written communication as "elaborated," as against spoken. (Various writers have done so.) A main basis is the assumption that written communication is *ipso facto* context-independent. That assumption, of course, is false. Our traditional stereotypes about the functions of writing perpetuate it, but an empirical examination of the uses and interpretation of writing would falsify it. A written document may be dependent on knowledge of non-linguistic context for its interpretation just as speech may be. One may need to be present, or privy to a description of the scene, in order to know the referents of pronouns in spoken narratives (this kind of example is typical of work in the Bernstein vein). One may equally well need to be privy to an implicit scene to know the true referents of norms in a written narrative or document.[2] Personal letters afford many instances. Even written documents in the most formal style may be deceptively explicit. A diplomat, a bureaucrat, a college administrator has to learn to interpret written communications as if present to a drama in which they are context-dependent utterances. In other words, it would work against adequate understanding of the cognitive uses of language to treat difference of channel as a fundamental difference. Actual uses of writing may not have the properties conventionally attributed to them. To think of spoken narrative as cognitively inferior to written statement, because less independent of context, is to rely unreflectingly on a stereotype.

Again, if one applies Bernstein's contrast to everyday genres, then one is likely to take discourse employing abstract terms, definitions, numbers, and statistics as self-evident examples of a cognitively superior ("elaborated") orientation. But the form is not a necessary evidence of the function. Abstract terms, definitions, numbers, and statistics may be present as a consequence of rote learning, rather than complex creative thought. One may find abstract, analytic forms that are bound to their immediate context, unable to transcend it, and one may find concrete narrative uses of language that leap toward alternative futures.

In sum, our cultural stereotypes predispose us to dichotomize forms and functions of language use. Bernstein's contrast of codes, distinctions between spoken and written, between narrative and non-narrative, tend to be absorbed by this predisposition. And one side of the dichotomy tends to be identified with cognitive superiority. In point of fact, however, none of the usual elements of conventional dichotomies are certain guides to level of cognitive activity. In particular, narrative may be a complementary, or alternative mode of thinking.

Even if dichotomous prejudices were overcome, so that narrative, even oral narrative in non-standard speech, were given its cognitive due, the greater equality that resulted would be an equality of modes and genres, not of persons. The stratification of our society, including its institutions, such as schools, would favor the telling of some stories over others, because of the position of the teller. The structures of relationships and settings would discourage some displays of narrative skill, inasmuch as true performance of narrative depends on conditions of shared background, similarity of identity, and the like (cf. Wolfson 1978). Some evidence and thinking in narrative form would not be admitted, or not counted. If reasons were to be asked, or given, very likely they would draw on the dichotomizing stereotypes just sketched. Narrative forms of evidence would be dismissed as "anecdotal," even where narrative might be the only form in which the evidence, or voice, was available. But the dismissal would be an application to others of a principle the user would not consistently apply to himself or herself--a principle, indeed, that no one could consistently apply, if I am right in thinking that narrative forms of thinking are inescapably fundamental in human life. The truth of the matter would be that only the "anecdotes" of some would count. Even if overt performance of anecdote (narrative) were to be excluded, there would still be covert appeal to narrative forms of understanding. Terms, formulae, data, statistics, would be interpreted silently in terms of "representative cases," and representative cases inevitably embody representative stories, what Kenneth Burke (1945:59, 324) has called "representative anecdotes." From Burke's point of view, every pattern of thought and terms must appeal to such anecdotes. One's choice is not to exclude them, but to chose ones that are appropriate and adequate. To exclude the anecdotes of others by a rule against anecdotes in general is in effect to privilege one's own anecdotes without seeming to do so.

In sum, if one considers that narrative may be a mode of thought, and indeed, that narrative may be an inescapable mode of thought, then its differential distribution in a society may be a clue to the distribution of other things as well--rights and privileges, having to do with power and money, to be sure, but also rights and privileges having to do with fundamental functions of language itself, its cognitive and expressive uses in narrative form.

Cazden's account, and the uses to which Bernstein's categories have been put, suggest that we do indeed tend to think of our society, and our educational institutions, as stratified in ways that define certain kinds of narrative as inferior, and people to whom such kinds of narrative are natural as inferior as well. Certainly the students at Harvard that Cazden discusses are being encouraged to repress or abandon personal narrative in certain settings and roles. Very likely something similar happens in many schools at many levels of education. The student or child is told in effect that his or her own experiences do not have weight (except perhaps as diversion). Not that there is not an essential purpose to going beyond individual experiences. But if, as the Bromberg-Ross recordings indicate, narrative of individual experience is a complementary mode of solution of cognitive questions, then a pattern of discouraging it is a pattern of

systematically discouraging what is at least a valid starting
point, and may be an essential means of thought.

The irony, or better, contradiction, is of course that academics are not themselves like that. Consider graduate work, or
teacher training. When a student is considered a candidate or
initiate for a profession, he or she becomes the recipient of
gossip and lore of the field, of insight and orientation passed
down in narrative form, of personal experiences that were meaningful to those who tell them, that have shaped understanding of
the field. What many of us know about our subject comes in part
from conversations with colleagues, from the stories they have
told us, not from reading and evaluating published works. And
from those accepted as co-members of the profession we do not
discount verbal interest and effect. Indeed, we may relish it,
if the result is a good story that makes a point with which we
agree. We pay it the compliment of introducing it into our lectures.

The implication of such observations is that the narrative use
of language is not a property of subordinate cultures, whether
folk, or working-class, or the like, but a universal function.
The great restriction on its use in a society such as ours has to
do with when it is considered appropriate and legitimate. Generally speaking, it is considered legitimate, a valid use of language
in the service of knowledge, when it is used *among co-members of
a group*.

If the narrative function is excluded in an institutional setting,
such as a college or school, the implication is that the students
are defined as NOT co-members of a group with those who teach
them.

Perhaps some of the decline in education in the country is
connected with this suppression of the narrative function. Certainly it is more and more the case that teachers come from districts outside the district in which they teach, even from outside
the city. Possibly schools worked better in the past when staff
and students shared more of the same world of experience, and
narrative use of language was more acceptable between them.
This factor could only be a partial one, but it may nevertheless
be significant.

Students may come from homes in which narrative is an important way of communicating knowledge. They may take part in
peer groups in which experience and insight is shared through
exchange of narrative. A classroom that excludes narratives may
be attempting to teach them both new subject matter and a new
mode of learning, perhaps without fully realizing it. Again,
difference between the culture of the teacher and the classroom,
on the one hand, and the culture of the children outside the
classroom, on the other, may be a problem. If so, a teacher may
not be able to be an ethnographer in the community, but she or
he can be an ethnographer of what is present in the classroom
itself. Giving children turns at narrative may allow them to bring

the outside culture inside. Finally, a teacher who permits herself or himself personal narrative, but not the children, may not
be bringing children closer but underscoring the barrier (as well
as being perceived perhaps as wasting time).

Consider graduate studies again. Success on the part of a
graduate student, in the eyes of the faculty, is in part a matter
of socialization into the profession. That socialization is a matter
in part of acquiring the lore and outlook of the profession, an
informal education. A student who had mastered facts and
theories and methods, and who had no stories, and no interest
in stories, would trouble a faculty. On the one hand, the already
initiated want to be considered entertaining or at least useful
sources of lore that is of interest; on the other hand, the initi-
ates at appropriate steps should show themselves to be entertaining, or at least useful, sources of lore in turn (as when having
returned from field work). There is a desire on both sides perhaps for the link between generations to be more than names of
documents and in bibliographies.

(Fame can be defined simply as the case in which a larger,
non-professional circle knows some of the names and is interested
in some of the stories. Others not themselves the object of interest find audiences for whatever narratives they themselves can
tell that involve the name. Stories could be studied in terms of
their range of distribution: department-wide, campus-wide, pro-
fession-wide, general intellectual circles.)

This argument goes somewhat against the grain of a major
thrust of our society for generations. That thrust has been to
transcend the parochial, the local, the rural, in the interest of
the opportunities and accomplishments of a general public sphere.
The often told journey to the city, or the larger city. (Though
even in the city one finds the successful able to indulge their
sentiment for their starting point and the events along the way,
others wanting or required to listen.) But perhaps this argument also helps to point up a major dilemma of our society: success in technical, professional fields is defined in such a way
that someone cannot both stay at home, or return there, to serve,
and feel successful. This is a major problem for persons with
strong ties to their communities of origin, such as Native Americans. One needs advanced training in order to be competent, to
be able to cope with problems faced by the community of origin,
but the advanced training embodies a message of on, upward,
and away. Perhaps the fundamental failing of higher education
in the United States is to educate for status and not for service.
Or to define service without regard to considerations of locality,
so that local is inevitably seen as lesser. Perhaps the treatment
of personal narrative in educational settings plays a part in all
this.

WARM SPRINGS INTERLUDE

Much of my sense of this problem comes from experience over the
years (over the summers, mostly) at Warm Springs in Oregon.
Let me try to convey something of this experience. In doing so,
I draw on a letter written (24 August 1976) to Dennis Tedlock,
responding to questions about the directions of the journal he
edits, *Alcheringa*, and leading into general questions about the
role of language in poetry, ethnography, and social life. Just
before writing, my wife, Virginia, and I had been reflecting on
a quality of the use of language in the life of Indian people we
know. It is a quality one comes to have a sense of through being around them over a period of time. In one way it is a sense
of a *weighted quality to incident in personal lives:* as when one
friend, Hazel Suppah, told us that her son had been out to look
at a root cellar her family had built many years ago. He came
back to say, "You know, it's still good. I think we could use
it." All this in the context of a visit off the road to where an
old man had lived years ago, the house now fallen in, and the
barn, nothing disturbed but only gradually reassimilated to the
land. Hazel had lived nearby when young; the old man had come
over to their place when lonesome. One bike lay prone against a
slight rise, now a magnificent red bronze, green growing around
and through the lines of its structure, the lowest and nearest
point, a pedal, already partly within the soil. Hazel was looking
for an old-style wooden trough (resembling a canoe) that the old
man had had out for watering horses; it was gone, she realized
it must be the very one that the Tribe had installed in the resort at the other end of the reservation, with flowers planted in
it. If she'd known the land had been sold to the Tribe, she
would have come to get it herself. We rummaged all around
the land, nothing to be heard but insects, the white peak of Mt.
Hood just visible from certain points behind the high hills across
the highway from which we had come. All those old places are
vacant now and most everything in them taken, years ago, by
men who built power lines across. The Indians themselves didn't
take an interest then; Hazel said they all had the same things
themselves then. Now these old places, the isolated homesteads
allotted to families in the founding of the reservation more than
a century ago, to make Christian farmers of them, are another
world and time to the Indians themselves, who cluster mostly
around the end of the reservation where the Agency, the Tribal
administration, the mill, the restaurant, the housing projects are.
Places that one can go out to in order to find and pick up things,
memories, like berry patches. We brought back an intact old
kerosene can for Hazel; she was sure her daughter would want to
go out and get the two others there. A weather-polished twin-
pronged grey piece of wood, having nothing to do with the farm,
was found by Ginny, and now shows between two trees just

outside the window of our cabin back across the mountain. Two
matching bronze sections of a broken harness, metal, a few links
of chain on each, I carried about in each hand as we walked all
round the rises on which the buildings half-stood, up to the
fences, down to the run-off creek, and finally put in the back
of the car. Well, I got carried away with trying to convey something. And forgot to put in the sunlight, along with the stillness.
Back to functions of language.[3]

Virginia pointed out that in going around with a friend from
Warm Springs one often *saw* a bit of experience becoming an event
to be told, being told and being retold until it took shape as a
narrative, one that might become a narrative told by others.
Hazel had such stories about the old man who'd had that place,
Dan Walker, stories I had heard from others. Her son's remarks
had the weight of a theme, a kernel, of a story, the first act
perhaps. Perhaps we'll hear the rest after it has come about.
My oldest friend, Hiram Smith, once did this to me. We had
wandered about twenty minutes in a store in The Dalles, drifting
out at last; later, to his daughter, Hiram reported, "Oh, that
young guy in there, he didn't know nothin' about fishing equipment, Dell and I just turned around and walked right out." No-
nonsense partners, us.

Many must have had experiences of this kind. Such experiences seem to point to something a bit beyond our current concerns. There is a current movement to go beyond collection and
analysis of texts to observation and analysis of performance.
That is essential, but perhaps only the second moment of three.
The third is what Hazel Suppah often did, what Hiram Smith did,
what members of cultures world-wide often do, I suspect. Continuous with the others, this third is the process in which performance and text live, the inner substance to which performance
is the cambium, as it were, and crystallized text the bark. It is
the grounding of performance and text in a narrative view of life.
That is to say, a view of life as a potential source of narrative.
Incidents, even apparently slight incidents, have pervasively the
potentiality of an interest that is worth retelling. The quality of
this is different from gossip, or the flow of talk from people who
have nothing but themselves to talk about--their illnesses, their
marriages, their children, their jobs, etc. Not that the difference
is in the topics. The difference is in the silences. There is a
certain focusing, a certain weighting. A certain potentiality, of
shared narrative form, on the one hand, of consequentiality, on
the other.

If such a view and practice is the grounding of an essential
texture of certain ways of life, then it needs to be experienced
and conveyed if others are to understand and appreciate the way
of life. Indians do not themselves think of such a thing as their
"culture." They use "culture" as we do popularly, for "high culture," dances, fabricated material objects, things that can go in
a museum and on a stage. Norms for speaking and performance

go further into general norms of etiquette and interaction that are
at the heart of certain qualities and problems, yet not explicitly
acknowledged.

Ethnography is the only way in which one can find out and
know this aspect of a way of life. Of course one could ask in an
interview, or on a questionnaire: "Do you ever make up little
stories about things you see or do?" ("Oh, I guess so.")
"Could you tell me one?" ("Well, let me see, once....") Even if
successful in getting little texts--texts almost certain not to be
truly performed (see Wolfson 1978)--such an approach would not
discover the texture of the text, the way in which it is embodied
in the rhythm of continuing life and observation and reflection of
life. One has to go around and be around to come to see how the
world is a world closely observed.

CONCLUSION

All this offers folklore, as a discipline with a special interest and
knowledge of narrative, an opportunity for both many empirical
studies and a principled critique of present society. The narrative use of language seems universal, potentially available to
everyone, and to some degree inescapable. Humanity was born
telling stories, so to speak, but when we look about us, we find
much of humanity mute or awkward much of the time. The right
to think and express thought in narrative comes to be taken as
a privilege, as a resource that is restricted, as a scarce good, so
that the right to unite position and personal experience in public
is a badge of status and rank. *My* account is to be listened to
because I am an *x*; yours is of no interest because you are only
y. All this in independence of narrative ability. The one who is
y may be an excellent raconteur, *x* a bore. To be sure, the excellent raconteur may be enjoyed if he or she chooses time and
topic with discretion. But very likely we hear narrative as much
these days, and enjoy it less. The decline in narrative performance among ethnic groups assimilating to the mainstream of life in
the United States has been deplored often enough. On the thesis
of this paper, the result is not a decline in quantity, but perhaps
in quality. If the Michael of Cazden's account enters the security
of an established profession, and gains standing in it, probably
he will find that his narrative accounts of his professionally relevant personal experiences are considered appropriate, count for
something. Whether or not he tells them well. Successful people,
interviewed on TV shows, are recurrently asked to tell "how they
got their start." No doubt many develop a moderately interesting
narrative, if only because it is needed and they have opportunity
to practice it. But sheer narrative ability, apart from success,
seldom finds a place. Orson Bean is a superb narrator, and sometimes Johnny Carson gives him his head, but on other shows, he
has gotten short shrift from MCs looking only for short repartee,
and embarrassed by the presence of small works of art.

Study of the interaction between ability and opportunity with respect to narrative experience is very much needed. The findings have a special bearing on education. Folklore has a special role to play in providing such findings.

NOTES

1. More than the students are different in the two classes. During the double three-hour Extension lecture, we take a break for coffee and informal talk. The evening hour, and the second presentation of the same content, probably made me more relaxed as well. Participants and situation are thus confounded in their influence.

2. Thus, from White's essay on Metahistory (1973a):

...it can be argued that interpretation in history consists of the provisions of a plot-structure for a sequence of events so that their nature as a comprehensible process is revealed by their figuration as a story of a particular kind. What one history may emplot as a tragedy, another may emplot as a comedy or romance. As thus envisaged, the "story" which the historian purports to "find" in the historical record is proleptic to the "plot" by which the events are finally revealed to figure a recognizable structure of relationships of a specifically mythic sort. (291)

In other words, the historian must draw upon a fund of culturally provided "mythoi" in order to constitute the facts as figuring a story of a particular kind, just as he must appeal to that same fund of "mythoi" in the minds of his readers to endow his account of the past with the odor of meaning or significance. (294) One can argue, in fact, that just as there can be no explanation in history without a story, so too there can be no story without a plot by which to make of it a story of a particular kind. (297)

This perspective is developed in detailed analyses in the 1973 book, but these elements of the perspective are stated in clearer, more quotable form in the article.

3. Some readers may be embarrassed by this bit of personal narrative. If so, the embarrassment helps me make my point.

REFERENCES CITED

Bernstein, Basil, ed. 1973. *Class, Codes and Control II: Applied Studies Towards a Sociology of Language.* London: Routledge & Kegan Paul.

Bissex, G. 1968. *The Harvardization of Michael.* Unpublished term paper, Harvard University.

Burke, Kenneth. 1962. *The Grammar of Motives.* Cleveland:

World. (Originally published Englewood Cliffs, N.J.:
    Prentice Hall, 1945.)
Gouldner, Alvin W. 1975-76. "Prologue to a Theory of Revolu-
    tionary Intellectuals." *Telos* 26:3-36.
Horton, R. and R. Finnegan. 1973. *Modes of Thought: Essays
    on Thinking in Western and Non-Western Societies.* London:
    Faber & Faber.
Hymes, Dell. 1976. "Sapir, Competence, Voices." Ms.
Labov, William. 1972. "The Logic of Non-Standard English."
    In *Language in the Inner City: Studies in the Black English
    Vernacular.* Philadelphia: University of Pennsylvania Press,
    pp. 201-240.
Mueller, Clauss. 1973. *The Politics of Communication. A Study
    in the Political Sociology of Language, Socialization and
    Legitimation.* New York: Oxford.
Philips, S. 1974. *The Invisible Culture: Communication in the
    Classroom and Community on the Warm Springs Indian Reser-
    vation.* Unpublished doctoral dissertation, University of
    Pennsylvania.
Ricks, Christopher. 1967. *Milton's Grand Style.* London: Ox-
    ford University Press. (First published, Clarendon Press,
    1963.)
White, Hayden. 1973a. "Interpretation in History." *New Liter-
    ary History* 4(2):281-314.
_____. 1973b. *Metahistory. The historical imagination in
    nineteenth-century Europe.* Baltimore: Johns Hopkins Press.
Wolfson, Nessa. 1976. "Speech Events and Natural Speech:
    Some Implications for Sociolinguistic Methodology." *Language
    in Speech* 5(2):211-218.
_____. 1978. "A Feature of Performed Narrative: The Con-
    versational Historical Present." *Language in Society* 7
    (forthcoming).

language in education: forward to fundamentals

INTRODUCTION

I have been asked to speak about imperatives for change--
change in university settings such as this, and change in schooling generally. This I am glad to do. I believe profoundly in the
need for change in the way we understand language, and in what
we do with language in schools. I agreed to become Dean of the
School of Education because of that belief. But let me pause.
Some of you must suspect that you are about to hear another
lecture from a self-appointed bearer of light to the benighted.
Not so. Part of what we need to know in order to change is not
now known to anyone; teachers are closer to part of it than most
linguists. No one who gives priority in the study of language to
the needs of education could consider present linguistics a region
of the already saved, toward which educators must look for missionaries and redemption. I have argued against the mainstream
in linguistics for years, precisely because it has been inadequate
to study of the role of language in human life. It has made
assumptions, adopted methods, accepted priorities that prevent
the contribution to education that serious study of language
should make.

There are serious scholarly reasons for critique of the mainstream in linguistics, reasons that draw on traditions of thought
with roots in the anthropology of Sapir, the sociology of Marx,
the linguistics and poetics of Jakobson, the literary criticism and
rhetoric of Burke.[1] There are scientific problems internal to linguistics that cannot be solved without change in the foundations
from which they are approached. But there are civic reasons for
critique as well. One by one some of us find it intolerable to
continue a linguistics defined in a way that divorces it from the
needs of the society which supports us. The number of students
of language sharing this outlook grows. The time is ripe for a
relation between the study of language and the study of education
that is one of partnership, not preaching.

Please do not misunderstand. To criticize linguistics is not
to absolve education. The ability of schools to deal with the linguistic situation in the United States is severely limited. One
often says, start where the child is, develop the child's full potential. To do that, linguistically, one must have knowledge of
the ways of speaking of the community of which the child is part.
Very little knowledge of this sort is available. Each of us has
some insight into these things--some command of the ways of

139

speaking, but each of us is a poor judge as well. Just because
language is basic to so many other things, so presupposed, much
of our speaking is out of awareness; we may be ignorant of much
of it, or even in good faith confidently misreport it. Things we
are sure we never say may turn up on someone's tape; matters
of more or less may be assimilated to a sense of all-or-nothing.
Our impressions of the speech of others may be remarkably accurate for placing them, without our being aware that our own speech
may contain some of the same features. Recently a linguistic and
anthropologist in Montreal recorded the speech of two friends, a
man and a woman, each speaking sometimes in formal situations,
sometimes in informal situations in which the colloquial French
known as Joual was appropriate. She played samples to a distinguished Montreal audience. The audience heard four people,
not two. It could not be convinced that there were only two, so
strong were its preconceptions as to the categorical difference.

If we are to know objectively what speaking is like, there
must be ethnographies of speaking, open to discovery of facts
that are inconvenient for one's grammar, pedagogy, or social
assumptions. Educators and linguists alike have been remiss in
not thinking of such knowledge as needed. Where linguists have
pursued intuitions and universal models that ignore the realities
of speech communities and language use, many educators have
pursued notions of language and correctness that have had the
same effect. Why want to know more about something one already
knew was not really 'language'? that one knew was 'wrong'?

All this leads me to believe that there are three primary imperatives for change.

First, to *see* the need for knowledge of the language situations of our country.

Second, to *support* training and research to obtain such
knowledge.

Third, to *change* the relations between linguistics and education.

Let me elaborate on this last imperative for a moment. A new
relation between linguistics and education may be basic to all the
rest. The essential point is that the nature of the change that
is needed is not one-sided or one way. Linguists and educators
should work together and change together. Only thus can research on language be relevant to the situations faced by schools.

I shall return to the relation between linguistics and education. Now let me try to give substance to the need for knowledge.

WANTING TO KNOW

Certain goals on which we would probably agree should govern
imperatives for change. The treatment of language in schools
should help, not harm. It should help children, and through
them their families and communities, to maintain and foster

self-respect. It should be consonant with respect for diversity
of background and aspirations. It should contribute to equality
rather than inequality.

It is probably hard to keep from nodding to words like these.
Such words are familiar and accepted. Yet we face assumptions
and ignorance about language that contradict and work against
such goals.

Consider a school in a community. What would you want to
know, were you responsible for the linguistic aspect of the schooling there? There are many who would not think that there was
much that they needed to know, even how to use the language of
the children. Recently I was asked to a meeting at the Philadelphia School Board to help resist pressure to remove the requirement that a teacher in a TESOL class know the language of the
children being taught English, that is, be able to communicate
with them. Most teachers at the school in Madras, Oregon, to
which children from Warm Springs Indian Reservation go, do not
think they need to know anything about the Indian languages in
the homes from which the children come, or the etiquette of speaking there. By and large, indeed, knowing languages and knowing
about language is little valued in our country, if it involves acceptance of diversity. You and I may have no difficulty in understanding standard West Indian English, may even admire it--I
think it myself the most lovely English I have heard. But the
daughter of a family from Jamaica was just admitted to a state-
affiliated university in Philadelphia on the condition that she take
a course in English for foreign students. Have you not often
heard a proper middle-class white say in exasperation to a cab-
driver or voice on the phone, "Oh, I can't understand you", although the black or Spanish accent was entirely intelligible?
Identification of the difference having closed the listener's ear?

When educated, concerned people want to know about language, what is it they are likely to want to know? A graduate
student at my university reports that when she spoke recently to
the group that supports her studies, their serious, well inten-
tioned questions made assumptions about languages and their relations to human groups that a linguistics student could not even
have imagined entertaining. Recently I was asked by a cultured
voice on the phone to help with a program being planned for the
Canadian Broadcasting System, to view French in Montreal in the
light of similar situations in the United States and the Caribbean.
I began helpfully naming friends who know about such things,
when it came out that the premise of the program was that the
French-speaking lower classes of Montreal could not think right
because they could not speak right. (You can imagine the haste
and confusion with which I withdrew the names and tried to dis-
associate myself from the whole thing.)

These are merely recent instances that have impinged upon
me in the course of a month or two. It is almost too painful to
be a student of language attentive to such things--examples

accumulate so readily of prejudice, discrimination, ignorance
bound up with language. It makes one wonder if discrimination
connected with language is not so pervasive as to be almost im-
pervious to change, so deeply rooted as to almost preclude support for the asking of questions that might lead to change. To
be sure, some may be sure that children would be fine if left
alone, and be glad to learn what is wrong with schools. Others
may be sure that schools are doing what is right, and be glad
to learn what is wrong with children and the homes from which
they come. It is hard to find people who sense a need to understand objectively the school child's communicative world, a world
seriated into a multiplicity of contexts of situation and ways of
speaking suitable to each, a world of a plurality of norms for
selecting and grouping together features of a verbal style, of a
plurality of situation-sensitive ways of interacting and interpreting meaning in terms of styles, such that a type of situation such
as classroom interaction with a teacher or formal test-making has
meaning in terms of its relation to the rest. Such that each involves a spoken or written genre that has a place in a series of
such, a possibility of performance dependent on particular rules
for commitment to performance. So that to understand the part
of a verbal repertoire that appears in educational settings, one
needs to be able to compare choices of communicative device and
meaning, displays of communicative and cognitive ability, across
a range of settings. So that to understand the part of a child's
(or teacher's) ways of speaking one sees in school, one needs to
understand the whole. One needs to do or to draw on linguistic
ethnography.[2]

As you know, there is little done and little on which to draw.
What I have sketched in general terms is what one might reason-
ably ask about if concerned with the role of language in schooling in another culture or country; expecting things to be strange,
one wants to know. In a sense, we need to be able to stand
back from our own situations so as to see them as strange and
as needing to be known.

BLACK AMERICANS, NATIVE AMERICANS, SPANISH-SPEAKING AMERICANS

I should not suggest that nothing at all is known or being done.
Certainly there has been a good deal of attention in recent years
to patterns of speech associated with some of the major groups
that make up this diverse country. Yet the research is scattered
and spotty with regard to both geography and class. The case
of 'Black English' is instructive. In the 1960's the ways of speaking of Black Americans attracted attention. The research has
been important in demonstrating the systematic, rule-governed
nature of the vernacular spoken by many Blacks, as against
notions of it as an incoherent corruption. Notions of Black children practically without language were shown to be functions of

intimidating formal situations in schools, to be situational, not
general.   Some of this work helped as well to highlight the respects in which distinctive features of the vernacular point to the
wider spectrum of Caribbean Creoles and their West African elements.   Awareness grew of the place of the vernacular in peer
group interaction against the background of Caribbean and African traditions of spoken artistry.   Still, research focused mostly
on the variety of speech most strikingly different from the public
standard, the vernacular of adolescent urban males.   Much less
analytic attention was given to the speech of Black women, of
preachers and ministers, of established upper-class families, or
to the Caribbean and African background of elaborated 'talking
sweet' and public oratory.   And some explanations of what became
known were so partial as to be false.   Some linguists wished to
treat the vernacular as only superficially different and formally
derivative from standard English, for reasons having to do in
part with convenient simplicity of a grammatical model.   Others
wished to treat the vernacular as so distinct that it might require
its own textbooks.   There are indeed places where people want
their variety maintained independently in print from a closely related one (in Czechoslovakia Slovaks feel this way about the relation of their variety to Czech).   In the United States such a conception fails to take into account the actual attitudes of many
Black people who want the variety of English in the classroom,
especially the written variety, to be the common standard.   Still
others drew from this isolated fact the inference that Blacks depreciated the vernacular, even speaking of 'self-hatred'.   In point
of fact, there is widespread acceptance of the vernacular variety
at home and in informal situations generally; [3] it retains a special
place even among Black students at a university such as Prince-
ton.   Yet sympathetic interpretations of Black speech can be inadequate too.   Many come to know Black terms for uses of language, such as 'shucking' and 'jiving', and regard them entirely
as an Afro-American ethnic heritage.   Yet analogous genres of
language use can be found among lower class white youths, and
such ways of coping verbally may have their origin in subordinate social status as well as in ethnic tradition.
    The relation between varieties and uses of English, on the
one hand, and being Black, on the other, is complex and only
beginning to be adequately known.   The situation is little better
with regard to other major groups.   We think of Native Americans
in terms of the many languages lost, and of efforts to maintain
or revive those that remain.   The relation of schools to these
efforts is of the greatest importance.   My own anger and passion
about the treatment of language in schools comes largely from
experience of local schools and educational research institutions
that affect Indian people at Warm Springs Reservation in Oregon.
But these situations must not be oversimplified.   Indian Americans
themselves may differ in their views as to what is best in terms
of language.   And aspects of language that are crucial to the

success of Indian children may not involve the traditional Indian language at all. Where the Indian children are, linguistically, may not be an Indian language, but an Indian variety of English. There are probably several dozen such Indian varieties of English in the United States. They play a significant social role. Someone who has been away, and who returns to a local community, must take up the local variety of English or be judged snobbish. Features of children's speech that seem individual errors may in fact reflect a community norm. They may reflect a carryover into English of patterns from an Indian language. In the English of Indians at Isleta pueblo, south of Albuquerque, New Mexico, a double negative contrasts with a single negative as a carryover of a contrast between two types of negation in the Isleta language. There are doubtless other such examples, but the fact is that Isleta English is the only form of Indian English carefully studied and reported on in print, and that only in the last few years.[4]

The language situation of an Indian community will be still more complex, in having standard as well as local vernacular English present, and a vernacular, even reduced, variety of an Indian language as well as or even instead of its 'classic' form. In the Southwest Spanish may be a factor as well. Yet we have hardly more than a few sketches of such cases. With Indians as with Blacks, research has not attempted to provide systematic knowledge of the language situation of the communities experienced by children. Research has focused not on social reality, but on the exotic. To say this is not to condemn study of traditional Indian languages. Much of my work continues to be devoted to the study of one group of languages, now nearing extinction. I and a colleague are the last to work intensively with fully fluent speakers, and like others in such a situation, we have obligations both to those who have shared their knowledge with us and to those who later will want access to it. The work has its contribution to make to respect and self-respect for Indian people. The disproportion between what most linguists do and what most needs to be done is not here. There have never been trained scholars enough, and much has been lost unrecorded in consequence. With all its wealth our country has sparsely supported knowledge of the language that first named the continent. The fact is telling. We have barely managed to study languages that fit our image of the noble Redman, let alone begun to notice the actual linguistic makeup of Indian communities.

The knowledge one needs to start where Indian children, any children, are goes beyond varieties of language, of course, to patterns of the use of language--customary community ways of answering questions, calling upon others, taking turns in conversation, speaking or remaining silent, giving instruction by verbal precept or observed example, all the ways in which etiquette of speaking and value of language may take distinctive shape. Many Indian children come to school, speaking only English, yet encounter difficulty, not because of language difference, but because of difference in patterns for the use of language. Children found 'shy' and non-talkative in class may be as talkative as any, if observed in situations where the rights and duties of speaking are those of the community from which they come. In such a case one needs to know not a language, but a community way of speaking.

The issue and language most prominent today are bilingual education and Spanish. I cannot attempt to treat this complex situation here, except to note that the general difficulty is the same. Too little is known as a basis for policy and practice in schools. The widespread resistence to such a thing indeed may cause bilingual education to be attacked as having failed before it will have had a chance to be understood and fairly tried. Efforts to provide equal educational opportunity to Spanish-speaking children must proceed with a minimum of information as to the Spanish the children speak, in relation to the varieties and uses of Spanish in the community from which they come. No simple general answer can be laid down in advance. There are several national and regional standards, Cuban, Puerto Rican, northern Mexican, Colombian, etc.; in many communities there is a range of varieties from a standard to colloquial vernacular and an argot, as well as a way of mingling Spanish and English in conversation that can count as a special variety among intimates. The attitudes of Spanish speakers toward the elements of this complex language situation are themselves complex. Clearly it is not enough to advocate "Spanish." It is possible to have Anglo children doing well, Spanish-speaking children doing poorly in a Spanish class in a school. There are problems of the fit or conflict between the Spanish spoken by children and the Spanish taught, between community and teacher attitudes, between the language-linked aspirations of cultural traditionalists and the job-linked aspirations of some of the working class; the desire of some speakers to institutionalize Spanish as a language of higher education and professional activity, versus the needs of children for whom Spanish is primarily a vernacular of the home and community; problems of children educated in Puerto Rico coming to the mainland with inadequate English and children educated on the mainland going to Puerto Rico with inadequate Spanish.

There are problems of assessing the language abilities of children both for assignment to classes and for evaluation in programs. Assignment to classes is sometimes being done under mandate of law in a begrudging rough-and-ready fashion, minimizing the number of children to be assigned. Sometimes the availability of monies to a district prompts forced assignment to special classes of bilingual children who have no English problem at all. Valid assessments of language ability require naturalistic observation across a range of settings, but such methods have been little developed in explicit form. Formative evaluation of programs in bilingual situations needs ethnographic knowledge of the community

language situation, and summative evaluation needs ethnographic
monitoring of the process by which a program comes to have
particular meanings and outcomes for participants and community.
Such success as bilingual programs have will be best attested in
the debates ahead, not by test scores, but by case-history accounts that show convincingly the benefits to children and communities, and how they were achieved.[5]

ETHNIC HERITAGE AND USAGES OF LANGUAGE

The situations of Black Americans, Native Americans, Spanish-
speaking Americans are salient but not unique. Bilingual education is an issue for communities of Chinese, Japanese, Filipino,
and others. Many European languages in addition to Spanish are
maintained to a significant extent. Immigration renews some of
these communities. All of them participate in a climate of opinion
that is world-wide. The general truth would seem to be that
about twenty years ago, when those who spoke in the limelight
foresaw an end to ideology, and an endless technocratic future
whose chief problem would be leisure, many ordinary people
around the world were drawing a different lesson from their
experience. They had been caught up in such a vision of the
post-war future for a while, only to begin to find that their
place in it was not worth the giving up of all that they had been.
'Progress' came more and more to seem the 'dirty word' that
Kenneth Burke has called it--less an engine carrying them onward
and upward, more a juggernaut about to run over them, their
place, their customs, their speech.
    This general revival of concern with ethnic heritage is not
merely a part of the annual tourist laundry ring around the
world, each countryside emptying out in summer to take in someone else's carefully staged culture while on vacation. It is a
shift in outlook that has to do with what one is for oneself, as
a member of a family with a certain name, a certain history, a
knowledge of certain places, certain ways of meeting sorrow and
sharing joy. Many of you may know personally the price that can
be exacted in acquiring a lingua franca at the cost of a language
of the home.
    Some repudiate concern of this kind as nostalgia and senti-
mentality, even as a dangerous refusal to face present realities.
I think that something profound is involved. Any one concern
may seem particularistic and limiting; when all such concerns are
considered together, one sees something general, a deep-running
tide. It is a vision limited to a national lingua franca that begins
to appear old-fashioned, limited, sectarian.
    The deep-running tide seems to me a shift in what is regarded
as the dominant obstacle to a way of life in balance with human
needs. A century, even a generation ago, it was common to think
that the dominant obstacle consisted of traditional ideas and customs. Except when compartmentalized in diminished form, as

objects of intermittent piety and curiosity, specific cultural traditions, beliefs, conventions, identities seemed brakes from the past
on progress. The future lay with a science and mode of production that could realize the control of nature, and the plenty, of
which mankind was capable. Now we are far less sure. Some
critics of contemporary society consider the very idea of incessant
technological change to be itself the dominant obstacle to a way of
life in balance with human needs. Not that material progress is
irrelevant, but that the quality of life is seen more clearly to depend on other things as well. What seemed a policy in the interest of all has come to seem an instrument of profit to some at the
expense of others in many cases. Uncontrolled, it threatens community today and even sustenance tomorrow.

There is an essential linguistic dimention to this. It is hard
to specify, but necessary to address. Let me try to suggest
something of its nature.

The internal structures of language and the structures of use
to which languages are shaped alike show two fundamental, complementary general kinds of function, of meaning, at work. They
are intertwined in reality, but our way of thinking about language
has separated and opposed them.[6] One can be roughly indicated
as concerned with naming, reference, sheer statement, the technical, analytic, logical uses of language. Modern linguistics has
built its models on this aspect of language. Modern science,
technology, and rationalized bureaucracy give it pre-eminence.
For a time the uses of language characteristic of literature, religion, personal expression were neglected and on the defensive.
For a time the pinnacle of knowledge appeared to many to be a
single logical language to which all science and legitimate knowledge might be reduced. That ideal has been largely given up and
replaced by recognition of a plurality of legitimate uses of language. The seminal figures in philosophy of course were Cassirer
and Wittgenstein, and there have been related developments in
poetics, anthropology, sociology. Interpersonal, expressive,
aesthetic uses of language come more to the fore. In part it is
because an ideal of language that seemed the touchstone of progress, of the advance of reason, has been too often traduced.
The idioms of objective knowledge, of science, mathematics, logic,
experiment, statistics, contracts, regulation and control were once
seen as common bases for progress for us all. We have too often
seen claims to authority, couched in such idioms, turn out to be
rationalizations of special interests, elite excuses, outright decep-
tions, as with the Vietnamese war. Idioms of moral concern and
personal knowledge that had at first no standing came to be seen
as more accurate guides than the trappings of elaborate studies
and reports. A little later it was general discovery of the personal voice through transcripts of tapes that decided, I think,
the public verdict on a president. I could not prove the point,
but I think these two experiences have had complementary, decisive effect on our sense of validity in the use of language.

I sense a more general drift as well. Increasingly we are concerned to have a place for things that cannot be said without distortion, or even said at all, in the idioms of elaborated, formal, purportedly rational and referential speech that take pride of place in public science, public government, linguistic and pedagogical grammars. There are things we know and need to be that have no standing there. A sense of this is a reflection of the central problem of the role of language in modern society, the crisis of language, namely, what the balance is to be between modes of use of language. The old dichotomies--correct vs. incorrect, rational vs. emotional, referential vs. expressive--fail to capture the nature and complexity of the problem, for it is not a matter of mutually exclusive opposites, but of the interweaving of mutually indispensable functions.

EDUCATION AND LINGUISTIC FOUNDATIONS

I am sorry not to be precise, concrete, and clear about this. It would require far more than one lecture to try to explain the ramifications of this point for the study of language, to trace the implications at different levels of the organization of language, to appraise the efforts that are being made now to devise an adequate general model. I can try to say clearly what this complex situation means for the future of language in education. It is this. Linguistics developed out of a situation in which the study of language was loosely distributed across a variety of disciplines. It became the central discipline by development of general methods for the formal study of language structure. The methods and the associated conception of language structure focused on an essential, but partial, aspect of the organization of language. Other aspects remained secondary or eschewed. The focus of attention, having started with phonology, and proceeded through morphology and syntax, has now reached semantics and even 'pragmatics' (that is, the interpretation of meaning in context of use). From every side it begins to be recognized that linguistics as we have known it is inevitably part of a larger field.[7]

At the first, language structure was divorced from language use. Now language use is included along with language structure by most. Eventually it will be generally recognized that it is not use that is a derivative of structure, but structure that is dependent on use. That one can never solve the problems of the organization of language in social life without starting from social life, from the patterns of activity and meaning within which linguistic features are organized into styles and ways of speaking. A linguistics that is truly the science of language, linguistics that is truly a foundation for education, will be a linguistics that is part of the study of communicative interaction. It will understand linguistic competence as part of communicative competence. It will understand the character of competence in relation to the social history and social structure that shape it in a given case.

Such a linguistics, should the day arrive, will have an essential property. Its practice and theory will be adequate to all the
means employed in speech and all the meanings that speaking (or
another use of language) has. Its theory of English phonology
will attend not only to the features that make a consonant /p/
instead of /b/, but also to the aspiration that can make the word
angry. Its theory of syntax will attend to isolated grammatical
sentences as but a special case among the intelligible, acceptable
sequences of discourse. Its theory of meaning will attend not
only to words and constructions, but also to the meanings inherent in choice of dialect of variety, of conversational or narrative
genre, of occasion to speak or be silent. Its theory of competence will go beyond innate and universal abilities to the kinds of
competence valued and permitted in a given society, to opportunities and obstacles of access to kinds of competence. It will recognize that the very role of speaking, of language and use of language, is not the same in every society; that societies differ in
their ideals of language and ability in language; that use of language, like sex and eating, is a universal possibility and necessity of society, but without power to determine its place or meaning. Its relative importance among other modes of communication,
its role as resource or danger, art or tool, depends on what is
made of it. [8] Two things follow. First, the relation between education and linguistics cannot be a matter simply of joining the two
as they are now. We do not yet have the kind of linguistics just
described. Second, we are not likely to get it if linguistics is
left to itself. The prestige of formal models as against empirical
inquiry remains strong. The pull to continue to concentrate on
familiar ground will be great. To get the linguistics we need will
take pushing by others. Educators ought to be in the forefront.
If you should remember just one thing from this occasion, please
remember this: Do ask yourself what linguistics can do for you,
but even more, demand of linguistics that what it can do *be* done.
And do not apologize for the demand, or assume that it diverts
the study of language from pure science to murky application.
The fact is that the study of language does not now have the
knowledge on which much of application should be based, and
cannot get it without new theoretical, methodological, and empirical work. To demand attention to the needs of education is not
just a demand for applied linguistics. It is a demand for change
in the foundations of linguistics. The struggle for educational
change with regard to language, and the struggle for scientific
adequacy in the study of language, are interdependent.

I have used the word 'struggle' advisedly. It would be misleading to suggest that the kind of linguistics we need is an apple
almost ripe, ready to drop at a tweak of the stem. There is indeed a diffused slow drift in the right direction, such that work
entwined with practical problems has low status. Still, work
more abstract and remote from practical problems, the higher the
status. Some leading linguists, such as William Labov, want to

reverse this polarity. Educators can help, and may have some
leverage these days when conventional positions for linguists are
hard to find. The fact that linguistics itself is evolving in a
direction that makes work in educational settings germane is a
help, as is the fact, just mentioned, that new theory is part of
what is needed. Still, a second great difficulty remains. This
is the difficulty of seeing language in education in the context
of American society, steadily and whole.

SEEING OUR LANGUAGE SITUATION

The history of attention to language situations within the country
points up the difficulty. Black uses of English have been evolving in the United States since before the Revolution, but have
begun to be adequately studied only as a consequence of the Civil
Rights Movement and the federal attention and funding that re-
sponded to it. Spanish has been here for centuries as well, but
Spanish bilingualism and language situations have begun to be
studied adequately only as a result of the socio-political mobilization of Spanish-speakers. American Indian communities have had
multilingual situations and distinctive ways of speaking for generations without much attention. The interest of many Indian people in maintaining and reviving traditional languages fits into the
traditional approach to the study of Indian languages, but it has
taken the Native American mobilization of recent years to make
academic scholars think of the preparation of materials useful in
education as something they should do. Indian English and ways
of speaking still remain relatively little studied.
    In general, educationally significant aspects of a language
situation have come into focus only after the community in question has been defined as a social problem, and more especially,
as a social force. Previous attention to the languages involved
focused upon what seemed most exotic and remote. Immigrant and
Indian languages alike have been viewed mostly as something
lingering from the past.
    We need to begin to think of the linguistic heterogeneity of
our country as continuously present. The United States is a
multilingual country, with great numbers of users of many languages. American multilingualism is not an aberration or a resi-
due. If anything, it has increased in recent years, especially
with regard to Spanish, Vietnamese, and perhaps a few other
languages. We need to address the linguistic heterogeneity of
our country as a permanent feature of it, discuss what shape it
will and should have, anticipate the future. To do so, we have
to address the linguistic ethnography of the United States as a
sustained, central scientific task. Ad hoc responses after the
fact of social mobilization connected with language come too late
and provide too little help. And ad hoc responses are too easily
distorted by the immediate terms of social and political issues.

Members of language communities themselves may have a partial view. We need sustained work that provides both knowledge of language situations and an independent, critical assessment of language problems.

Educators have a stake in the mounting of such a program of study, since mobilization around issues of language so commonly turns attention to schools. Educators have a special stake in making sure that a sustained program of study includes independent, critical attention to the nature of language problems. That attention should include study of the process by which something having to do with language does (or does not) become defined as a problem in our country in the first place. It is not to be assumed that there is a fit between public recognition of problems and actual language situation. (To repeat, teacher failure to recognize the structure and role of Black English Vernacular still handicaps many Black children, and did even more before it became recognized as a 'problem' in the 1960's. Some of those who resist such recognition continue to be Black.)

I suspect there are four kinds of case. That is, there are indeed situations recognized as problems that are genuinely problems (bilingual education, for example); there may well be situations not defined as problems that can be left alone. But I suspect that there are also situations not now defined as problems that ought to be so defined--situations taken for granted but at possible cost. For example, very little has been done to study communication in medical settings, especially between professional personnel and patients.[9] What are the effects of difference in idiom, terminology, semantic system? or even of difference in native language, there being so many medical personnel of foreign origin? and in some regions so many patients with little command of English? Perhaps there is no recognized problem because those affected have little visibility or consciousness of common concern. Yet a series of articles in the New York Times might make this situation, itself unchanged, suddenly a 'problem'. Finally, there may be situations defined as problems that ought not to be, the issue being falsely or superficially posed--e.g., the supposed problem of children with practically 'no language'. Any of us may be subject to cultural blinders and public fashions. We need comparative, critical, historical perspective to transcend them.

We need, in short, to be able to see our country in terms of language, steadily and whole. To do so is to go beyond questions of diversity of languages and language-varieties. Black English, Navajo, Hopi, Zuni, Spanish, Italian, German, Slovenian, the many, many languages of this country are salient and important. The diversity they comprise is so great, so neglected, as to be almost overwhelming by itself. Yet there is something further. There is a unity that has also escaped us. I do not mean political and social unity. That is not in question. To be sure, the drive for homogeneity has been so great that even today the thought of diversity being accepted can frighten some. Street signs in

Spanish, even in a Spanish-speaking neighborhood, can attract
ire. A telephone company may refuse to hire a Spanish-speaking
operator, to answer emergency calls, in an area with many Spanish dominant speakers. To argue for recognition of ethnolinguistic diversity seems troubling to many, as if the ties between us
were so fragile as to break beneath a crumb of difference. But
the forces making for integration, the economic and communicative
ties of the country, are irreversibly dominant. To argue the
right to diversity is to argue only for breathing space within the
hive.

The unity in terms of which we need to see our country is
the unity in its dominant groups and institutions that gives it a
certain cut and pattern, regarding language, regarding the value
on language, the way in which language enters into life. We need
to be able to imagine the United States sociologically as if it were
a small country, a Belgium or Switzerland, a single entity of
which one could ask, as one can ask of any society: what are the
basic patterns of the use of language? what are the values, rights,
responsibilities associated with language? what is the outlook of
the culture with regard to language? how did it come to be that
way? how does it seem likely to change?

We are able to think of the Navajo or the French in this way.
We need to be able to imagine ourselves in this way as well, to
find, through comparative, historical, and descriptive study, a
mirror in which to see the United States as possessed throughout
its history of language policies, of predominant attitudes towards
language and its role, that give it one place among many possible
places in the roster of the world's cultures.

Even if there were only English the unity to be seen is not
simple. Imagine that the only language in the country was English, even standard English. Situations, roles, activities, personal characteristics such as age and sex would still affect and
shape ways of using language. The occupational and class structure of the society would still be there as a source of heterogeneity, on the one hand, and hegemony, on the other. Let us
consider heterogeneity first.

Inherent Heterogeneity. Even if everyone used some form of
standard English, all the manifold ways of talking as a person of
a certain kind, of using language to do a certain kind of thing,
would be present, needing to be discerned and described and
their consequences considered. Many of the judgments made of
persons in everyday life, many of the opportunities one has or
does not have, involve command or lack of command of these
styles and genres, of being able to talk like an X, or being able
to use language to do Y. Such diversity is inherent in social
life. Research has barely begun to address it adequately, relating linguistic devices and patterns to social meanings and roles.
It is the same here as with differences of whole language or
language-variety. Research mostly follows the flag of social
mobilization. Sex-related differences in language hardly appeared

for the first time a few years ago. Yet until recently one would have had to conclude that men and women talked alike in every society except for a few American Indian tribes, the Chukchee of Siberia, and some scattered others, so far as the published literature could show. Again, status-related differences in language are hardly the monopoly of the Japanese, Koreans, and Javanese, yet until recently linguistic theory treated them as fascinatingly special.

There is a general lesson to be drawn. A linguistics that starts from grammar can see socially relevant features only when they intrude within the grammar. If the very units of phonology or morphology cannot be stated without reference to the sex or status of a participant in speech, then the social fact is taken into account; indeed, the case may become celebrated as an instance of "men's and women's speech" or special concern with the expression of status. Yet sexual roles and status differences are universal in society, and assuredly come into play when people speak to each other. Starting from grammar, one does not see how they come into play; one has to start from the social feature itself, and look at the use of language from its vantage point. Then the features of language that are selected and grouped together as characteristics of speaking like a woman, speaking like an elder, and the like can be seen.

A final example: many are aware of the interesting ways in which choice of second person pronoun in French (tu: vous), German (Du: Sie), Russian (ty: vy), etc., can signal lesser or greater social distance. Many is the paper written on such pronouns and related forms of salutation and greeting. Yet it is a safe assumption that variation in social distance is universal, and universally expressed in one or another way in use of language. Management of social distance may well be one of the most pervasive dimensions of language use. One has to start from recognition of social distance to begin to see thoroughly and accurately how it is accomplished as a function of language.

Even if only standard English were found in the United States, then, there would be many socially shaped patterns of language use to discover and consider. Still, the diversity would have a certain unity. Not "English", but the history, values, and social structure of the United States would give a characteristic configuration to them.

Hidden Hegemony. Schools would not find their problems of language resolved in the situations we are imagining now. Concern to develop the full potential of each child would lead to recognition of language as involving more than command of a standard. For example, I suspect that there is a pervasive dominant attitude that discourages verbal fluency and expressiveness in white males. It ought to be food for thought that in most known societies it is men who are considered the masters of verbal style, and indeed often trained in its ways, whereas women are subordinated and even disparaged. In our own country, as we

know, it is commonly girls who show most verbal ability, who
learn to retain foreign languages, etc. Men in public life whose
work depends on use of language may be heard to disclaim any
special knowledge or command of it. The hint of homosexuality
seems not to be far from aesthetic mastery of language in a man.
Again, I suspect that many persons spend much of their lives in
what might be called 'verbal passing', the maintenance of the
public verbal face that is not chosen, but imposed. And what is
the fate of narrative skill in our society? There seems some reason to think that the expressivity of traditional narrative styles
has often been disapproved by the upwardly mobile and middle-
class. One sees a loss between generations of a vital narrative
style in some people of Indian communities. People continue to
relate accounts and narratives, of course; are we storying more
and enjoying it less?

Most serious of all, and most difficult for schools perhaps to
accept: I suspect that our culture is so oriented toward discrimination among persons on the basis of language that even a society
of 200 million speakers of standard English would show a class
and occupational structure much like the present one, matched by
a hierarchy of fine verbal discriminations. In other words, we
must consider the possibility that schools, along with other institutions, have as a latent function the reproduction of the present
social order on the apparently impartial ground of language.
Given the inherent variability in language and language use, even
a society of standard English speakers would show detectible
differences in pronunciation, diction, preferred constructions,
and the like. Are we so convinced that language change is language decline (as many of our educated elite appear to be), so
predisposed to correctness and correction, that most of that
society of standard English speakers would still leave school with
a feeling of linguistic insecurity and inferiority?

Perhaps not, but in order to see our society, and the place
of language in it, especially the place of language in education in
it, we have to ask such questions. To what extent are the inadequacies and senses of inadequacy about language in the society
to be explained by the backgrounds and characteristics of those
who pass through schools? To what extent are they unwittingly
produced by schools themselves?

EQUALITY-IMPLEMENTATION

Perhaps our society can never come closer to equality of opportunity, to a treatment of language in schooling that starts where
the child is, that develops the fullest linguistic potential of the
child. Still, those are the goals in terms of which one often
speaks. It is only that the change required to come closer to
them is so pervasive--change in knowledge, change in attitude,
ultimately change in social structure itself. Change in what we
know can never be enough, yet without it the other changes are

impossible. One sees some change in the treatment of Black English Vernacular that would not have come about without the research of the past decade or so. Knowledge of other situations can have effect too, especially in the context of a view of the history and direction of the role of language in the society as a whole.

My call for such knowledge in relation to schools amounts to a call for an educational linguistics, as a major thrust of schools of education, departments of linguistics, and all concerned with language and with education. Let me add that it should be shaped not only by educators and linguistics, but also by members of the communities concerned, teachers and parents both. It is inherent in adequate study of language that one must draw on the knowledge that members of a community already tacitly have, and the same is true for ethnography, for knowledge of ways of speaking in relation to cultural contexts. And insofar as the work to be done involves policies and goals, members of the communities affected must necessarily play a part. The educational linguistics envisioned here is in part a community science.

Such an educational linguistics entails change in both linguistics and education. In a sense, its goal must be to fill what might be called a 'competency' gap. There is a gap in the sense of a lack of persons able to do the kind of research that is needed. The gap exists because the need to fill it has not been recognized, and recognition of the need depends on overcoming a 'competency' gap in another, theoretical sense. Both linguists and educators may use the term 'competence'; the gap between their uses is at the heart of what needs to be changed.

In linguistics the term 'competency' was introduced by Chomsky a decade or so ago. Its ordinary meaning suggested a linguistics that would go beyond language structure to the linguistic abilities of people. The promise proved a bit of hyperbole. The term was used in a reduced sense as equivalent to just that portion of competence involving knowledge of a grammar, and grammar itself was defined in terms of an ideal potentiality, cut off from any actual ability or person. Grammar was to explain the potential knowledge of an amalgamated everyone in general, and of no one in particular. Social considerations were wholly absent from such a 'competency'. The result has been conceptual confusion that has led some to abandon the term altogether; others to tinker with it; still others to denounce its use as partisan apologetics ('that's not 'competence' was used to mean 'what you are interested in is not linguistics!). In Chomskyan linguistics, in short, 'competence' has meant an abstract grammatical potential, whose true character and whose relation to realized alike remain quite uncertain. The image of the language-acquiring child has been one of an immaculate innate schemata, capable of generating anything, unconstrained and unshaped by social life.

In education the terms 'competence' and 'competency-based' have become associated with a quite different conception. The emphasis is upon specific, demonstrable, socially relevant skills. No one can be against demonstrable skills, but there is fear that the notion reduces education to a very limited conception of ability and potential. It suggests an image of an externally shaped repertoire of traits that does not allow for going beyond what is already given. It suggests that success in transmitting basic skills is something that was once in hand, lost, and now to be gone back to.

Each polar notion of 'competence' treats as basic something that is derivative. The simple linguistic notion treats formal grammar as basic, and use of language as unconnected, or dependent, whereas in fact the opposite is the case. What we conceive as grammar is a precipitate of a normative selection from among the ways of speaking, the true verbal repertoire, the full organization of means of speech. Grammar began that way in the service of Hellenistic cultural hegemony and continues that way in the service of a certain conception of science. A valid notion of verbal competence reaches out to include the full organization of means and meaning of speech, and becomes part of a notion of communicative competence.

The notion of 'competence' that has gained currency in education treats distinguishable skills as elementary, underived, whereas any prescribed set of skills is a precipitate of a complex of assumptions and understandings as to the nature of society, its present and future opportunities, and the probable or prescribed relation of a group of students to it. There is a tendency to focus on instrumental, vocational ingredients of verbal skills, perhaps at the expense of the full range of verbal abilities valued and possible.

In both cases the limited notion of competence is bound up, I think, with a limited ability to see the nature of the language situations in the United States. That limitation is academic. I want to suggest that the problem of language in education is not to go back to basics, whether in the grammar of the linguist or the grammar of the schoolbook, but to go forward to fundamentals. How does language come organized for use in the communities from which children come to schools? What are the meaning and values associated with use of language in the many different sectors and strata of the society? What are the actual verbal abilities of children and others across the range of settings they naturally engage? What is the fit, what is the frustration, between abilities and settings--where is an ability frustrated for lack of a setting, a setting unentered for lack of an ability, in what ways are patterns of personal verbal ability shaped by restrictions of access to settings, on the one hand, culturally supported aspirations, on the other?

When we consider where a child is, what its potential is, we are considering abilities for which 'competence' is an excellent word, if we can understand it aright, in something close to its

ordinary sense, as mastery of the use of language. To use the
notion in education, we need to know the shapes in which mastery
comes in the many communities of speaking that make up the
country, and we need to be able to relate those shapes to the
larger historical and social factors that constrain them. Ethnolinguistic description can at least enable us to see where we truly
stand with regard to linguistic competence in the United States.
The knowledge it provides is indispensable for those who wish to
change where we stand.

To see the need for knowledge of the language situations of
our country, to support training and research to obtain such
knowledge, to change the relations between linguistics and education, so as to bring into being an educational linguistics that can
foster all this--these are the imperatives for change, the fundamentals to which we must move forward.

The key to implementing such changes, I think, is in the
hands of Schools of Education. There is little chance of success,
little chance of results relevant to schools, if educators do not
play a principal role in shaping the growing concern of students
of language with the social aspects of language. At the University of Pennsylvania we are expanding a Reading and Language
Arts program into a general program of Language in Education,
and including in it a specialization in Educational Linguistics as a
foundational field. The purpose is both to train researchers and
to influence the training and outlook of those in other parts of
the School. The new program is possible partly because of the
cooperation and support of some linguists outside the School.
Each School of Education may find its own particular pattern, but
a successful pattern ought to have these three ingredients mentioned: training of research specialists, influence on the training
and outlook of others, cooperation between educators and linguists.

The greatest challenge to research, the research of greatest
benefit to schools now, will be to domesticate and direct the skills
of ethnography and descriptive linguistics, of sociolinguistics or
ethnolinguistics in broad senses of those terms. We need programs
of research that can function within a limited frame of time, say a
year, and provide through linguistic ethnography a usable sketch
of the ways of speaking of a community or district served by a
school. For the most part linguistic ethnography has flourished
abroad with studies of cultural uses of language in Mexico, Africa,
Panama, the Philippines. We need to bring it home to Pittsburgh
and Philadelphia. The support of Schools of Education will be
essential for this. The models of research that are needed are
not wholly ready to hand: practical relevance and research development must grow together, in the sort of environment that a School
of Education can provide.

It is not too much to imagine, indeed, that language in education can be an integrating focus for many aspects of a School.
The ties with Reading and Language Arts, with developmental

psychology, with English studies are obvious. When one considers the way in which problems of language are shaped by cultural assumptions and attitudes, it becomes apparent that there are ties with the historical, sociological, and anthropological foundations of education. There is a complex of spurious and genuine problems of language diversity in relation to special education and school counselling. Issues of curriculum and instruction arise as well. With a bit of luck and a lot of initiative, education might find itself a major force in shaping the study of language in the United States.

NOTES

1. The contribution of each of these men, and something of my debt to them, is indicated in Hymes 1970, 1974, ch. 8, for Sapir; Hymes 1974:85-86, 121-122, 204, for Marx; 1975, for Jakobson; 1974, ch. 7, for Burke.
2. This point is developed more fully in my Introduction to Cazden et al. (1972). In introducing my lecture, Donald Henderson quoted a very apt passage from that essay, framing what I had to say perfectly, and I am grateful to him for it.
3. See Hoover (1975).
4. The pioneer in this work is William Leap. See his article (1974); a book-length collection of studies of Indian English is now being edited by Leap.
5. I try to address these issues in some detail in a paper called 'Ethnographic Monitoring', written for a symposium on 'Language Development in a Bilingual Setting', March 19-21, 1976, organized by Eugene Briere for the Multilingual/Multicultural Materials Development Center of California State Polytechnic University. Plans for publication are not yet definite. (See pp. 104-118 in this volume.)
6. Let me stress that I do not suggest that every aspect of language structure and use can simply be assigned to one or the other of the two generalized types of function. They are not either-or catch-alls. They are interdependent; their nature is not quite the same at one level of language as at another; their manifestations enter into a variety of relationships as between levels of language. The essential point is that an adequate study of language cannot be built on attention to just one of them. I speak of generalized types of function because there is no agreement on the specific set required in a model of language structure, and a good many specific functions may need to be recognized, some universal, some local. I do think that at any one level there are fundamentally just two kinds of means, and organization of means, roughly a 'what' and a 'how'. The principle of contrastive relevance within a frame that is basic to linguistics applies to both: the 'same thing' can be said in a set of contrasting ways, and the 'same way' can be used for a set of contrasting 'things'. A key to the organization of language in a particular culture or

period is restriction on free combination of 'what's' and 'hows', the things that must be said in certain ways, the ways that can be used only for certain things. The admissible relations comprise the admissible styles. In effect, the study of language is fundamentally a study of styles. There is further discussion in my Introduction to Cazden et al. (1972) and my essay, 'Ways of Speaking', in Bauman and Sherzer (1974).

7. See Hymes (1968).

8. This point should be obvious, yet seems hard to grasp, so deeply ingrained is a contrary assumption. I have been trying to make the point for almost twenty years. See Hymes 1961a, 1961b, 1964a, 1964b, 1974, ch. 6.

9. Roger Shuy has pioneered in this regard. For discussion of the general issue of language problem, I am indebted to members of the Committee on Sociolinguistics of the Social Science Research Council, especially Rolf Kjolseth.

REFERENCES

Bauman, Richard and Joel Sherzer (eds.). *The Ethnography of Speaking.* New York: Cambridge University Press, 1974.

Cazden, Courtney; Vera John-Steiner; Dell Hymes (eds.). *Functions of Language in the Classroom.* New York: Teachers College Press, 1972.

Hoover, Mary E. R. "Appropriate Uses of Black English as Rated by Parents." Stanford University, School of Education, *Stanford Center for Research and Development in Teaching, Technical Report No. 46*, 1975.

Hymes, Dell. "Functions of Speech: An Evolutionary Approach." In Fred C. Gruber (ed.), *Anthropology and Education.* Philadelphia: University of Pennsylvania, pp. 55-83. Reprinted in Yehudi A. Cohen (ed.), *Man in Adaptation.* Chicago: Aldine, 1961, pp. 247-259.

_____. "Linguistic Aspects of Cross-Cultural Personality Study." In B. Kaplan (ed.), *Studying Personality Cross-Culturally.* Evanston: Row, Peterson, 1961 (later: New York: Harper and Row), pp. 313-359.

_____. "The Ethnography of Speaking." In T. Gladwin and W. Sturtevant (eds.), *Anthropology and Human Behavior.* Washington, D.C.: Anthropological Society of Washington, 1962, pp. 15-53.

_____. "Directions in (Ethno-) Linguistic Theory." In A. K. Romney and R. G. D'Andrade (eds.), *Transcultural Studies of Cognition.* Washington, D.C.: American Anthropological Association, 1964, pp. 6-56.

_____ (ed.). "Introduction: Toward Ethnographies of Communication." In J.J. Gumperz and D. Hymes (eds.), *The Ethnography of Communication.* Washington, D.C.: American Anthropological Association, 1964, pp. 1-34.

Hymes, Dell. "Two Types of Linguistic Relativity." In W.
     Bright (ed.), *Sociolinguistics*. The Hague: Mouton, 1966,
     pp. 114-158.
_____. "Linguistics--The Field." *International Encyclopedia
     of the Social Sciences*. New York: Macmillan, 9:351-371,
     1968.
_____. "Linguistic Method of Ethnography." In Paul Garvin
     (ed.), *Method and Theory in Linguistics*. The Hague:
     Mouton, 1970, pp. 249-325.
_____. *Foundations in Sociolinguistics*. Philadelphia: Uni-
     versity of Pennsylvania Press, 1974.
_____. "Pre-War Prague School and Post-War American Anthro-
     pological Linguistics." In E.F.K. Koerner (ed.), *The Trans-
     formational-Generative Paradigm and Modern Linguistic Theory*.
     (Amsterdam Studies in the Theory and History of Linguistic
     Science, IV; Current Issues in Linguistic Theory, I.)
     Amsterdam: John Benjamins B.V., 1975.